D0501963

TREASURE IN CLAY POTS

To Sam and Wanda
With deep appreciation.
Love,
Richard + Nancy
Jan. 1982

TREASURE IN CLAY POTS

An Amazon People on the Wheel of Change

MILDRED LARSON AND LOIS DODDS

Person to Person
—*BOOKS*—

Palm Desert, California / Dallas, Texas

Treasure in Clay Pots

Copyright © 1985 by Mildred Larson and Lois Dodds

All rights reserved. No portion of this book may be used or reproduced in any form without written permission of the publisher except in the case of brief quotations within critical articles and
reviews.

Person to Person Books
Palm Desert, California
Dallas, Texas

Photos courtesy of Wycliffe Bible Translators,
Don Hesse, Mildred Larson, Lois Dodds, Doug Denning.

Library of Congress Cataloging in Publication Data

Larson, Mildred L.
  Treasure in clay pots.

  Bibliography: p.
  1. Aguaruna Indians—Cultural assimilation. 2. Aguaruna Indians—Religion
and mythology. 3. Larson, Mildred L. 4. Summer Institute of Linguistics.
5. Wycliffe Bible Translators. 6. Evangelistic work—Peru. 7. Indians of
South America—Peru—Cultural assimilation. 8. Aguaruna Indians—Religion
and mythology. I. Dodds, Lois. II. Title.
F3430.1.A35L37 1985   303.4'82'08998   85-21406
ISBN 0-933973-01-2 (alk. paper)

First Edition
1 2 3 4 5 6 7 8 9 10

Printed in the United States of America.

Contents

Supplemental Information

Preface

For several years a faint urge drifted around in the back of my mind—an urge to write a book about God's ways among the Aguaruna people of Peru.

One evening in late 1972, after a weekly prayer time, Jerry Elder, director of the Summer Institute of Linguistics in Peru, began to encourage me to write a book. In January of 1973, God again confirmed to me, through a most extraordinary time of prayer, that I was to write it.

At the end of 1974, I organized the material from the files of our Tribal Affairs Department and the Peru Branch Publicity and from my newsletters. I also gathered information from my personal files, which included correspondence between my team workers, letters from hundreds of Aguaruna friends, my diary accounts, my yearly calendar records and my collected letters home.

Then I spent six weeks in Aguaruna communities taping interviews with Dantuchu, Alias, Chamiquit, Miguel, Tomas, Abel and others who remembered the "old days."

Far more happened in the twenty-plus years I spent with the Aguaruna than I have included here. I leave a great part for my colleague, Jeanne Grover to tell—especially the medical aspects of the story.

I am deeply indebted to Jeanne and my other team workers, Martha Jakeway and Dennis and Susie Olson, for making valuable suggestions, and to many others, such as Jean Bates, who typed much of the first draft.

In 1980, my friend and colleague Lois Dodds eagerly agreed to research various matters and to organize and rewrite the material for me, since my academic responsibilities kept pushing the book out of my schedule. Her enthusiastic and careful work has brought it to its final form.

I extend special thanks to each person who has faithfully supported me since I became a member of the Wycliffe Bible Translators and the Summer Institute of Linguistics in 1952. Your gifts and prayers have been a vital part of this story. Thank you, each one.

MILLIE LARSON

Introduction

"Change the indigenous culture! Make all the nations become as one!" cry some people. Others protest, "Don't destroy the past. Preserve the cultures of primitive peoples!"

But what of the persons themselves who are the object of this fierce controversy? What of the man and woman still immersed in their so-called primitive culture, who may know little about the world outside their cultural boundaries? Does anyone ask them about their own destiny? Sadly, no. Seldom are they given the opportunity to speak or to choose for themselves, to help determine their own future. They are like clay, molded and shaped by outside forces—sometimes gently, but more often ruthlessly, by hard blows that make them lose all resemblance to what they once were. They are pummeled and pounded, and are often ground down or ground out by the swirl of forces impinging upon them. Will the wheel of change never quit spinning them? Will the pressures never cease? Is the man and woman in a technologically primitive culture destined to extinction by forces beyond their control? Should they be isolated and "preserved," static in time? Or is there some other, more hopeful, alternative?

To speak of culture change, or to promote it in any way, is not popular in some circles today. Yet change is inevitable in every culture; it cannot be ignored. Like it or not, change is a fact of life. We can either pretend it does not exist, and thus permit it and promote it in our blindness, or we can choose to recognize it and seek to guide it into the most helpful channels. To take the former position is to leave the unprotected to the exploitation of forces and people who care nothing about them. Thinking, sensitive people can only choose the second alternative—for other cultures as they do for their own—of trying to peacefully halt destructive changes and to promote those which will preserve both the individuals and the societies they compose.

For more than twenty years I lived with a people caught on the wheel of violent cultural change. I saw and felt firsthand what they experienced. I saw the changes—some thrust upon them, others chosen by them. I felt the pressures that squeezed them. Often I found that I myself was one of the forces shaping the people. One day I would find myself pulling them towards the outside world, and the next day I would be urging them to hold onto the ways of their forefathers. I looked with them for answers, sometimes making decisions without knowing what the answers ought to be. I had to face the fact that I, too, was the instigator of change—and sometimes of change that I didn't like. At other times I tried to bring about change which from my outside perspective seemed beneficial. Yet I found the ancient beliefs of the Aguaruna so deeply entrenched in their minds that change seemed impossible. But then again I would see change take place so rapidly that I wanted to yell, "Stop! Not that way!"

This book is an account of changes I have seen taking place in the Aguaruna culture, and those which continue to affect the people. It focuses on changes in the lives of individual Aguaruna and in my own life as I have worked in Peru with them and other indigenous groups. Though it has been difficult to assess all the forces acting upon the Aguaruna, from my perspective as a Christian I have tried to see a larger view. Behind the conflicting pressures creating change, I have seen the hand of God—working deliberately and skillfully—fashioning, from Aguaruna clay, vessels which are destined by Him to be the recipients of His treasure, to be used in His eternal purposes.

Scripture tells us that our substance is but clay. Yet God has fashioned us into useful vessels, and into these He pours the treasure of His own Spirit. From us He then pours forth His treasure in a never-ending stream—into still more pots made of the same clay. He is the potter, the in-filler, the pourer-forth, whether for the Aguaruna on the jungle trail or for the person on the city street far away. My desire is that this book bear witness to the reality of God's work in all of us involved in this account.

MILLIE LARSON

TREASURE IN CLAY POTS

Part I

Mixing Clay and Ash

O Lord, you are our Father.
We are the clay
and you are the Potter.
We are all formed by your hand.
Isaiah 64:8

1

Man of Many Names

The palm switch stung the calves of the young boy. He jerked awake and shifted on his sleeping mat so he could see his father standing over him. It was 3 A.M., and like all good Aguaruna men devoted to rearing their sons in the wisdom of the ancestors, Yashurai's father had been up for an hour or two before the rooster's first crow. He had already washed out his stomach by drinking and then vomiting up tea made with boiled *wais*[1] leaves; now he was ready for the day's lecture and scolding. Today Yashurai was lucky; he had done nothing to merit being switched with nettles or having boiling water splashed on him. The sting of the palm switch was not so bad compared to those punishments, which some Aguaruna fathers used to castigate their sons.

"Yesterday, you went to a house where you weren't invited!" his father scolded. "Don't do that! Children don't go visiting here and there." He spoke forcefully, displaying his spirit strength.

"Children stay at their father's house. If an adult invites you to visit in his house, you may go. If not, don't go. When you do go, don't ever sit where a woman has sat!" The father cleared his throat and spat vigorously at the corner of the earth floor. He would teach his son by example as well as with words. He must never swallow his saliva, for it was, like other bodily wastes, something repulsive; he would be ashamed to swallow it.

"You must never be lazy. Don't be idle either. You must work hard and earn the respect of the others. Don't play— especially don't play with girls! Don't ever be a coward. You must have courage. Don't let yourself get spoiled or be seduced. You must be

7

respectable and never corrupt. Work hard, and earn respect. Don't ever take things that belong to others."

These early morning lectures usually lasted an hour, while the father sat on his low wooden stool weaving cloth or spinning cotton. As time passed, they changed according to Yashurai's needs.

"Don't drink too much fermented manioc drink. Don't eat too much. Don't watch other people eat. Don't go around looking at girls. Stay away from where the women are. Don't ever touch your sister in any way. Don't ever go into a planted garden. Someone might see your footprints and say, 'Who was walking in my wife's garden?' or 'Who was talking to my daughter?' Only walk where people don't go, out in the jungle. Don't steal women. If you want to steal a woman, don't do it here in our community. If you get caught, where will you live? All will be angry. But when you go to another place far away, it's okay to do wrong, but stay good in your own community."

On some days, the lecture focused on kinship relationships. Yashurai, like all Aguaruna boys, must be drilled in family and clan relationships. His life would depend on knowing how he related to each person he met. He must be able to recite his genealogies and the history of wars, revenge killings, retaliations. He must learn when to kill everyone in a war and when to kill only his personal enemies. He must learn the secret war songs and those for shrinking heads to get their power and force. He must know the songs to drive away the demons. He must know whose house to burn down and whose house to spare.

One morning, when Yashurai was about nine, his father said to him, "My son, listen to my dream! We must change your name again! Your uncle gave you your first name the fourth day after you were born when we let you down through the roof and chanted and sang for you. He named you 'Tuyas,' for a tall man who was brave in war. Your nickname has been Yashurai because when you were a baby your lips curled out when you cried. But now we must change your name again. Now you will be Egkeash, 'One who joins hands.' Egkeash was a very respected man, famous for his bravery in war. You will be like him," he told Yashurai, never knowing how prophetic this new name would be. "Soon it will be time for you to go to the jungle to sleep alone by the sacred waterfall to encounter your *ajutap*[2] spirit. Thus you will have power and will become strong and brave."

At about the age of twelve, the time did come for Egkeash to be sent alone into the jungle, for only there could he find the *ajutap* spirit and become a man ready for war. He had already been preparing for this for years. At age five he had begun to restrict his diet by eating no sweets, and since age seven he had slept in the jungle with only one companion. At age eight he had begun to drink belladonna.[3]

"You must go out alone now," his father said. "Go down the trail where you will encounter no one else. Go deep into the jungle, by the sacred waterfall. Every day you must make yourself a shelter of leaves; don't sleep in the same one twice. You must sleep alone, night after night, and wait for the spirits to come. Drink *datem*[4] and tobacco tea, belladonna and the other drugs. They will help you to have visions and to find the *ajutap* power. He will protect you and make you invincible. You will be strong in battle.

"You must not have sex with any woman before you marry. If you sleep with a woman before your visions, you will have no power; you will die young. When you see a woman on the trail, get away from her! Hide! If you must talk to her, cover your face and nose. Her *etse* may enter through your mouth or nose. If you breathe a woman's breath, or you smell her sweet seed collar, you will want her. If you smell her odor you will become a coward. Don't use any seeds that smell sweet; you will smell like a woman and *ajutap* will not come to you. You must be pure and disciplined in these things if you expect to get power. When you do marry, never touch your wife's breasts. You will lose the power for your blowgun if you do. Be sure you don't sleep with her for six months after you kill, or allow her to touch your private parts, because this will cause you to lose your power to kill. Don't ever ask about not-to-be-known things. Some things are secret, not known to men."

Thus Egkeash went off alone into the deep, dark jungle, far from all his people. For days he roamed through the thick woods, searching for the plants he needed to prepare his hallucinogenic drugs. Laboriously he prepared them, gathered what food he could, and built his small sleeping shelters. Each night he slept in a different place and drank the *datem* drug, hoping the *ajutap* spirit would come to him in the form of a jaguar, a boa, or an eagle—perhaps even as a dead person (in the form of an owl) or in a ball of light. He dreamed about the dramatic change he would undergo when he saw his first vision. He would never have to tell about it; people would know by his happiness, his vigor, his sudden desire to kill, that he had *ajutap*.

Yet Egkeash feared the many other spirits and demons who might also come. Darkness was the time they liked best to roam the jungle and to snatch away people or eat their dogs. He was especially frightened to hear an owl hoot, for that meant someone would die. At night he thought of his relatives who had died, wondering if their spirits would come to him. He listened to what various spirits had to say in the thunder, lightning, fog, and wind. Such events were always generated by the spirit world, portents of coming events. He waited for the violent wind on which his *ajutap* spirit would come and thought of how he would answer bravely when the spirit questioned. "Are you afraid?"it would ask, pacing back and forth in front of him. When he caught glimpses of the stars through the canopy of trees high above him, he shuddered to think of his own soul burning as those souls above him in the sky did. He wondered what effect their doings had on him and his people.

At the end of seven days, Egkeash drank *baiku*,[5] the strongest of the drugs. He knew that when *ajutap* came to him in the blast of wind, appearing as an animal or a spirit, he would become very powerful. He would kill many enemies. He would be able to speak forcefully. People would listen to him and obey him; he would command respect.

During these days, Egkeash talked to no woman. He ate very little—no sweet-smelling food, no pineapple, crab, boiled eggs, peanuts, or soup made with meat. Grated green bananas were also taboo. He could take along nothing his mother had prepared. He ate only wild potatoes and bananas which he roasted for himself in the coals.

Periodically for months Egkeash repeated his vigils, which lasted for weeks at a time. When he occasionally visited home, he lay motionless on his bed most of the time, dazed by the drugs, caught up in his search for visions, withholding himself from family involvement.

Egkeash had many dreams during this period. He thought of his initiation, when after his first vision he would be regarded as a man. What a day that would be! His uncle would cut his hair for the first time, just below the shoulder blades so it would still properly cover his neck. The elders would place the adornments of manhood on him: earrings, a wrist band, and seeds on his chest. They would paint his face and give him his own painted drinking bowl. He wondered too what his destiny would be.

But Egkeash was disappointed. The hallucinogens never gave him a vision; he never enountered his *ajutap* spirit. For several years he repeated his search, his vigils, his visits to the sacred waterfalls, living the rigorous, monastic life of one searching for spiritual power.

Finally, Egkeash gave up his search. He made a daring decision; he would do things a new way. He would gain his power by killing other warriors! If the *ajutap* would not come to him in the jungle, he would gain him by killing others who had power, even though he would be vulnerable at first, not having the power to protect himself. He would take a wife and join revenge parties, as any initiated Aguaruna youth could do.

Egkeash chose himself a "wild pig" (secret girl friend). As he crept into her house to visit one night, he sneezed. The girl's father woke up.

"Who's that?" he asked, startled.

"Oh, it's just Jiukunch," his wife assured him, thinking it was the family dog.

Somehow the story got around, and the nickname stuck. Egkeash became Jiukunch, meaning 'Boney Eyes.' But his position and the respect he gained belied the name.

Before long, Boney Eyes had killed five people. His power grew. No one could kill him when he had gained that much power, the strength of so many *ajutap*!

Later, Boney Eyes' name changed once more—this time to the Spanish *Arias*, pronounced *Alias* by the Aguaruna.[6] But he did not count on anything else in his Aguaruna world changing, as it soon would.

Some of Alias' enemies decided to avenge his latest killing in a new way. They wouldn't go after him with spears; instead they would report him and his cousin, who had collaborated with him, to the Spanish-speaking authorities!

Soldiers came in search of the criminals; they captured Alias and his cousin and took them to an army post downriver. There seemed to be no way of escape, as the only door leading out of the jail was constantly guarded.

The captors decided that the best punishment for the Aguaruna killers would be to send them further downriver, to be inscribed into the Peruvian army for three years without pay. As Alias and his cousin discussed their unhappy prospects, Alias remembered once having heard a missionary talk about prayer.

"If you pray to God for forgiveness, He will forgive your sins and help you," the man had said. Alias' cousin agreed to try praying with him. For the first time in their lives they talked to God, confessing everything they thought was sin that they could recall. They asked God to forgive them, and to help them escape from jail.

Many days later, Alias somehow knew the day of their escape had come. In the evening the captain asked the two men to entertain the soldiers with Aguaruna dancing. Expertly, Alias and his cousin danced and drummed, on and on, singing the repetitious five-tone dance tunes.

One by one, the drunken soldiers fell asleep. Even the captain and the guard succumbed. The two men continued to sing. They danced their way back into the jail, picked up their blankets, and danced on out the door to freedom. Their first encounter with God seemed to them a great success.

2

One Who Joins Hands

I met an Aguaruna for the first time in 1953. I had no idea then that my life would soon be immersed in the Aguaruna world. I never dreamed I would learn to speak their language, to put it on paper, and to write books for them.

The Aguaruna, I found out, were one of more than forty indigenous groups living in the tropical rain forest of Peru, South America.[7] Before coming to Peru, I had heard about the "head-hunters of the upper Amazon." That day as I met Daniel Dantuchu, I saw only a young man, dressed in baggy pants and a wrinkled shirt, barefoot and smiling. He certainly gave me no reason to think about head-hunters. I saw him as someone with whom I could practice a few words of beginning Spanish.

Dantuchu was one of sixteen young men and women from various jungle groups who had recently come to Yarinacocha,[8] the center of the Summer Institute of Linguistics in Peru, to learn to become a school teacher. He seemed excited about his opportunity.

How differently I would have reacted to Dantuchu had I known then that I would spend many hours in his classroom, many days traveling the headwaters of the Amazon with him, and much, much time conversing about the changes affecting his people so drastically. Had I seen in him the first hopeful teacher candidate, the beginning of an educational program that would later extend to 25,000 Aguaruna scattered over more than 20,000 square miles of jungle, I would have treated him with awe.

That I would translate the New Testament into Dantuchu's language didn't even occur to me then. Ray and Alice Wakelin were already busy studying the language, preparing an alphabet and making primers for Dantuchu's future school.

"Aguaruna is the toughest language in Peru," someone commented to me.

"Well, I'm glad it's taken!" I said. Clearly, there was no danger of my being assigned to such a highly complex language.

But I was wrong. Soon after that, Cameron Townsend, our director, talked to me.

"Millie," he asked, "how would you like to give the Wakelins some help on grammar analysis while you're waiting for your permanent assignment?"

"Okay," I agreed. What a crucial decision that would prove to be! More than twenty years later I was still on my Aguaruna assignment. Before I could even help them, the Wakelins had to leave because of illness. I took up the study of Aguaruna while I waited for their return. But once I began to study the language and to get involved with the people, there was no stopping! So much more needed to be done! When I found that the Wakelins could not return, my choice was clear. I had my permanent assignment! "Millie," God seemed to say to me, "the Aguaruna are my special people for you. Show them how much I care for them. Translate my Word for them, so they can know me as you do." Of course, I didn't know then how important this sense of God's call would be in sustaining me through many discouraging times.

Jeanne Grover, a nurse in our center clinic, gladly agreed to join me for a time out in the Aguaruna area that first year. Outgoing, dedicated and enthusiastic, Jeanne also got caught up with the people. She not only launched into the medical work, but also took on many responsibilities relating to the schools. Gradually, these took up more and more of her time; her temporary assignment became permanent also. I was glad God so early gave me a partner whose training and roles filled in where mine were lacking and shared my love for the Aguaruna as well.

Jeanne and I inherited the Wakelins' village house, with miscellaneous food supplies as well as notebooks and files of language materials. The house was built Aguaruna style, with walls made of split palm bark staves and a thatched roof, but it was more open than theirs. Since we didn't have to worry about evil spirits coming in over the wall and we wanted to promote friendship, an open house served our purpose better than a totally closed one such as the Aguaruna used. We were glad for the extra light too.

Some of the linguistic work we inherited had been done by the

Wakelins, and some by Titus and Florence Nickel who preceded them. We even found materials collected by Roger Wynans, a Nazarene missionary who had first contacted the Aguaruna in 1925 and worked with them until 1947.

Titus and Florence agreed to spend a couple of months helping Jeanne and me get acquainted with the Aguaruna. They had begun their linguistic work in 1947, at the invitation of Mr. Wynans, but because of Titus' administrative duties at the SIL center, the Wakelins had taken over from them in 1950. Now, Jeanne and I were to take over where the Wakelins had left off in 1954.

Jeanne and I first lived in Nazaret, a community far upriver, named by rubber hunters at the turn of the century. From this location we would be able to supervise Dantuchu and the five other new bilingual teachers during our many long months each year away from Yarinacocha.

We loved Nazaret. It was set on a high bluff above the river, surrounded by rugged mountains covered with lush, dense, tropical vegetation. We enjoyed hiking from house to house and visiting the garden clearings scattered through the jungle. We explored trails with our new friends, picking our way over ragged roots and mudholes, and through vines hanging from the trees that towered over us. Once away from the village, we found a hushed world of awesome beauty, different from any world we had known. It seemed God had poured out His best creative efforts in this world of green backdrops accented with brilliant birds, exotic flowers and changing skies. He had created a whole new world of sound, orchestrated by nature itself, to accompany this lush world. Crickets, frogs, cicadas, clicking butterflies, rustling leaves and dozens of bird songs make the jungle one of the richest and most alive parts of God's creation. It reminded me of strolling through a huge cathedral, and filled me with awe.

When we arrived in Nazaret Dantuchu was downriver, opening a school in a new area. But his brother Alias, director of the school in Nazaret came to visit one afternoon. We did our best to communicate.

"How many students do you have?" I asked him, hoping to make the conversation simple because of my limited knowledge of Aguaruna.

Alias was silent for a moment. He bent each finger into the palm of his hand, sealed them with his thumb, and said, "One hand finished." He repeated the count on his other hand.

"Second hand finished," he said. As he thought of the next

child, he reached down to touch his little toe. Suddenly he stopped short; his look of consternation quickly turned into an embarrassed grin and a chuckle. Shoes! You can't count on your toes with shoes on! He resorted to hands again and concluded that he had two complete hands, two feet, and four again on his hand, or twenty-four children in school.

We soon became enough a part of the community that Alias didn't find it necessary to put on shoes when visiting us, as he had on that first visit in order to make a good impression on the new foreigners. As Alias learned to feel at home with us, and as my ability to communicate increased, I found out more about Alias' life.

He told me of his childhood, of the lectures by his father and of his search for his *ajutap* spirit. He told me how he had decided to gain power by killing rather than by waiting for the *ajutap* spirit to come to him, of being turned in to the authorities, and of the way God helped him and his cousin to escape.

"What happened then?" I asked, fascinated by his story.

"We took a machete and canoe from the army post, and we poled up river for many days. At night we traveled and in the daytime we hid in the homes of relatives. Finally we arrived safely back in Nazaret," he said.

"But I forgot about God, then," he continued. "I didn't remember what He had done. I began killing again. The constant threat of revenge filled my mind. But I had killed five, and so I was invincible. I had plenty of time for fiestas and women, as well as for hunting and fishing. I was young, but my fame had grown."

"When Ray and Alice came to Nazaret in 1950, I went to visit them. They had heard of my fame as a hunter, and Ray asked me, 'Alias, how would you like to hunt for me? I'll provide the shotgun shells; you hunt, and we'll share the meat.' So we became friends, because I liked hunting and the extra meat this gave me."

During this time, however, Alias became increasingly tired of the constant threats and having to hide from his enemies. Finally, he thought of a solution. He would go away and join the army—of course, not downriver where he had escaped, but up in the mountains to the west.

And so he made another daring decision. He went to Ray with his plan.

"I'm going into the army," he told him. "Please cut my hair."

"Are you sure?" Ray asked him. This would be no ordinary haircut; Alias' hair hung halfway down his back; it was black, thick and wavy—the pride of his life since boyhood. To cut it off short, exposing his neck as the outsiders did, would be contrary to all he had been taught, to all he respected.

"Cut it off!" he insisted.

As soon as he thought he looked sufficiently "civilized," Alias took off on the trail up into the mountains, through the cool tropical foothills into the hot, dusty desert west of the rain forest.

Such a daring move, I continued to discover through the years, was typical of Alias. His early names—"brave, strong man" and "one who joins hands"—proved to be prophetic. He was the first Aguaruna to own a motor boat, the first to learn to type, the first to own a cow, and the first one to help many Aguaruna know Jesus Christ. He indeed became brave and strong, turning away from killing to promote a kind of unity and cooperation previously unknown to the Aguaruna. He joined them to each other and to the outside world in new and unexpected ways.

"I have come to join the army," he told the soldiers in the small mountain post.

"But we can't take you," they insisted. "We have already filled our quota for the year. There is no more room."

However, the soldiers took Alias' picture, filled out papers, and said they would call him the next year. That was definitely not what Alias had in mind! Now he would have to go back to the jungle, filled with his enemies. And he would be embarrassed by his short hair.

When he returned to Nazaret, something new altered Alias' Aguaruna world. His brother Dantuchu had just returned from the first teacher training course and was beginning his bilingual school.[9]

"Don't join the army, my brother," he said. "Become a teacher! I'll teach you to read and write at night so you can take the training course next year."

Alias, bold again, agreed. Thus he too became a bilingual school teacher, destined to be woven more tightly into the fabric of change for his people.

3

Clay Pots

One day not long after our arrival in Nazaret, Jeanne and I decided to go up the hill to visit our neighbor, Mamai. When we arrived she looked up with a pleased smile and greeted us as we entered. She sat on the dirt floor, busily mixing clay on a large flat board. We managed our greetings quite well, and she was obviously pleased at our progress in learning her language. Our understanding was still very limited, but there was no doubt about what she was saying. With many gestures and a constant stream of explanation, she told us that she was making pottery today. As she worked she gave us words, which we quickly wrote down in our notebooks and tried to repeat back to her.

Mamai's friendliness and composure impressed me. She was not accustomed to outsiders at all. Like other Aguaruna women and girls, she had been reared almost exclusively in the presence of her immediate family, seldom being allowed to spend time with other people. As a child she had never gone out of the house alone, even for personal needs. She had always been accompanied by another relative. Her childhood had been spent working in the garden with her mother, babysitting the younger children, and learning domestic chores. She had married early, perhaps before puberty, and even now had little social life. Yet she was willing to be our friend.

Mamai told us more about pottery making. She had gathered her clay from the bank of a stream nearby, carefully choosing the earth that would be most uniform, cohesive and malleable. It seemed an ugly gray mass to me! She had mixed it with the ashes of a special tree bark in order to strengthen it. After firing, the ash would make the clay much more durable; resistant to chipping, cold nights, and the heat of cooking fires. Now she was rolling it into long strings about a quarter of an inch in diameter. With these strips she built the sides of her pot, winding them around and around on top of each other, smoothing as she worked with a piece of clam shell. She worked quickly and skillfully, having made pottery all her life. Her five-year-old granddaughter sat beside her making her own little pots from the same lump of clay, imitating everything she saw her grandmother do.

When Mamai finished the shaping, she showed us that the pot was indented on the bottom. Thus it would sit on the head easily when used for carrying water. Then she took us outside to see the line of pots drying in the sun. Pointing to a pile of sticks and logs she had prepared, and then to the sun, she told us that she would be firing the pots in the late afternoon. Would we like to come back and watch?

Mamai gave us a tour of her house, showing us the pots already in use. On a high rack above the split cane sleeping platform were cooking pots turned upside down. On the floor a very large red pot, perhaps three feet in diameter at the widest point, held fermented manioc[10] drink. A pot full of bananas was boiling on the fire, supported by three large logs whose tips were burning. She showed us another pot, like a gourd, with just one small hole near the top on the side. This was filled with clean drinking water. A number of smaller bowls, used for eating and drinking, were stacked in a basket hung from a pole near the fire logs. I noticed another, a bit different in shape, and darker in color. Mamai demonstrated that this was a special bowl used for rinsing the mouth with warm water early in the morning or after eating. On one of the posts of the platform bed hung a very small pot, tied by a palm fiber string and covered with a leaf. Mamai showed us that this contained a thick black poison, used on the darts of the blowgun when hunting birds and small animals. Even the dog had his own clay pot. He was eating from a broken one, filled with pre-chewed chunks of manioc.

"No wonder Mamai has to take a day or two off every now and then to make pots!" I thought. She seemed to make all sizes and shapes to accommodate any use. Obviously she was proud of her skill as a potter and was pleased at our interest in her work. I couldn't help reflecting on what God says about Himself as the potter and us as His clay. He carefully chooses our substance. He mixes us with the ash of adversity and suffering to strengthen us. He molds us individually to just the right shape and size to suit His purpose. And He fires us in temptation and trial to make us durable containers for His Spirit.

When Jeanne and I returned in the afternoon to watch Mamai fire her new pots, the other members of the family were home. Mamai's husband, back from his day's hunt, was tying his 10-foot blowgun[11] to the main pole of the house, where it would stand up straight, carefully resting the mouthpiece on a small piece of wood. He had stopped at the stream to bathe on his way home; his thick black hair hung dripping down his back. He wore a single garment —a handwoven, wrap-around skirt. It reached just below his knees and was held in place by a handwoven belt. Near the fire lay a number of small birds, shot with his blowgun, and a large rodent which the dogs had discovered and helped to kill. The children eagerly examined them, trying to name and identify each one.

Mamai's oldest daughter, still in her early teens, was emptying a large pot of boiled manioc into a round wooden trough, three feet in diameter. First she mashed the cooked tubers with a pestle. Then she scooped up a handful of the mash, chewed it, and spit it back into the trough. She kept chewing, spitting, mixing, chewing, spitting, mixing, until she had all the mash thoroughly mixed with saliva. Then she transferred it to a large pot and began a new batch.

"It will take a lot of chewing to fill that large pot!" I thought.

"Don't you want to help her chew?" Mamai asked us. But we just laughed.

"We don't know how!" we told her.

The cooking fire and sleeping platform of the daughter and her young husband were next to those of her parents. Her husband was expected to live there for the first few years of their marriage, fulfilling certain duties. He had to keep his mother-in-law supplied with fire logs, bring her the hearts of palm trees and palm grubs to eat whenever she asked for them, and serve his father-in-law in various ways. Hopefully he would also help to increase the meat supply by being a good hunter and fisherman. Meanwhile, Mamai would teach her daughter how to be a good wife. If she and her husband were not satisfied with their son-in-law's development as a husband, they might send him away and look for a new one.

Two other sleeping platforms and fires occupied the space on the other side of Mamai's house. Two older sons, having served their in-law time, had returned with their wives and small children to again live with their parents.

Mamai reminded us that it was time to fire her pots. She led us outside to the pile of waiting sticks and logs. Carefully she arranged the firewood and each pot that she wanted to fire, building each stack very carefully so that the heat would be even. She lit the fires and watched intently as the burning wood engulfed the pots in flame and then slowly turned to coals. At just the right point, imperceptible to us, she pulled the glowing logs away. Carefully she cleared away all the fire and ashes, leaving the pots to cool without disturbance. Jeanne and I were fascinated and impressed that Mamai's handiwork emerged so useful and attractive from such a simple setting.

With the help of Mamai and others, Jeanne and I continued to learn to live among the Aguaruna, in a world radically different from our own. Our Aguaruna friends were always willing tutors. They helped us to discover the hazards of traveling by canoe and balsa raft on dangerous rivers and to learn to hike over mountain trails and eat strange foods such as grubs. Yet we found that the material adaptations they helped us make were inadequate preparation for the pressure that we felt from our intense involvement with people those first years. Learning to live without privacy and any time to call our own was extremely trying.

Before I came to Peru I had been warned about loneliness. My training had prepared me psychologically to cope with that. I had visions of long hours all alone. I would work long days at my desk on language materials, with no one but my partner to talk to. I would get used to having no diversions. But what a shock I got! By the end of the first few months in Nazaret, I longed more than anything else just to be alone. I thought of what our colleagues at Yarinacocha had said.

"Living in a village will be like living in a fish bowl," I remembered one of them saying.

"You'll feel like an animal in the zoo," someone else had said. But that wasn't half of it! Our observers were in the cage, in the fish bowl, with us! They inspected us from head to foot, felt us all over, and then inspected everything in the cage with us. Our half-open, thatched roof house didn't help; it was like a stage on which we were the continual entertainment.

During the first few weeks, we had found it interesting to be the center of so much attention. Since we couldn't understand what the people were saying, it wasn't too frustrating. Besides, we were busy looking at them, too. But we got tired of staring long before they did. Because the Aguaruna are great travelers, and prize hospitality to friends and relatives, they came in droves to visit us—so there was always someone new to stare at us. People we had never seen just popped in any time, assuming we would welcome them. Those from far away or families with a sick person would spend the night—or several nights. Many times people shared our house twenty-four hours a day.

During the day the Aguaruna watched everything we did. They talked, laughed, pointed, and generally had a great time. They asked questions constantly. As we learned more of the language, we found their most frequent question was, "How much does it cost?" They were shocked to find we didn't know the exact price of every item we possessed. We soon learned to take nothing but the essentials when we went left Yarinacocha to go out to the village. But even our "essentials" seemed like a lot of rare new things to them—typewriter, tape recorder, kerosene pressure lamp, two-way radio, air mattress, mosquito net, pressure cooker. We were indeed wealthy and the possessors of many things! Often I wished I could live without these things so there wouldn't be so much for our new friends to ask about.

Lack of sleep added to the pressure. Often I couldn't sleep because someone was always stirring up the fire at the foot of his bed. Of course, I sometimes forgot that I didn't need to stir up a fire because I had a nice warm sleeping bag. Even dreams kept me awake. If someone had a dream, it had to be told immediately in a loud voice. Then it provoked great discussion on the meaning of the dream and whether it meant someone was going to die.

The constant stream of people and interruptions put enormous pressure on our time. We felt keenly the need to get our "work" done. When I arrived in Nazaret the schools already needed more books. The students had quickly mastered the three primers prepared by the Wakelins. But there would be no books unless I wrote them. But how should I spend my time? The language analysis also needed to be done, and I needed to become more fluent in speaking. Yet day after day my time was taken up with visitors from all parts of Aguaruna territory. How could we ignore someone who came three days by canoe or five days by trail, just to visit us? As far as the Aguaruna could see, we had plenty of time; we obviously weren't doing anything except sitting and staring at paper.

As the days went by, so filled with people and so lacking in time to think even about my assigned responsibilities, I began to resent the people I had come to serve. It was an awful feeling. Didn't I love the Aguaruna? I found the vociferous and aggressive weren't easy to love. I felt irritated with their questions about my personal affairs; I couldn't get my work done! God began to show me in deeper ways how impossible it would be for me to do His task with the Aguaruna in my own strength, that I *must* draw on His strength to get through. I had to trust Him with the ashes of adversity in my life too, if I wanted to become fully useful to Him.

4

They Have My Words

In spite of inner frustrations, I kept working with my language helper Kunyach on material for the schools. Once he understood that I wanted stories for the children to read which came out of their own familiar beliefs and legends, he was able to give me just what I needed, like this story about the hummingbird:

> Long ago man had no fire. A bird brought it to man this way. The bird was sitting on the road, all wet. A man happened by and said to himself, "The bird is cold. I'll put it by the fire." He took it into the house and put it alongside the fire so that it would get dry. And it became dry. Then the bird's tail caught fire and so it flew away. As it flew away the man said, "The hummingbird takes fire; the hummingbird takes fire."
>
> The hummingbird set the trees on fire as he flew. In that way people received fire. As a favor, the hummingbird gave it to the ancestors because they didn't have fire.

Through our visits to Mamai and other neighbors, Jeanne and I got better acquainted with them and progressed in learning the Aguaruna language. Of course, we didn't always preserve our dignity.

"Can you give me some *pampa*?" I asked our next door neighbor one day. She laughed and laughed; finally she got some cooking bananas for me, saying emphatically as she gave them to me, "*paampa!*" stressing the long vowel in the first syllable. Then, picking up a smooth rock, she informed me that I had asked her for *pampa*, a rock.

These two words gave me an important clue for language analysis. I learned that I must listen carefully for the length of vowels, because the longer ones must be written double. We found many other words in which the double vowel was important— words like *tajai* meaning "I say" and *taajai* meaning "I arrive back."

Another day I asked a friend to bring me some *tsangku*. Doubtfully she brought me some, but she wondered if I was going to visit the shaman, as only shamans use tobacco! I had wanted *sangku*, a plant whose leaves make a delightful substitute for spinach.

"*Ijakun*," I said brightly to the neighbors on the trail one day. To my embarrassment, I found out later that instead of saying, "I'm going visiting," I had said, "I'm having diarrhea." They didn't know whether to laugh at my mistake or to sympathize with my illness. I had failed to add the nasal quality to the *j* sound!

Jeanne and I continually came up against cultural differences that made our work challenging. For instance, Alias' teaching style didn't conform to our ideas. He would never get an "A" in pedagogy, I decided. As I supervised his teaching, his seeming lack of organization astonished me. He impulsively jumped from one thing to another. But this didn't seem to bother his students at all. Whenever I tested the children, I was always amazed to find that they knew how to read. They knew what they ought to know, even though I was never sure how Alias had gotten them there. I was supposed to help him improve his methods of teaching. He was quick to accept my suggestions—and just as quick to abandon them for his own comfortable approach.

Fortunately, at times the cultural differences allowed us to learn from each other more rapidly, and even humorously.

Jeanne and I had inadvertently brought a new entertainment to Nazaret—one in a brown box. Some thought our tape recorder was even more fun than fishing! We recorded many legends and songs, to help us analyze the language and to understand and preserve the history of the people. If our neighbors heard our small generator start, they would come running down the hill, hoping it meant we would turn on the tape recorder.

One day Kuyach said, "There's a man visiting in the house up on the ridge who is from way back in the interior. He has never seen a white person. This afternoon he wants to come to see you."

"Fine," I said. "Do you suppose he knows the legends just like the ancestors told them? Could we record him telling them?"

"I'm sure he does. I'll ask him," he replied.

A couple of hours later our visitor arrived. His face was painted with red achiote[12]; his hair was tied in a pony tail, adorned with bright red and yellow toucan feathers attached to long fish bones. His handwoven skirt was set off by several strands of bright red seeds criss-crossing his chest.

Kunyach explained to the visitor how the tape recorder would preserve his words so we could all listen to them again later. The man told us many stories. I could understand only a little, but I knew his stories would be good material for study.

When our guest finished, I thought it would be nice to play a little of the tape back for him to hear. At first he didn't seem to respond. Then suddenly he became very excited.

"Waa! It's my words! They have my words!" he shouted. He stood up and left abruptly. He had had enough of these white women and their machines.

Not all our days in Nazaret were spent working. Village life provided many diversions for us. We learned a great deal by joining in the daily life of the Aguaruna. Through sharing in their practices and work, we increased our knowledge of their beliefs and thinking as well as of their material culture.

One very rainy Saturday morning we were awakened early by yelling down at the river. The night before, the men had put a split cane fence across the river, in preparation for fishing. As we cleared away the breakfast dishes, people streamed by on their way to the river. The men carried spears, harpoons or machetes. The women carried baskets. Many also carried banana leaves, umbrella style, to keep their babies dry until they could tie up the baby's hammocks in the temporary leaf shelters on the beach. Everyone talked excitedly.

"Come on! Come with us!" they urged us.

Jeanne and I threw on our rain coats and, slipping and sliding down the trail, descended to the river where the whole community was gathered. We decided to leave our tennis shoes on the big rock and go barefoot in the sand.

I never dreamed my feet could be such a fascinating conversation piece.

"How big! How white!" the women gathered around and exclaimed. One of them got up the courage to feel our feet.

"They're soft, oh, so soft. How can they walk on them?"

As the men pounded away on the *barbasco*[13] roots they had gathered to poison the fish, the women waited, trying to keep warm by the fires they had built in the shelters. The men talked and laughed loudly as they pounded the roots until the milky poison oozed out of them. Their faces glowed from the red *achiote* seed paste smeared on them.

For this work bee everyone wore his oldest, most patched skirt or sarong. Some barely hung together. Several men also had vines tied around their heads, crownlike.

The men scattered along the beach for several hundred yards, each with his bundle of beaten roots. Then, with much more yelling and laughing, they all dove in, swimming back and forth to wash the poison out of the roots into the water. Others in canoes reached over the edge to swish out their poison.

The *barbasco* poison stunned the fish, so that they were unable to breathe. As they surfaced for air a few minutes later, they were easy prey for spears and harpoons.

The women and children ran down to the water's edge with baskets and machetes in hand. Some men jumped into canoes; others worked from the shore. A young boy stood near his father, stringing the fish onto his unwound vine crown as his father harpooned them. Another man slashed the heads of the fish with his machete as he stood in knee-deep water, then grabbed the fish and threw them to his wife to collect in her basket. Everyone was grabbing fish. Jeanne and I busily snapped pictures, while trying to keep our cameras dry.

We had brought our own basket, however. First our "grandfather" put two fish in, then a woman gave us another. When it was all over, we had eight big fish. I actually grabbed one myself when it flipped out onto the beach.

Fishing was not always that successful, however. A few weeks later we all went again, with the same anticipation. But nothing happened. The fish did not jump. We waited in vain.

"There is some pregnant woman here. That's why there are no fish. Who kept the fish away?" someone finally said.

"Maybe only her husband is here," someone else suggested. No one wanted to admit who was guilty, but everyone knew that a pregnant woman and/or her husband had come and spoiled the luck of the day.

Our neighbors' favorite diversion, even more popular than fishing, was the fiesta, or *nantsen*, characterized by abundant fermented manioc drink and dancing. If a man needed to build a house or clear jungle for a new garden for his wife, he could count on the help of his friends and relatives. He would tell his wife to prepare for the work party. This meant hard work for her. She had to dig up baskets full of manioc root, peel it, and boil it in a huge pot. Then she had to chew each piece and spit the mash into another large pot. After she had chewed it all, she added water and left it to ferment for two or three days.

When the *nijamanch* drink was ready, her husband invited his neighbors to come and work by beating the signal drums early in the morning. These drums were huge, hollowed out logs with openings like a flute. The sound from them carried for miles, from ridge top to ridge top.

After a hard day of work and a cold dip in the river, the men dressed in their finest skirts and ornaments. Their feather crowns were made of orange, white, blue, black and yellow feathers woven on to bands and glued with pitch. Their long, dangling earrings were made from iridescent beetle wings. They came with their wives for their day's pay—abundant drink and dancing.

"Would you like to go upriver with us to a fiesta this afternoon?" Alias asked Jeanne and me one day.

"Oh, yes!" we assured him, not wanting to miss an opportunity to learn more about our Aguaruna friends.

Alias expertly poled his dugout canoe, as his younger wife, two children, and Jeanne and I perched on pole benches in the middle. We admired his skill at maneuvering the heavy canoe in the rocky river. We soaked in the beauty of the lush tropical rain forest edging the river banks.

"This has got to be one of the most beautiful places on earth!" I thought as I scanned the billowing cumulus clouds drifting in a clear blue sky above the Andes Mountains in the west. But we were learning that the Aguaruna had different thoughts and feelings about the world around them. Even the beauty of rainbows and sunsets, which provided rich touches to our lives, caused great fear for the Aguaruna. When a rainbow arched across the sky, the people became afraid. To them, the great *pangki*, or the spirit of the boa in the rainbow, is an ominous sign of imminent death for someone. If it is a small *pangki*, a child will die; if a large rainbow, an adult will die. Death has been a constant visitor to the Aguaruna; rainbows are also seen frequently. Who could say there is no connection? Our attempts at scientific explanations did little to change the reactions of our neighbors when the fearful serpent appeared in the sky.

"Don't do that!" one friend had said to me, horrified as she saw me point at the rainbow. "Don't you know your finger will rot and fall off? Everyone knows that if you point at a rainbow, your finger will fall off!" She was amazed when her prediction didn't happen. Maybe white-skinned people were different? Or—could it be that the ancestors were wrong?

I remembered an afternoon when dark clouds had rolled up the valley toward Nazaret. A neighbor woman, wearing more necklaces than I had ever seen on any woman, turned to face the oncoming storm. Her hair flying in the wind, and her arms waving wildly against the foe, she shouted, "Go back! Go back!" Her orders went unheeded, and wind and rain soon hit in full force. The storm settled down to a steady rain, with the constant rumbling of thunder. She instructed her daughter on the meaning of the storm.

"There has been a war. Someone was killed and now they are boiling him in a big pot. Hear it boil? Don't go outside when it's boiling like that!"

Even the sounds of nature which Jeanne and I welcomed were sources of fear for the Aguaruna. If an owl hooted long before dawn, it meant someone would die. It if hooted at dawn, a child would die, if at dusk, an old person. Other sounds, especially at night, meant that demons were near, waiting to bother someone or disturb his possessions.

When the setting sun turned bright red, Jeanne and I would exclaim, "How beautiful!" But our neighbors would be saying, "How fearful! There has been an accident. Someone has been killed!" If the sunset turned red slowly, the people quietly chanted in sing-song melody, "There has been an accident today and now they are crying." We discovered that they sang many such songs on many different occasions. They were fond of making up ditties or chants for even simple, everyday affairs. These served to reassure them, to verbalize their fears and to mobilize them against the horde of supernatural events and forces which seemed to rule their lives.

We finally arrived at the small village set high on a bank above the river. We entered a huge oval house, built of saplings and hard palm bark staves. The huge thatched roof was held up by several large central logs. The whole house was tied together with vine;

there wasn't a nail in the structure. It was cool and dark inside, as the walls reached all the way to the roof—to keep out jaguars, possums and owls, which might be embodied spirits.

Our host invited us to sit on the edge of one of the many sleeping platforms which lined the walls. Soon his wife brought a dish of boiled wild potatoes for us. She thoughtfully peeled them with her teeth before offering them to us. While I struggled to get down one cold, mushy potato, Alias and his family finished off a plateful. I was grateful that at least Jeanne seemed to be struggling with me.

Two fifteen-gallon ceramic pots of fermented manioc drink stood ready for the guests. As each one arrived, the host greeted him loudly for several minutes, while the visitor simultaneously responded with equal vigor. (Such greetings often went on for an hour or two, I found out later.) The host's wife then offered the guest a large bowl of *nijamanch* to drink. About twenty people, all adorned in feathers and necklaces, with hair freshly blackened with *suwa*[14], made up the party. They continued to drink, the men and boys sitting on logs in the husband's end of the house, and the women, girls, and little children gathered at the other end. As the hostess kept the drinking bowls full, the men's laughter and talking became louder and louder. After several bowls full, the men started stomping around the big house, beating drums made of monkey skin stretched over pieces of hollow log. Soon they began singing as they moved. Every once in a while, someone would yell, *"Jai, jai!"* Soon they were all bouncing up and down, back and forth. Women danced with women, and men with men, in pairs.

The women wore their best sarongs, rectangular woven cloths tied over their right shoulders. The stripes on their sarongs were horizontal, while those on the men's skirts were vertical. The women wore dancing belts adorned with triangular pieces of shell cut from fist-sized snails. These rattled pleasantly as they moved. They also wore aromatic seed necklaces, and bits of sweet-smelling wood tucked between their breasts. Men wore anklets made of nuts, which rattled in a lower pitch as they danced. Each person sang, but each one sang his own individual song.

"They aren't singing in unison. Don't they all sing the same song?" I asked Alias. Only the drum kept them together.

"Each one sings his own words. How could they all sing together? One might be happy and another sad," he explained.

The dance was well underway. The rhythm of the drum and the harmony of the clinking shells and rattling nuts filled the house.

The men's bare backs glistened as they danced back and forth, back and forth. The shaman came in, looked a little surprised to see us there, and sat down with his big spear in front of him. I couldn't help wondering if he was the policeman come to keep order. I noticed, however, that he was soon drinking as much as everyone else.

"We'll have to go now to get back downriver before dark," Alias told us, interrupting my observations. As we left he told us the party would go on and on—all night and for several days. Some woman might pull a lock of her hair over her shoulder, or touch a man's hand as she served him drink, signaling she wanted an affair. Or a man might put love potion on the edge of his drinking bowl so a woman he wanted would touch it and want him. With the drinking, this would probably lead to sexual liaisons, then to fighting, and perhaps to killing.

While Jeanne and I were learning about the Aguaruna, they were also learning about us. One woman just couldn't believe we came from a land where no one spoke Aguaruna. Could there really be such a place?

They never tired of asking us about our families.

"Is your mother living? What is her name? Is your father living? What is his name? Do you have brothers? What are their names? Do you have sisters? What are their names?" On and on the questions went. It was terribly important to them to know who we were—and the way to find out was by asking! That was their pattern; only then could a person find out if someone was relative or enemy. When they found that Jeanne and I weren't related and had never even *seen* each other in our own country, one woman was incredulous. "Are you enemies?" she asked.

5

Sickness Is More Than Germs

Alias made his way up the difficult trail with his fellow teachers to a dusty mountain town several days' hike away. It was 1956 and they were to be the first Aguaruna to cast ballots in a national election in Peru. But their trip proved to be memorable for other reasons too; the town had other attractions for them besides the voting booths.

While he was there, Alias heard of a man who could actually predict the future. He hastened to find the man who could have such power. The diviner told him many things about his past as well as his present.

"You are an orphan," he told him. "You are a teacher, and if you continue this work you will live well; but if you ever stop teaching you will have problems. You were a killer and have many enemies, but now you are a Christian."

Alias listened, amazed, as the man continued.

"Your trip up here was easy. But on the return trip you will have many problems." The diviner rounded out his prediction with a final warning.

"You have a very bad disease," he cautioned him. "Perhaps you won't live very long."

Alias paid the high fee of fifty *soles*, about two dollars or two days wages, for this terrifying information. Hastily he found his friends and they began preparations for the arduous trip home. They had planned to float downriver with the supplies they had bought, but at first they couldn't find balsa logs to make a raft. When they finally found logs and had tied together their raft, they headed downriver. But it seemed the diviner was right. They had one mishap after another, fighting the rising river. They overturned and lost all their purchases.

Alias was relieved to arrive back at his own house in Nazaret. But his relief was short-lived. The next evening he stepped out of his house for a few minutes. Suddenly a bright beam of light flashed into the clearing near his house. His heart pounded. Who could be shining a light from above? Again the light flashed on; again there was darkness. Then a third time the light came on, like someone playing with a huge flashlight. Alias called his wives and they searched for the source; they found nothing to account for the light.

Surely it was a sign! The words of the diviner rang in Alias' ears. "You won't live long!"

Alias stretched out on his sleeping platform, but he couldn't sleep. He was filled with fear and sought constantly to understand the meaning of the light. The next morning he came to our house to tell us about it.

"What can this mean, sister?" he asked urgently.

"There has to be an explanation," I assured him. I suggested all sorts of natural possibilities; I wasn't at all ready to admit that it might be something supernatural.

A month later Alias began having fevers. His ankles and knees swelled. He stopped teaching school and prepared himself for what he believed was inevitable death. Jeanne and I were very concerned about him and wanted to treat him, but whenever we would go to his house to visit, he was not there. His wives said, "He's gone hunting," or "He's gone visiting." Finally, when we saw him, we told him, "If you aren't well enough to teach, maybe you should stay in bed and rest. What would the minister of education think if you were hunting instead of teaching?"

In spite of our advice, Alias kept hobbling around. He sent a note down to us with one of the school boys, saying, "Please advise the minister of education that I am not going to teach any more because I am not able."

Alias packed up his few belongings and moved back to his mother's house, about a half mile upriver. Several days passed before we heard any news of him. When a report did come, it was that he was no better. Then one night we heard wailing from that direction. We feared the worst.

"Has Alias died?" we asked a passerby in the morning.

"Oh, no," he said. "The wailing was for his wife's grandmother. She is very sick!"

"I think I had better go and find out what is happening," Jeanne said, getting her medical supplies together in case she could help. Of course, I wanted to go along.

We crouched under huge leaves, held over us like umbrellas, to keep dry in an incessant drizzle as two teenagers poled the canoe upriver.

As we neared the house, we could hear more loudly the slow, rhythmic wail. It seemed so hopeless. Even though we were now accustomed to hearing wailing every sundown as people mourned for their dead relatives, I still found it hard to bear. I shuddered as we entered. Inside, the windowless house was even darker than usual due to the rain. The natural darkness amplified the darkness of oppression that I felt as we watched the people crying, clapping their hands in agony, pleading with the sick woman, "Don't leave us! Don't go!"

At last I realized, through the confusion surrounding the dying woman, that Alias was in the far corner of the large house. He lay groaning on his mat, while his mother paced back and forth wringing her hands. "My son! My son! You are dying! You are dying!" she wailed. A chill went through me. I wanted to run and leave this eerie scene behind me.

First Jeanne checked the grandmother. She was suffering from a stroke, and we could do nothing for her. Jeanne predicted that she would soon die.

She turned her attention to Alias. A look of relief swept over his face as he recognized us. Jeanne said over her shoulder in desperation,

"We've got to get him out of here!"

"Alias," she asked, "would you like to come and stay in our clinic house to be treated?"

"Oh, yes!" he said. He didn't need a second invitation. In spite of his mother's protests, he immediately ordered one of his wives to carry him to the canoe. She was large for an Aguaruna woman, and strong from carrying heavy baskets of manioc every day. She grabbed a few necessities—a couple of pots, some bananas and manioc, and their blanket. She threw these into a basket, which she carried in front of her as she carried Alias piggy-back. She hurried him down to the canoe; they were waiting before we even finished our good-byes.

I was relieved to be going, but as much as I wanted to leave, I felt overcome with deep sorrow for this household. I knew the people would spend the rest of the day, and maybe the next and the next, in darkness and misery. They would mourn, calling out to the spirit of their dying grandmother to return and not to harm them. They might even get sick from exhausting themselves in mourning. My own inability to cope with their gloom and hopelessness stung me. Did we really have a message of hope for the Aguaruna? When would we ever be able to make it plain to them?

"Grandmother has died," they told us the next day. Meanwhile, Alias relaxed on the platform bed in the clinic near our house. What a relief he felt. He was free from the confusion and oppression of his mother's house. But day after day his fever continued to rise; the swelling and pain in his feet and knees remained. Jeanne consulted by two-way radio with the doctor at our center, seeking his help in diagnosing and treating Alias. Alias agreed he would count on the medicines to heal him, rather than resorting to the shaman. Alias' mother, after overseeing the preparation of an underground chamber, the burial of her mother, and her purification rites, moved into the simple, thatched clinic with Alias. She urged him to call for the shaman. He refused.

"If you won't go, I'll go see the shaman as your proxy and find out myself who is causing this sickness," she finally said.

So she went to see the most powerful shaman in the area. He took drugs, chanted, and had visions on Alias' behalf. In his visions, he could see the phosphorescent darts implanted in Alias' body, alleged to be the cause of his illness. His mother returned, confirmed in her point of view; her son was indeed under a curse! The shaman's vision proved it was true! Alias would be healed only by going to the shaman himself; only he could extract these weapons of the sorcerer.

"No, my mother," Alias told her, "I will not go. I will trust the medicine to heal me."

However, many times during the days that followed, Alias was tempted to give up and to go to the shaman. He asked us to pray that God would heal him. We explained that if he wanted God to heal him, he must not be thinking about going to the shaman, as God had said that it was wrong to use Satan's power. But in spite of prayer, days went by with little improvement. My own faith fluctuated as I expected God to act, and yet He seemed to delay. In spite of my weak faith, God began at last to work; slowly, slowly Alias began to recover.

During these weeks when Alias was confined to the clinic, he began helping me translate Bible stories into Aguaruna. I was eager for him to know and understand more about Jesus' suffering, death and resurrection. The day our work brought us to the story of Jesus praying in the garden, and His betrayal by Judas' kiss, Alias was profoundly moved. In fact, he was speechless. He sat for five minutes, tears running down his face.

"How could anyone do such a terrible thing?" he choked.

I realized then how very much Alias loved Jesus and that he considered Him as his Lord. In spite of his recent suffering and struggles over sorcery, he was still awed that Jesus had died for him.

A few days later I heard Alias singing quietly to himself. When I visited him later, he showed me a hymn he had written about the death and resurrection of Jesus. He sang it with an Aguaruna melody he had composed. I was elated; our being in Nazaret *was* making a difference!

Despite my elation over Alias' progress, the months of his illness had been very trying for Jeanne and me. Though our first two years had gone fairly smoothly, and 1956 had started out the same way, the last couple of months had been very depressing. It seemed that there was one death after another. Everyone was either sick and dying or running to the shamans to see who caused the sickness of someone else, and therefore should be killed next. It seemed they talked only of death, revenge and killing. We understood the language well enough by then that we could no longer live in blissful ignorance of the fears that plagued our neighbors.

The stream of patients coming to us with malaria, vomiting, headaches, infections, cuts, and other complaints never ceased. But treating them was sometimes extremely frustrating. Jeanne began treating a baby, only to have its mother carry it away the next day before treatment was complete—because the baby was under a curse and our medicine would not help. A week later the baby died.

Alias was just beginning to feel better when Jeanne came down with malaria. She had to spend three days in bed. I had already had several rounds of it; the medicine had left me feeling dizzy and depressed.

At what seemed like the worst possible time, our most challenging patient was brought to us—a woman with severely burned feet. She had come several weeks earlier with what seemed like a bad cold. Jeanne had treated her and she returned home. However, a few days later she became paralyzed and lost all feeling below her waist. One day as she slept, the fire at the foot of the bed flared up and burned her numb feet severely.

In spite of the terrible smell of burned, rotting flesh and the horrible sight of the charred and draining burns, Jeanne bravely and patiently cleaned the woman's feet. I served as nurse's assistant, handing her bandages and medicines, but only the cloth tied over my nose made it possible for me to hold the woman's legs as Jeanne treated her.

For ten days the woman lived next door to us in the clinic house. We were never free of the smell of rotting flesh or of the woman's constant moaning. Both Jeanne and I found it difficult to sleep.

Our patient seemed to get no better, and we could do nothing more for her. Finally we decided her family should take her home. But first, somehow, we wanted her to hear about Jesus coming to earth to forgive us and change us. The teacher, David, talked with her. He explained in detail how God had sent His Son into the world and how he had died for our sins. But the only response our patient ever made was, "I'm not a sinner."

During these last months I had also been very frustrated in my language analysis. It was difficult to get it done. My language helper was never around. Even his son, an excellent language teacher for me, couldn't help me. He had just gotten married and was busy keeping his mother-in-law happy. Bringing her fire logs, searching in the jungle for palm heart and helping his father-in-law make a house and clear jungle took up all his time.

We began to think that no one cared enough to help us learn the language; perhaps all they wanted was our medicine. It seemed they thought only of sickness, sorcery, and revenge. In my fatigue and depression it seemed to me that no one wanted to hear about God. Why should I bother to tell them anyway?

When the float plane landed to take Jeanne and me back to Yarinacocha, we were more than ready for a change. I wondered whether we would ever want to come back. After long and difficult months in Nazaret, it seemed that Alias and his love for the Lord was our only real encouragement. How grateful we felt that he was well enough to steer the canoe as we went out to meet the plane.

6

Measles!

A month of vacation in Lima and the prayers of our colleagues was just what Jeanne and I needed. We felt restored; we had a renewed vision for our work with the Aguaruna. It came just in time to meet another crisis.

In January, 1957, the teachers came again to Yarinacocha for their annual three-month training course. We were delighted to see Alias arrive and to see that he had completely recovered from the fevers and swelling. He greeted us enthusiastically. He was eager to learn more!

But Alias' happiness soon turned to terror. He heard that someone had brought measles to Yarinacocha! The words of the diviner rang again in his ears. At last, death would catch him! He wrote his last will and testament in the form of a letter to his cousin back home.

Many times on the Marañon River, rumors of measles had sent the Aguaruna running away into the jungle. But first they would kill all the roosters so they couldn't crow and let the measles spirit know where they were hiding. The old ones always said that it was the crowing of the roosters that let the spirit of measles find them. They had to run away to escape the terrible death that measles brought. But now, Alias and the others felt trapped. There was no remote, uninhabited jungle to which they could run and hide. They were four hours away from home by airplane, and all the jungle around Yarinacocha was occupied by other indigenous groups. Where could they go?

Day after day the men waited in fear for the time when the fevers would begin, when the terrible rash and nosebleeds would plague them, when pneumonia and finally diarrhea would weaken them. They knew that only a few of them would survive. They knew of the houses full of dead bodies found along the river a few years before when one rooster after another had crowed and passed on the deadly spirit of measles.

Alias' fear was not in vain. He and sixteen other Aguaruna came down with measles, all at once. Jeanne nursed them constantly, giving out aspirins and checking temperatures. But her job was much more than physical care. She had to constantly reassure each teacher that there was plenty of medicine, that the doctor was taking good care of him, that no one was going to die. Dr. Ralph Eichenberger, the SIL center doctor, made rounds twice daily to check for pneumonia, deciding when to switch from aspirin to sulfas and penicillin. I had not been trained in nursing, but I helped as I could. I filled water jars during the day and accompanied Jeanne on her night rounds. I encouraged each teacher as much as I could, especially to drink water and to eat well. But they steadfastly refused to eat meat, because the old ones always said, "If you eat meat when you have the measles, you will die."

Amazingly, all the Aguaruna teachers had their turn with measles—and survived! They were very weak—but they survived! They could hardly believe they were all still alive.

We could always tell when one of them was feeling better by his request.

"Will you bring me soup—chicken soup with lots of meat, sister?" they would ask as soon as they knew they would live.

Of course, no one learned any pedagogy during the teacher training course that year. But each teacher learned a great deal about treating measles. This proved to be the most important lesson the Aguaruna needed for the year ahead.

Returning home late in March, the teachers found an epidemic of measles raging along the river in the Nazaret area. Many people were already sick, and many more had been exposed to the virus. Alias wondered what he should do. He had learned to give injections from the doctor and Jeanne during his own illness, and had learned much during the Nazaret epidemic three years earlier. But he knew the meager supply of medicine he had brought back from Yarinacocha would not be adequate. He visited each sick person and told him how the doctor and Jeanne had treated his own illness at Yarinacocha, and that he had recovered. Couldn't they see he was well? He would treat them, and they would get well, too.

"You must not bathe in the cold river when your fever is high," he told each one. "Stay in the house and cover up if you can borrow an extra piece of cloth from someone. You must drink a lot of water. I will give you medicine when you need it," he assured them.

"What shall I do?" Alias asked himself. "My medicine will not last for all the people." And then he thought, "I'll ask the officials in the government center up in the high mountains for help!"

Alias' request was sent on into Lima, and a doctor was sent out by helicopter to investigate the epidemic. He brought a large supply of medicine—and even a stethoscope for Alias. They made rounds together to visit the sick. The doctor showed Alias how to listen to the lungs of each patient.

"When it sounds like this give the person an injection," he said. "When it sounds like that, he doesn't need one yet." And so, patiently the doctor taught Alias how to know when pneumonia was developing.

"Do you know how to give an injection?" the doctor asked.

"I have been doing it the way the doctor and Jeanne taught me to do it at Yarinacocha," Alias replied.

"Good! I will teach you more about it now." And so he gave Alias further instructions on how to prepare and inject the medicines.

The doctor returned to Lima, and Alias was left on his own with a hundred patients, a stethoscope, a syringe, and ampules of penicillin and other drugs. He couldn't even begin to think of teaching school. Even if he had had the time, all his students were in bed or hiding in the jungle.

Day after day Alias hiked many miles, visiting every house scattered around Nazaret, carrying the medicines and stethoscope. He listened to lungs, dispensed pills or gave injections, checked the water jugs, and prayed for the ill.

The shaman's daughter was Alias' most ill patient. While Alias was visiting another house one day, her father called him.

"She is dead. My daughter is dead!" he wailed. Alias hurried back down the trail to her house. But it seemed he had come too late.

"She is dead," Alias thought. "Her hands are black; her eyes are rolled back." The people were already wailing loudly.

Alias remembered the story in Mark 5, which he had translated, of Jesus healing the little girl. He had a copy of this scripture with him, so he said to the people, "Don't cry. If you want her to be well, don't cry. Just think about God." Then he pulled out his papers and read to them:

> When they arrived, they heard the noise and the people wailing loudly. Going inside Jesus spoke to the people saying: "Why do you make so much noise? Why are you all crying? The little girl isn't dead, but only sleeping." The people laughed at Jesus very much, but He said, "You all leave." When they had left, taking the little girl's father and mother and his three disciples with him, Jesus went into the room where the little girl was on her bed. Then taking hold of her hand He said to her, *"Tabitha kumi"* which means "Little girl, get up." After he said that, she quickly got up and walked.

When he finished reading, Alias prayed simply, "God, you heal her. Raise her up so these people will believe and say, 'God really lives!'" He put the paper down and waited to see what God would do. The child opened her eyes. She looked around at them.

"Now, right now, I'll commit myself to Jesus," the shaman shouted. "She was truly dead; now she is alive. I really do believe God." His wife also agreed to trust in Jesus. Alias helped them to make a personal commitment to Christ. He was deeply grateful that God had again answered his prayer.

The people at Nazaret were getting better. The worst was over. Amazingly, only a newborn baby died—and that was because the mother was sick with a high fever when the baby was born and thus had no milk. Then a call came from upriver.

"People are dying up here. Please come to help us."

Alias took the remaining medicine and all alone went upriver to see what he could do. He had been the first Aguaruna to buy a motor for his canoe; now he put it to use, glad that he had bought it.

No one was around when Alias arrived at the first house. He pulled out the upright balsa poles that closed the doorway and went inside the seemingly empty house. A bit of light seeped in through the canes of the walls. As his eyes adjusted to the darkness, he began to realize that the house wasn't really empty. On the first sleeping platform lay a man—dead. Alias' eyes adjusted further to the darkness. He saw another platform; on it lay a child —already dead. Then he saw another man—dead. And a woman— dead. The house was full of dead bodies. Alias became afraid; their spirits might still be there! He hurried out, quickly replacing the logs in the doorway.

Farther on Alias came to a second house. He heard talking inside; it sounded good to hear voices! He relaxed.

Alias found his uncle Japa, who had survived measles years before, in this house trying to care for the sick. But he was very old, and the task seemed hopeless. Mostly he buried the dead.

"Grandchild[15], you have come!" Japa said. "How good that you have come!"

Alias immediately checked over the people who were still alive. From house to house he went with Japa, treating the survivors while Japa continued the miserable job of burying the dead. No one died after Alias arrived with his stethoscope and medicines, but Japa buried thirty-five of his relatives during the epidemic. "If only Alias could have come sooner," he thought. "If only more men knew how to cure measles!"

These exhausting, demanding weeks had a profound impact upon Alias. He became convinced that measles was not passed by a spirit or summoned by the roosters' crowing. Measles was a disease—spread by people who had the disease; and it could be cured with medicines and prayer. People didn't have to kill their roosters or die from measles. And he, who had been taught so much of hatred and revenge, discovered that he found more happiness in serving and in helping than he had ever found in killing. Praying and working with God's power was the kind of life he wanted—for himself and for his people.

7

Taking Roll Without a Pencil

During each training course at Yarinacocha, Alias and his fellow teachers learned the basics of school administration. Such matters were new and confusing to these novice teachers from the jungle. Paperwork was especially difficult for them. They were expected to jump from illiteracy, from being the first readers ever of their people, to keeping complex records in just a few short years.

One day Alias' administration teacher checked his school records. Mystified, he asked, "Wasn't anyone sick this year? You haven't marked any absentees in your register for the past school year."

Astonished, Alias replied, "Yes, but you wouldn't mark the students absent for being sick would you? They couldn't help that!"

The teacher of the course then called on a Cashibo student teacher.

"Why haven't you filled in all this part of your attendance record during the past year?" he quizzed him. The Cashibo teacher stood up, and after a long pause he said in faltering Spanish, "I called roll every day—but I didn't have a pencil to write down who was absent."

These revelations prompted a long discussion on the whys and wherefores of taking attendance and keeping class records. A Bora student teacher got up and explained that it was much easier to do the monthly reports if all the students came to school every day. That way the average daily attendance would be the same as the number of students.

"I tell all the children at the very beginning they can register only if they promise to come every day, all nine months," he explained.

"If you do that too, it will make it much easier for you to count."

What these novice teachers lacked in sophistication of records and paperwork, they more than made up for in zeal. They were eager to teach their own people, and this was the most crucial quality they needed for such an heroic undertaking. Helping to create the very first literate generation among their people was no simple matter!

Jeanne and I spent many hours sitting in on classes with the Aguaruna teachers. They were often entertaining. But we were also learning, acquiring more Spanish along with them. For years we spent every January, February and March at Yarinacocha with the bilingual school teachers.

More and more Aguaruna communities were wanting to have schools. This meant we had to constantly find new prospective teachers. Often some new man would turn out to be a long–standing enemy of one of the other teachers or prospects. One year we unknowingly invited one of Alias' enemies. Revenge killings between the two families had been responsible for Alias and his cousin going to jail. Their feud had never been terminated, yet now they found themselves side by side, studying together.

When it was Alias' turn to lead the Aguaruna teachers' Sunday meeting, he decided to teach from the newly translated Scripture.

"Do we Aguaruna ever forgive?" he dramatically opened his talk. In chorus, the thirty teachers shouted back, "No!"

"What a start for a Sunday sermon!" I thought.

Alias opened his typed booklet to the gospel of Mark. He read Mark 11:26: "If you do not forgive others, neither will your Father in heaven forgive your sins." He expounded on this text, applying it to the lives of the Aguaruna. Alias had his audience's attention to the end. When he finished speaking he went and sat down with his long-standing enemy. He put his arm across his shoulders.

My eyes filled with tears as I watched.

"At last, here is a man willing to practice what he preaches!" I thought. "God can even break through the Aguaruna's deep-seated patterns of hostility, mistrust, and revenge!"

Every minute I was not attending classes with the teachers, I was preparing more books for them. It was hard to keep ahead of the demand. Primers, writing guides, and arithmetic and social studies textbooks all had to be written or translated into Aguaruna. Those for the fourth and fifth grades had to be bilingual—written in both Spanish and the idiom, to help the children make the transition into Spanish. This way they might be able later to continue their education by attending a secondary school in Spanish, and they would know more of the Peruvian national life.

Each book had to be prepared, checked, typed, illustrated, and reproduced in the print shop before the teachers completed their training and returned to their villages in late March.

Along the way, I was continually working on language analysis. I needed to give it much more time—time that I didn't have. I was eager to get enough of it done so that I could spend more time translating the New Testament.

Jeanne and I, as well as the teachers, welcomed the end of each training course in mid-March. We all enjoyed the finale. As soon as classes were over, we all began preparations for the closing program, which would be presented to an airplane load of guests from Lima, including the minister of education, other presidential cabinet members, and various additional dignitaries. Many local officials and visitors were also invited each year.

The teachers would often spend their first salary advance from the Peruvian Ministry of Education to buy new pants and shirts for the occasion. They wanted to impress the officials from Lima, to look as though they belonged to the outside world now that they were teachers.

One might expect that in the presence of such important people the jungle teachers would be fearful or bashful. Yet they were neither afraid nor backward. They enjoyed all the pomp and ceremonies. They clapped loudly for the many lengthy speeches, even though they understood little.

Perhaps the most fascinating portion of the program for the guests from the coast was the demonstration of traditional Aguaruna greetings. Alias and his cousins dressed in native skirts, crowns, and earrings and painted their faces with red *achiote*. Then carrying spears, two of them would act out the role of visitors. Two others acted as hosts. In loud, rhythmic voices they shouted at each other alternately, repeating all their news and family genealogies. As they shouted, they swayed and stomped back and forth rhythmically, their shaking spears punctuating the air as they did their speech, and their earrings and seeds rattling. These greetings usually last an hour or two, but for the demonstration, they shortened them to ten or fifteen minutes.

After the demonstration of greetings, the Aguaruna entertained the guests with singing and dancing. It was hard for the visitors to believe that these men, who seemed to them to be wild, boisterous savages, were the same ones who had stood earlier, quietly dignified in white shirts, to receive certificates. The change of clothes and the face paint made them seem like different people.

During the afternoon after graduation, everyone enjoyed the contests between various teachers. Blowgun and archery competitions and a game of soccer were followed by canoe and swimming races.

The Aguaruna usually won the blowgun contest. They could hit very small targets many meters away with a forceful puff of air directed through their ten-foot guns.

In canoe racing, however, the Aguaruna were complete failures. The canoes provided for them were the shallow, round bottomed ones designed for the tranquil lake. They tipped easily compared to the heavy, square-bottomed and high-sided canoes built for the rocky, swift rivers in the Aguaruna area. Once when the starting "Go!" was given, the contestants dashed down to their canoes and jumped in. The two Aguaruna shot out onto the lake with a couple of powerful pulls on their paddles, only to find themselves swamped and sinking. They came up laughing uproariously.

"How can anyone go any place in a canoe like this?" they laughed.

"I'd like to race a Shipibo in one of *our* canoes on the Marañon River," one of them remarked. While they were swimming back to shore, the Shipibo contestants, used to the dainty canoes, were gracefully skimming over the water, out to an island and back.

The next day after the ceremonies, the guests would always enjoy a leisurely return to Lima. But for Jeanne and me, this was often the most hectic day of the whole year. We had to help each teacher and his family prepare to fly home. Blackboards, boxes of books, notebooks and other school supplies, medicines, all the personal belongings—including chickens, dogs, cats, plants and whatever else a teacher wanted to take back to his village—had to be weighed and readied for the flight. We could never be sure two days or even a week later, if the weather was bad and the plane couldn't fly, that the cargo would still weigh fifty-four, and only fifty-four, kilos. It was so easy to add a little something here and there.

When the last flight of Aguaruna teachers took off for the north, Jeanne and I would go home and collapse into the first comfortable chair. Peace and quiet! Wonderful silence!

We enjoyed the quiet for an hour or so—and then suddenly we really missed our noisy friends, who now seemed like family to us.

By mid-April, Jeanne and I headed back out to the Marañon. By then each teacher would have arrived in his village and enrolled his students, ready for another nine-month session.

I often marveled then, as I do now, at God's answer to the problems of bringing literacy to the many indigenous groups in the Peruvian jungle to prepare them for the day when they would fluently read His Word. Jeanne and I would never have been able to teach all the Aguaruna to read! But God, through the cooperation of SIL and the Peruvian Department of Education, was making literacy possible. The government not only paid the bilingual teachers' salaries, but also paid for their training and transportation. They even funded the printing of the books we prepared. Our task was thus simplified enormously; we prepared books, assisted during the training courses, and supervised the teachers in their villages.

When the Aguaruna teachers returned to the villages after the 1957 course, for the first time in four years I didn't follow them out. It was time for furlough to the U.S. A temporary partner replaced me, and continued the school supervision with Jeanne while I was gone.

But it seemed like I was returning to another world. After years in the tropics, Minnesota was cold! I wanted to crawl into bed and stay there all day—not just because of the cold, but because I felt so out of place. Except for my relatives and close friends, I couldn't remember people's names. Half the conversations I heard were meaningless after five years of very little U. S. news, and even less local Minnesota news. What should I talk about? My world of bilingual schools, linguistics, primer-making, and life in a jungle village seemed as remote as Timbuktu—and just as unimportant to the people around me. I felt isolated and odd. The loneliness I had so long anticipated in the jungle finally caught up with me in my own country.

Then a letter came from Jeanne. It wasn't full of joyful news, but at least it sounded real. Jeanne included a letter from David, the teacher at Nazaret that year. He wrote:

> Millie, I really like this letter you wrote to me. Jeanne is truly helping those who read and write Aguaruna words. All the Aguaruna at Nazaret want you to come back

quickly. They say, "Quickly, Millie, come back." Nazaret is better. Let's eat fish, palm grubs, greens, and palm heart.

I did adjust back to the U. S. By summertime, I was ready to teach at the Summer Institute of Linguistics held at the University of Oklahoma where new workers were being trained—a most refreshing time. I spent the school year studying at the University of Michigan, working on Aguaruna language material and cultural descriptions for my course papers. Then I returned to teach linguistics again at the University of Oklahoma. Letters from Peru helped to liven up those months of teaching and study, and kept the Aguaruna world alive in my heart and mind.

8

Who Listens to Women Anyway?

On November 7, 1958, I returned to Nazaret. It was already late afternoon when we circled the village and landed on the river. But the usual crowd of our friends eagerly waiting on the river bank was not there. Only a handful met the plane. The absence of so many worried us.

"Where are the others?" I asked as we finished our greetings.

"They are all at home in bed, very sick with the measles," they told us. "All those who killed their roosters and ran off to the jungle to escape last year are now very sick."

Another epidemic! And Jeanne had gone on furlough. My temporary partner, Lila Wistrand, and I hurried to our rather run-down house and dropped our gear. We quickly ate some of our left-over lunch and set out up the mountain side to visit our sick friends.

In each house we were greeted with, *"Jakattajai. Jakattajai."* ("I'm going to die. I'm going to die.") We assured our friends we would do everything possible so they would not die.

Twenty-four people had already died in the area, we found out.

Getting back to our house at nine, we blew up our air mattresses, hung our mosquito nets, and crawled in.

"What a reception!" I thought. "Sickness and death still reign. Satan seems determined to snuff out every life before the people can hear and understand the Word of God. If only I can get time to translate. Lord, please give me time to translate!" And so I fell asleep, exhausted my first day back.

During my absence, Alias had come a long way in his understanding of the small portion of the Word which he had. He was firm in his desire to follow Christ. He had gone to another area, Chiangkus, to teach school so that he might also teach the people what he had learned about Jesus. But after only two months, word reached him that his sister had died. He rushed back to Nazaret to the house of his brother-in-law Tomas, his fellow teacher at Nazaret. Thoughts from the past dominated him.

"We Aguaruna, when our sister dies we cannot forget it," he kept thinking. "She died of diarrhea and vomiting. Who caused her death? Someone is responsible. No one just dies." He felt anger, mixed with his sorrow.

Alias called in many of his relatives. Surely they were responsible to avenge this death; it was their duty.

"We will kill three people," Alias announced, and readily everyone agreed.

"Okay, tomorrow we will kill." And thus the constant wailing of the women was accompanied by the animated planning of the men.

But later Alias began to think. "Can God forgive me such great sin? If I do it, surely I will be lost. I must get away and pray."

Alone in the jungle Alias cried in desperation, "God, give me power over this sin!" But at dawn he and the other men were busily preparing for their revenge raid into enemy country. They checked over their feather crowns; they painted their faces with red *achiote* and their bodies with black *suwa*. They exchanged stories of their latest visions to bolster their spirit power.

"Okay, let's go," Alias said. But as they were leaving, ten-foot long spears and shields[16] in hand, Alias' little old mother came up to him. Even in her grief for her daughter, she felt concern for her impulsive son.

"My child, where are you going? What are you doing?" she asked.

"My mother, we are going visiting," Alias replied. But his mother knew the truth.

"You are going to kill. Don't do it. Don't go. All the fighting will start again. They will kill you. Don't go, my son."

Alias turned to the waiting men.

"Let's not go. Let's not kill," he urged them. But this change angered them. When did an Aguaruna ever turn on his word— unless of course he had had a dream? But this was not a dream; Alias was just listening to his mother. Who listened to women anyway? Everyone knew their opinions didn't count when it came to killing.

"Why did you say 'Let's kill,' if you didn't mean it?" they argued.

Alias calmly listened to their words of disgust and protest.

"God has truly helped me in this thing," he thought. "Before, once I had said, 'Let's kill,' I never turned back. But now I don't feel that I can kill any more. God saved me from that sin. I can't do it again." And so Alias persuaded them to abandon their plan.

Alias returned to teaching in Chiangkus. But he kept thinking about his sister's death and about his niece who had almost died the year before. Everyone had said his niece was under a curse.

"It's *tunchi*," they all had said. And the shaman had agreed. He even named the one who had had her cursed so they could avenge her when she died. But her father had decided to take her to the Nazarene mission. The missionary said that she was sick because of parasites. He gave her medicine and she got well.

This thinking led Alias to another remarkable conclusion, fitting for one so early named "the one who joins hands."

"When we could be getting well with medicine, we just kill other people because we don't get well," he decided. "What we need is a doctor and medicine. I will study medicine and cure people. Then there won't be any more killing. When the shaman says, 'It's *tunchi*,' I'll say, 'Maybe not. Why don't you try this medicine?' And then when the people get well the *tunchi* will be forgotten and no one will be killed."

Thus it was that Alias undertook another key step. Jeanne had gone home on furlough, so he decided to talk to me about his decision.

"Sister," he asked when he came back to Nazaret to see me, "can I study medicine at Yarinacocha? I can study at the clinic in the mornings and help you translate in the afternoons."

Dr. Ralph Eichenberger happily welcomed Alias to the clinic at Yarinacocha. In early December, 1959, Alias began studying medicine with him. Day after day Alias stood by the doctor and together they saw many patients. A very apt pupil, Alias soon began to recognize the symptoms of parasites, amoeba, and malaria. He learned how to treat infections and many communicable diseases.

In the afternoons, true to his word, Alias helped me translate. I enjoyed working with him; he was fun and challenging. I could see he had grown in his faith in Christ.

On Sundays Alias taught each new translated portion of Scripture to the teachers and their families. Everything was going beautifully.

But in January, Alias began to talk about going home soon.

"I can't figure out what the problem is, my brother," I said. "You are so happy at the clinic, and you wanted to translate." Then I thought, "Maybe it's money. Maybe I should pay him. He has his salary from teaching and I pay for his food. Maybe he wants more."

"Could it be that you want me to pay you more?" I decided to ask.

Alias looked shocked. "Sister, you can't pay me for helping write God's Word. That's what I want to do."

The next Sunday morning as Alias was teaching, he told the teachers about his sister's death.

"But I failed to help her know Christ," he said sadly. And my mother..." He couldn't hold back his tears. "I have heard that she is sick. I know that she has never committed herself to Jesus. My brothers, I am going back to Nazaret tomorrow and I'm going to tell her again that Jesus died for her sin."

At last I knew what was driving Alias from the clinic and translation which he loved so much. His sister's death had been a deep experience for him; he didn't want his mother to be lost too.

I returned to Nazaret on the plane with Alias to look for someone to replace him. I didn't know who would help me.

"If only David would come in," I thought. "He is one of our best teachers. He's finished the training course, so he's on vacation." But when I talked to him, David told me many reasons why he couldn't come to the center just then.

"Lord," I prayed, "will you find someone to go with me—or better yet, will you change David's mind?"

Five minutes before we were ready to take off, David ran up to the plane and said, "I'll go!" So with nothing but the clothes on his back, he climbed into the small plane, and we returned to Yarinacocha.

For a month David and I worked seven hours a day on translation. His brilliant mind often ran far ahead of mine. Like Alias, he had taught himself to type. He often typed up the material we worked on. In the evenings he supervised the study hall for the other teachers, especially helping the new ones. His own five years of training and teaching qualified him well to understand their problems.

I was thrilled with the way David took over the evening devotions and Sunday meetings for the other Aguaruna. He picked up right where his cousin Alias had left off. It was clear that his decision to give his life to Christ had been very real. One night his prayer touched me deeply.

"God, when we pray, even the hard things become easy." During his month of work we finished a draft of 800 verses for selected passages on the life of Christ—a feat which normally takes many times as long.

David returned to Nazaret in mid-February. I worked until early March polishing the material with a second language helper. But then I was convinced I needed Alias back; he was so good on details. But Alias had gone back up into the mountains to Chiangkus. Even if a plane went out to Chicais on the main river, it wouldn't be able to contact him—a day's hike away.

Then I heard of an emergency flight going to Chicais! A young man studying in the Swiss training school for indigenous pastors had received word of his father's death; they were sending a plane to take him home to Chicais.

"Lord, maybe it seems ridiculous to ask you for Alias to come back on that plane," I prayed, "but I've asked you for some pretty ridiculous things before, and you've done them. I know you have given me this job of translation. You're responsible to provide the way for me to do it. You know I need Alias right now. Please bring him in on this flight."

The day before the plane left for Chicais, Alias decided he needed to see his brother Dantuchu, at Chicais. He took off by trail, planning to spend a day and then return to Chiangkus. On that one day, the plane arrived. Instead of returning to the village, Alias got on the plane and came to Yarinacocha.

How delighted I was to see Alias!

"Sister," he beamed, "I have good news! My mother and many others have come to know Jesus! Now let's work on the translation!" And work we did. The life of Christ was born into Aguaruna words, so that He might live in Aguaruna hearts.

9

Pouring Water on Fire

In the three years since 1955, when Dantuchu had left Alias and their cousin David to teach at Nazaret, his school downriver at Chicais had grown to 140 students, with five teachers. The community had built five dormitories to house boys from distant rivers.

The increasing prestige and remarkable growth in the educational system were destined to play a key role in the age-old conflict between Aguaruna and outsiders, as Dantuchu began to discover.

Dantuchu skillfully took advantage of the patterns of his own culture to strengthen loyalty to the schools. By regularly putting on school assemblies for the constant stream of visitors from other areas, he showed how much the children were learning. The people begged him to let their boys come to school too. As they saw more and more results of having a teacher in the community, they pleaded for schools in their home villages as well. They realized that a school brought medicine, help in coping with outsiders, and the knowledge of God, as well as literacy.

"I don't go in and tell them they should build a school," Dantuchu explained. "I just plant the idea, and let them decide they need it. If it's their idea, then it will be their school. I don't put myself up as the big boss. When there are fights, I try to stay neutral so that I can help everyone."

"But what shall I do, sister?" he asked. "Requests for schools keep coming. Where can I get more teachers?"

Dantuchu's own ingenuity solved the problem. He invited young men who had in previous years studied in Spanish at the Nazarene mission to come to Chicais so they could be ready in a couple of years to begin as teachers.

As new schools started in community after community, it was the older teenagers who were most eager to learn. With books in their own language and enthusiastic teachers who saw nothing unusual about seventeen-year-old first-graders, many of these older students learned quickly. Many begged Dantuchu, "Help me become a teacher!"

Dantuchu's leadership was widely recognized; he was indeed like a chief. Aguaruna came from all over to consult him. Where should their children go to school? Was it true that 5,000 colonists planned to move into Aguaruna territory? Would he help them get justice from a trader who had taken their rubber but had never paid them? On and on they asked, wanting help with many problems. All up and down the main river people formed new villages to be near the schools and the teachers with their medicines. The traditional independence began to be tempered by a sense of cooperation.

Dantuchu encouraged the cooperation and the desire to learn.

"The man who has a machete is able to do something," he said. "The man who has both an ax and a machete is able to do much more. In the same way the person who speaks two languages can do much more than the man who speaks only one language." Dantuchu told both students and teachers this often as he encouraged them to learn Spanish.

Dantuchu himself was the perfect example of using both "ax and machete." With his own language he taught school, pastored the community, encouraged his countrymen to ask for more teachers, explained to them the need for getting land titles, and showed them how the traders were cheating them by underpaying them. With Spanish he defended their land rights, stood up against the abuses of the traders, reported to his supervisors the need for schools, and negotiated in Lima when necessary on behalf of his people.

Jeanne and I could see that Dantuchu had not just become a teacher. He was also the proverbial "doctor, lawyer, merchant, chief"—and pastor too!

Dantuchu put in long, busy days. Along with the constant interruptions for help, he had to direct the five-teacher school and care for the many boys away from home. He knew he must keep them busy and happy. He was most concerned to teach them, as well as the community, all he knew of the gospel. Each Wednesday evening, he held a very down-to-earth prayer meeting for interested students. He prayed for them, and they prayed for him. They enjoyed singing very much and eagerly bought the Aguaruna hymn books he offered them.

By 1958, Dantuchu's spiritual work in Chicais was very evident. Believers gathered to hear the Bible stories Alias and I had translated. The student prayer meetings were well attended. One boy enthusiastically said, "I don't understand the Spanish Bible, but I understand the Aguaruna Bible stories well."

Many young men committed their lives to Christ as Dantuchu taught them. Some later became teachers, and took the Good News with them to other villages.

This new spirit of cooperation among the Aguaruna did not include everyone in the area, however. Serious conflicts were brewing between the Aguaruna and the Spanish speakers who had moved into the area, fueled by generations of misunderstanding, conflict and mutual distrust. These traders were fighting to destroy the bilingual schools. Their living depended on keeping the Aguaruna illiterate and ignorant of Spanish and arithmetic. Many never even weighed the huge balls of rubber, laboriously collected and prepared, that the Aguaruna brought them. The Aguaruna knew little of the value of their rubber, and less of the value of the items the traders gave them in exchange. They often paid many times the value of items they received.

If an Aguaruna wanted a box of shotgun shells, he would bring a jaguar skin. But he didn't know that a box of shells cost only fifty *soles* (two dollars) and the skin was worth four hundred *soles* (sixteen dollars)! A box of matches was clearly marked "fifty *centavos*," but many Aguaruna paid *twenty* times this price! Many times an Aguaruna would trade for a gun, bringing rubber for years, only to be told is wasn't paid for yet; he may, in fact, have brought enough rubber to buy ten guns!

Not all Spanish speakers were against the Aguaruna, Dantuchu discovered. As the coordinator of bilingual education in Lima heard more and more about these abuses, he was indignant.

"Dantuchu, you must organize a cooperative. You must help your people learn the value of their rubber and hides. Instead of coming to the teacher training course this January, work on the co-op. Get the people of the Chicais area to collect 5,000 kilos of rubber. Then take it by raft to Iquitos and sell it for eight *soles* a kilo.

With this, buy cloth, guns, shells, machetes and all the things the people want. This will be the beginning of the cooperative."

The Aguaruna were enthusiastic. Chicais became a hub of activity. The men built a warehouse and began to fill it with huge balls of smoked rubber and smelly hides. Dantuchu spent long hours weighing rubber and recording names and weights. Jeanne spent many days helping Dantuchu, both that first year and in those to come.

The coming of the *kistian*[17] (outsiders), who forbade revenge killing and head-slashing as punishment for adultery, had upset the old Aguaruna system of law and leadership. The Peruvian government began to see the need to reinstate order. They wanted the Aguaruna to follow the norms of the country, to have civil government. A government-appointed coordinator of bilingual education for the jungle was sent to visit each school, and to set up civil government in each village. The coordinator, with the teacher as translator, told them that they must select someone besides the teacher to be the mayor of their village; they must also select an assistant mayor.

The idea of democratic leadership was totally new to the Aguaruna; they were used to a system based on power, fear, and supernatural forces. Thus, the idea of *voting* as a means of determining leadership was scarcely fathomable to them. When it was time to vote, the first name was read, and everyone's hand shot up. The second name was read—and every hand shot up again. The third name was read; again everyone voted. It took much more talking to get the principles of election across. This experience was repeated in village after village, but finally a mayor and assistant mayor were named for each village.

These newly elected leaders gathered at Chicais for their first conference on civil government. The large, oval-roofed co-op warehouse buzzed with activity. Representatives from a dozen communities along the Marañon River, seated on balls of rubber, lined the walls of the large room, brightly lit with two pressure lanterns. Skins of various wild animals hung overhead, swaying in the breeze. Their shadows danced impishly, as though falling from some giant kaleidoscope overhead.

About fifty mayors, assistant mayors, and other delegates attended. Their head-pieces portrayed the mixture of old and new cultures: Daniel Boone style skin crowns, red and yellow toucan feather crowns, shell crowns, seed crowns, and even a handkerchief tied over the forehead in the fashion of the rubber-gatherers. Typical long-haired, skirted, gesticulating, shouting, old-time Aguaruna sat beside short-haired, trousered men of the younger generation. All intently discussed important civic problems; everyone talked at once. Now and then, with a shout and a whistle, Coordinator Dantuchu demanded the floor and restored order.

Actually reinstating law and order in so many scattered communities was not achieved as easily as were the elections, however. The unrest caused by the influx of outsiders continued; conflicts with the Spanish-speaking neighbors increased further.

A major confrontation followed the typical pattern of mushrooming revenge. It began when a teenager decided to exercise his prerogative as an Aguaruna man and object to his sister's marriage. Following tradition, he intended to insist that his sister return home because her husband was mistreating her. He got his friends together, and set out to bring his sister back home. He had no idea that the tempest he was about to create would reach the Lima newspapers, hundreds of miles away across the mighty Andes Mountains.

On his way upriver, the teenager and his friends overtook a soldier and some other Aguaruna traveling to the fort upriver. They invited the soldier and his companions to travel with them in their canoe. They accepted.

When they all arrived at his sister's village, the rescue party found it deserted. Everyone had gone hunting. So the boy and his friends entered his sister's house. They destroyed all the clay pots, and what little else they could find. Then, taking the soldier along, they all ran off to the jungle to wait for the return of the sister.

In the evening, the sister and her husband returned to their raided house. They began searching for the attackers—and find them they did. But they were able to catch only the soldier; their fellow Aguaruna were too swift for them. Since the soldier spoke no Aguaruna, and they spoke no Spanish, they could not understand his explanation of his happenstance role in the raid. In their anger, they beat him, and then let him go.

The angry soldier went immediately to the Spanish settlement downriver, and told his story to the authority, a man appointed as justice of the peace. The next day a revenge party of traders, Aguaruna acculturated to the mestizo culture, and soldiers from the fort, made their way upriver. By the time they reached the

Aguaruna village, the people had fled, knowing only too well that they would be punished for touching a Spanish speaker.

Unfortunately, two families, including the new village mayor, had been upstream for several days. They knew absolutely nothing about the rescue raid or the other events that had just taken place. When they returned to a deserted village, they assumed the others were out fishing or hunting. As these two families were innocently getting settled back into their homes, the revenge party arrived. Without asking any questions, the men from downriver beat the two men and raped the women.[18] Then they took the families as prisoners back downriver to Nieva. There they strung them up by the feet, naked, and beat them further. They tied just-boiled eggs into their armpits. Through an interpreter they taunted them.

"Millie and Jeanne have been forced to leave the country!" they lied. "The coordinator of bilingual schools is in jail in Lima. You should all quit working rubber for Dantuchu's cooperative; nobody will buy it from him anyway." On and on they jeered.

The torture went on for three days. Finally, not wanting the Aguaruna to die in their town, they let them go. Once back in his village, the mayor, who had suffered the most, sent word to Dantuchu.

The report confirmed the rumor that Dantuchu had heard. Once he got the story straight, Dantuchu left quietly for Lima to get help. He wanted to be sure the stories about Jeanne and me and the school coordinator were false.

When Dantuchu arrived at our group residence in Lima, our director, Mr. Townsend himself, was there. He went with Dantuchu to visit the school coordinator. Together the three of them called on the minister of war and the minister of education.

The minister of war sent a colonel to investigate the whole affair. Accompanied by Dantuchu and the coordinator, they flew in one of our SIL planes back to the Aguaruna area. They went to investigate one problem, and found another. Things had continued to mushroom. The Aguaruna told Dantuchu that the *kistian* had announced that there would be no bilingual schools, and that all the Aguaruna children must go to the Spanish school downriver. A boat had gone upriver to collect the children!

Dantuchu passed this information on to the startled coordinator. Both he and the colonel wanted to look for the boat immediately. All three hurried back into the airplane. Ten minutes' flight upstream they indeed spotted a boat full of children. The pilot set the plane down alongside it.

It was hard to tell who was most surprised. Two traders, with guns in hand, and two teachers from the Spanish school downriver sat amid crying children.

"The traders insisted we gather up the children," the embarrassed women argued.

"No," the traders insisted, "it's just the other way around. These women begged us to come and help them capture the children."

The bilingual school coordinator, a man of forceful personality, quickly dispensed with the accusations.

"You fly these women back downriver to Nieva," he ordered the pilot. Then he turned to the children.

"The bilingual school teacher will be there in your village when it's time for school to open in a few days. Don't worry." He then faced the traders. "You men! Take the children home right now!" he ordered them.

"I'm pouring water on fire," he sighed to Dantuchu, explaining his role in reducing the conflict.

After a thorough investigation of the original problem, the school coordinator wrote a detailed, fiery article for a Peruvian magazine. He decried the injustices against the jungle peoples. He also had newspaper articles published on the matter. From that day forward, the bilingual school system had new prestige among the Aguaruna, but increased opposition from the Spanish settlement downriver.

10

Roasted Frogs and Hummingbird Meat

The boundaries of Jeanne's and my education in the ways of the Aguaruna were continually enlarging; our classroom included the picturesque rivers and the dozens of thatched-roof villages and schools scattered along their banks. As we offered the teachers and others our help, we were continually enriched and expanded by their knowledge and encouragement. Riding the crest of a new wave, however, was never dull, neither for us nor for them.

During the first years of our visits for school supervision, Jeanne and I had given two weeks to each village. But as more teachers were trained and sent to new locations, supervision became a tremendous task. By 1960 we had to visit thirty-three teachers, with a thousand students; by 1963, we had to move every two or three days in order to visit each location in the two months we could give for this task. Such a timetable allowed no leeway for the state of the weather or the condition of the river. Our classroom without walls moved on schedule—no matter what.

In October of 1963 we started our trip in Nazaret, since it was the village farthest upriver. The men had built us a raft of ten large balsa logs lashed together with vines, which would take us downstream from village to village to the last school. Jeanne and I sat on the open side of the raft, with our belongings stowed behind us on a platform enclosed on three sides. Usually three older students from each village served as our guides. They would steer us through the turbulent waters to the next village, and then return home by trail.

Our river travels always proved to be very educational, in both natural history and the ways of the Aguaruna. Only a few places on the river were truly frightening. However, our steersmen usually entertained us with the history of all the river accidents they could remember. As we left each village for the next, the people would always playfully say, "If you don't drown, we'll see each other again."

On one leg of our trip that year, the river was especially turbulent. The joking stopped, and we learned more about the very real dangers of traveling in swift, rocky waters. The Aguaruna insisted we ride ahead of the raft in a canoe. Their foresight proved to be valuable.

The raft, carrying all our belongings, caught on the rocks in mid-river, and teetered precariously. Jeanne's frantic shouts of instruction were lost in the roar of the river. I stood on the beach, gripped with fear, tears running down my cheeks. All I could think of was my first complete book—the manuscript of the Gospel of Mark, lying inside my aluminum suitcase on the low side of the raft. I should have been thinking, "Thank God they insisted we come by canoe rather than riding the raft." But instead I thought, "Oh, God! Help us! We have the radio with us, but—oh, how stupid! The antenna is on the raft! Now we can't even call the center and tell them of our tragedy."

"God!" I prayed, "Have we come through the treacherous rapids only to lose everything on this rock right in front of our destination?"

Our Aguaruna friends did not panic as we did, fortunately. Masterfully and methodically they paddled canoes from the bank alongside the raft. To me, an apprentice in the ways of the river, each moment seemed an eternity. The raft looked as if it would turn over any minute and dump our precious equipment and supplies into the raging waters. But the men shifted the load from the raft to the canoes, and moved everything to the river bank. They even managed to drag the raft off the rocks and in to shore.

We breathed a prayer of thanksgiving. Everything was wet, but nothing was lost. After I dried out my precious manuscript, I discovered it was still quite readable.

Not all of the river trip was so eventful. For many long stretches it seemed we barely moved. The scenery passed like a slow motion movie, the sound track tuned to the Aguaruna sense of humor. We could easily see the people on the banks, some in their gardens, some fishing, and some working in their houses.

"Who are you?" everyone who saw us would shout to the steersmen.

"It's me. I'm Agkuash," they were expected to shout back. But our guides were usually tired of such a simple answer. Here was a great opportunity for fun! More often, they joked.

"I'm a *kistian*," or, "I'm a mechanic," or "I'm a pilot," they would say. One answered, "I'm your mother-in-law whom you love."

"Where are you going?" the people would shout next. But instead of the usual, "I'm going downriver," our guides would shout back, "I'm going to Lima to see the president," or "I'm going to Iquitos to buy a wife," or "I'm going to the city to buy a car."

"What are you doing?" our helpers would shout to the men on the shore, who countered with equally entertaining answers. One man yelled back, "I'm working here in my garden so the snakes can bite my child!"

Even having our everyday needs met was a source of learning for Jeanne and me. Since we visited many communities only once a year, everyone was eager to take care of us. Often when we arrived, the people were still making last-minute preparations—bringing mats for our beds and logs for our fire, putting up a shelf for medicines and books, walls to keep out the chickens, or a roof over a new outhouse hole.

Even taking a bath was a lesson in God's creativity in nature. We had a variety of bathtubs. At times we could have a lovely, clear stream; at other times deep, cold water. Sometimes we could sit under a tumbling waterfall for a good back scrub. At other times we could only dip water from a spring and throw it over ourselves. My favorite bathing spot was a huge waterfall, which crashed into a deep stone pool about ten yards across before rushing on into a lower waterfall. The lush ferns and brilliant flowers that thrived in the misty spray made it seem a paradise.

Our food too came in a variety of forms. When I visited one school by myself, the teacher asked the students to be sure and bring me food, so I wouldn't get sick. One small boy generously brought me special delicacies—one well-roasted frog, two juicy palm grubs, one black beetle, some delicious palm heart squeezed in his dirty little hand, six peanuts—and one very small hummingbird, only partially defeathered. He even promised me more for the next day.

The hummingbird was very special, I discovered.

"Men can't eat hummingbird," he told me. "They would become like it, always wanting a drink every little bit. But hummingbird is good for women because it will make them thirsty often, and they will remember to give the men something to drink. But they shouldn't eat the tongue; they won't be able to talk well if they eat that."

I might not have kept my good health so well if the boy's mother had not also brought me wild turkey and boiled manioc—less exotic but more appetizing staples. With these, and the bananas, corn, and sweet potatoes that others brought me from their gardens, I stayed very healthy!

Once in the classrooms, several problems inevitably caught Jeanne's and my attention. One was the tables and benches in every school. For people accustomed only to the simple furniture of platform beds and a few log stools, the idea of adapting a desk and bench to each child in school came slowly. Even though we had instructed the teachers many times, each year we found that many little children could hardly get their chins on their desks—much less write on them. I remember one child who watched his teacher from *under* his desk top, instead of looking over it.

So adjusting the furniture was usually our first task. One of us would spend a few hours with the older students and a teacher changing the length of the bench and table legs. This was simple enough. The legs were forked sticks pounded into the ground; the seats and desk tops were formed by laying old canoe sides on the sticks. Year after year we would show each crew how to measure the bench sticks by the back of the knees of each child. Then, with the child sitting down, they could measure the height for the desk by where his elbow came.

Jeanne and I enjoyed leaving each school knowing that every student's desk was the right height. But we also knew that by the next year the sticks would have rotted, and the new sticks would probably be too long again.

While one of us worked on tables and benches, the other often worked on book inventory, helping the teachers to figure out book orders for next year, and to discover any surplus books we could send to another school.

As school supervisors, we also reviewed many things the teachers had learned in the teacher training course, to see how they put them into action. We received the teachers' official reports, helped them with teaching methods and lesson planning, and worked together solving problems. We found many problems unique to a first-time, pioneer school system.

One problem was attendance—not absenteeism, but over-attendance. Inevitably we found that many little children, too young for school, had been sent by their parents; they were eager to get in on the action. The first year Alias taught at Chiangkus he had seventy-six students! We suggested he send home all those under ten years of age, as he couldn't possibly teach so many. Later, supervisor Dantuchu found that Alias still had fifty students, so he sent home twelve more. But even thirty-eight were a handful. The next year we assigned another teacher to help Alias, and the children all returned—with new ones to boot.

Keeping a proper register, full of unaccustomed details, was another challenge to the teachers. No one knew the children's ages or birthdates, since the Aguaruna had never kept birth records. We had to help the teachers become astute guessers. If a child could reach over his own head and touch his ear on the opposite side, we knew he was at least six. After guessing the child's age, the teacher would ask the parents which season he was born in. Those born in the dry season were assigned to July 28, National Independence Day. Those born in the rainy season took January 1 as their birthday. Anyone looking at early school registers on the Marañon would no doubt have wondered why Aguaruna babies were born only on those two days. To make things more accurate, the teachers learned to record all later births in their community for future school registrations.

Names were problems too. In Peru, the Spanish culture dictates using two last names, one from each side of the family. So we taught the teachers to use the child's given name, plus his father's name for the first surname, and his mother's name for the second surname.

Our work didn't end with the school, since we were concerned about the health and spiritual well-being of the Aguaruna too. Even after an exhausting day's work, the evenings had many challenges for us. Jeanne had to see all the medical problems the people had saved up for her visit. The teachers treated people as they could during the year, but the difficult cases they discussed with Jeanne. Often she would have to consult the doctor at Yarinacocha by radio. But sometimes, there was no way to help because the real problem was one of belief.

One such situation was especially disconcerting. The teacher's newborn baby had just died, and he was in despair.

"I didn't know she was having the baby," he said over and over, condemning himself. "When it was born I was out hunting. I didn't know the baby would be born that day. I shot a white crane. I would never have shot it had I known. And now the baby's dead."

It hurt us to see our friend so needlessly taking the blame for his baby's death. But nothing we said would persuade him he was not responsible for the death of his first child, his first son. Everyone knew that a man must not kill a white bird while his wife is giving birth.

Jeanne and I continually hoped, as well as prayed, that medical knowledge and training would soon help the Aguaruna relinquish such beliefs and thus lessen their fears and suffering.

Another time, when our canoe pulled up to the river bank near a village, our first sight was of a shriveled old man hunched up in a small leaf shelter near the river bank. I was startled by his appearance; I felt repulsed by it. He seemed too ugly to look at, yet I couldn't help staring at him. His nose, and part of his mouth, were completely gone. His throat had been eaten away. Now, since he could swallow little, he sat waiting for the inevitable: death by starvation.

Jeanne and I found that the old man was a victim of leishmaniasis. Jeanne had treated many patients at various stages of this disease. Treatment was lengthy, and costly beyond the resources of most Aguaruna. Sadly, for this man, the disease had progressed too far for any treatment to be effective.

A dreaded disease in the jungle, leishmaniasis seems innocuous in its early stages. An ulcer develops on some part of the body as a result of a bite by a sand fly. This lesion heals, only to reappear years later as the organism attacks the soft tissues of the nasal passages and eats away at them. It causes eventual disintegration of the tissues, with grotesque disfigurement. Our SIL colleague, Dr. Ralph Eichenberger, later conducted an extensive research campaign for this disease, and taught the Aguaruna themselves how to recognize and treat it.

We often chatted with the teachers in the evenings—and stretched our knowledge of their language and beliefs along with the teachers' minds. Questions about science, geography, history, and religion kept us talking. The more the teachers learned, the more they wanted to know. They began to wonder if their beliefs about earthquakes, rainbows, lightning and other natural phenomena were true.

After one such discussion about Scripture with the teacher and a group of older students, the teacher asked, "Can you explain this? A person is dying. He says, 'Tomorrow at sunset I'll beat a drum if I go to a good place.' He dies. He doesn't believe in Christ, but the next day everyone listens at sunset and they all hear the drum beating in the distance. How can this be if he didn't believe?"

"There are always people beating drums in the late afternoon," I suggested. "Probably if you listen, you can hear them almost any day." But no one seemed too satisfied with my answer—and I found myself wondering about it. Maybe the dead man's spirit *did* beat the drum and deceive them into thinking he was happy.

"How can you dream about a person who is dead?" The questioning continued. "Does his spirit still walk on earth? You said if he believed in Christ his spirit is in heaven. Then how can we dream about him?"

"But a dream happens in the mind; a person's spirit isn't really present," I tried to explain. But this didn't fit their idea of dreams—a matter of utmost importance to the Aguaruna. Each one told me many dreams that had come true. In fact, many times they were of me. One time when I had unexpectedly flown up to Nazaret with some guests from Yarinacocha, one of my closest friends greeted me excitedly, "I knew you were coming. I dreamed about you. I've already prepared the chicken for us to eat." And sure enough, I found a delicious dinner all ready!

Each year as Jeanne and I visited villages, we noticed more tension. Frustrations were building up. Many times our discussions turned to problems arising from the coming of outsiders.

"What do they mean, saying we must ask for our land? If it's ours, why do we ask for it? How can it belong to the government when it has always belonged to us Aguaruna?" Often they told us of their anger towards an outsider who had moved onto their land and was abusing the people.

Fortunately, the Aguaruna didn't come just for medicines or for discussions. Often in the evenings they would come, songbooks in hand, saying, "Let's sing." How exciting for us to come into a village and meet new people—and then discover that they were already believers! If I asked, "When did you commit yourself to Jesus?" they would often answer, "When the teacher taught us God's Word."

How grateful Jeanne and I felt! God was using the bilingual teachers, not only to educate their own people in reading, math and a knowledge of the world, but also in the knowledge of Himself. Our school visits, intended to help and encourage the teachers, became a rich source of learning and great encouragement to us.

11

Strange Customs

For several years, in addition to the bilingual teachers who came to Yarinacocha for training, a number of qualified young men came to study Spanish for a year. This study would prepare them for the next teacher training course. This final stage of Spanish preparation culminated their five years of primary education in their local bilingual schools.

Sharing in the students' lives during this time not only taught us about our differences but also that we had similar needs and problems. We found that like anyone in the process of learning a new language and a new culture, the Aguaruna had a great fear of failure. In their own culture they were relatively secure, just as Jeanne and I were in ours. They knew how to do anything that needed to be done, just as Jeanne and I knew how to do what our culture required of us. Now, suddenly they were meeting circumstances that could lead them to failure, to losing face. This had repercussions in their school performance.

Often when the Aguaruna were given an examination in the Spanish prep school, or later in the teacher training course, they would turn in an almost blank paper. Yet when we questioned them we would find that they knew the answers. When we would ask why they hadn't written the answers down, they would say, "I was afraid I might be wrong." They considered it better to have a blank paper than to put down an answer which might be wrong.

Just as Jeanne and I had experienced in learning both Spanish and Aguaruna, it was difficult for the people to move into a whole new world, where they did not know the language or culture.

Without these crucial tools, they felt stripped of their primary means of interacting with other people. They were, as we had been, subject to constant mistakes, placed back at the level of children once again. Limited in communication, their intelligence and ability which gave them status and security back home were not readily expressed. Their responses appeared childlike to others because of their limited Spanish, just as our meager Aguaruna had in the beginning often hampered our responses and made us appear childlike in their world. They had the uneasy feeling that people were laughing behind their backs—and often this was true, as the ignorant who did not respect their struggles made fun of them.

Even at Yarinacocha the Aguaruna often felt very keenly the strain of trying to communicate. They were never quite sure when and how to speak to strangers.

One day Spanish prep student Roberto began working for my colleague Kenny Gammon at the maintenance shop so he could earn money for clothes, books, and other spending.

"I'm afraid," Roberto told me as he left the house the first day. "I don't know any Spanish."

But that night he came back, elated.

"Kenny and I get along fine," he said. "He doesn't know much Spanish either!"

Kenny and Roberto became the best of friends and worked together at learning Spanish after that.

We—and the Aguaruna—discovered that our tastes in and beliefs about food could differ considerably.

One evening Kenny and his wife Ginger, invited all seven students and me for supper. Ginger served fried cubes of alligator tail. It tasted delicious—like deep-fried chicken. After dinner, Kenny asked the men if they knew what meat they had eaten.

"Maybe it was chicken," one of them suggested.

"No," Kenny said. "It was alligator."

They all turned green—and I thought for sure some of them would lose their supper. No Aguaruna ever ate alligator! But they admitted it had tasted good.

When Jeanne and I left Yarinacocha to make our school supervision trip, Ginger and Kenny looked after the men who continued to study at Yarinacocha. When a flu epidemic hit, the Gammons took care of them, to see that each one got medicine and plenty of fluids. One day Kenny thought, "If I were sick, what would I really like? Jello!"

"Ginger, fix a big pan of Jello, and I'll take it to the dorm for our friends. A refreshing bowl of Jello will be just the thing for them."

"Whatever is this?" the students protested. "It's alive! It jumps around on the plate and in your mouth!" None of them could manage to swallow even their first bites. Kenny, most disappointed, asked, "Well, what do you want?"

"A big bowl of boiled banana drink," they said. "That's what we need when we're sick!"

Another day Ukash complained about the food.

"I just can't eat that cow's meat. Where can we get some fish? How can anyone eat cow? It tastes horrible. It makes me nauseated. At home we don't even eat deer meat. How can we eat a cow? It's even bigger!

"You know, deer meat is taboo. After all, it is bigger than a person, and it might possess the spirit of your dead mother or grandmother. Spirits enter into deer. You can tell by the way they look at you with big sad eyes."

As for the cows, Ukash didn't claim there were any spirits in them; but he just couldn't get the meat down. I could see that his fellow students agreed.

Sometimes our strange customs actually seemed ominous to the Aguaruna.

"You should really be afraid of Cecil!" one of the students said to me one day.

"Why?" I asked, mystified that he could have such a view of our center director.

"Because he kills dogs. Anyone who kills dogs is a murderer. He might murder someone."

"Oh, Cecil is only getting rid of some stray dogs that are causing problems on the center," I assured him. "We have to protect people from rabies. These dogs might bite us." But the students weren't too impressed with my explanation.

"Anyone who kills dogs is wicked," they insisted. "We Aguaruna never kill dogs. We let them suffer and die of old age, like people. After all, dogs also go to heaven."[19]

The student told me a story from his ancestors which proved his point. God judged a man who had killed many people, including one whom he killed without a justifiable revenge motive. God ordered that a fire be built around him because of his sin. The man became thirsty and a black dog came and gave him a drink.

"You see," he said, "Our black dogs are the ones who refresh us when we burn."

"Well, that's humbling," I thought. "How quick people are to think badly of the Aguaruna for revenge killing, yet when they judge us by their standards, *we* seem to be the barbarous ones for killing dogs!"

Another time a young Aguaruna startled me with his frank comments about our customs.

"You don't love your families at all," he told me after attending the funeral of the child of one of my SIL colleagues.

"Oh, yes! We do!" I objected. "What do you mean?"

"You just throw them away in the ground," he said. "You don't even put a roof over the place you throw them in."

"But the person isn't really in his body anymore," I explained, "because he has gone to heaven." But my explanations didn't help.

"I didn't see anyone wailing—not even the mother!" he continued. "Americans don't even love their own children."

This experience, more than any other, reminded me how difficult it is for the Aguaruna to understand and accept another culture, so different from their own. "They judge the ways of our culture to be *wrong* and *inferior* because they don't understand the reasons behind the actions. Since what we do doesn't fit into their system, it creates all kinds of misunderstanding. They interpret what we do by the way they think, instead of by the way we think. But then! Isn't that exactly what most of us do too?"

I thought back to one dark night at Nazaret when Jeanne and I had been talking to our neighbor. The rain fell gently on the thatched roof as we all sat on the palm bark floor around a small, flickering kerosene lamp.

"You don't love your families, do you?" our friend asked after a pause in the conversation.

"Why, yes! Of course we do!" we objected.

"Oh, no, you don't," she insisted. "You just bury your dead relatives and abandon them. You don't go back and look at them again or even really cry."

"But what more can we do?" we asked her.

"We really love our families," she went on. "We never abandon them. We never forget those we love who die. We dress them in their best clothes and paint their faces. We wrap them carefully. We go every day to the place where they are resting and we think about them. If it is an adult, we put the body on a platform and keep the fire burning at the foot of the bed to keep him warm. Or we make a wooden box tied with vines to lower into a chamber in the ground so we can easily pull it up. We bring food every day for the spirit to eat. We look regularly to see how the body is decomposing. When only bones remain we put them in a clay pot and either put them in the rafters of the abandoned house in which we have guarded the body, or bury them in the pot. All this time we wail whenever we think of the dead person.

"When it is a small child who dies, we bury him right in our house, under our bed. We don't want him to be lonely. Until only bones are left we occasionally dig him up to see how the body is decomposing."

"But how can you do that?" Jeanne and I gasped, appalled.

"We cover our faces with cloths. When the flesh is all gone, we put the bones in a clay pot in an abandoned house. Some people even take the bones along when they move."

I was deeply moved by this account. It certainly did seem like love to pack up the bones of one's loved ones in clay pots to take along when moving. "How comforting it will be," I reflected, "for the Aguaruna to know that God has made *them* to be clay pots filled, not with dead bones, but with His own living Spirit—and that He will never abandon those who are His own.

12

Shall We Kill Again?

I can't go another step," I said to Jeanne as we stopped to rest had to once more. But I knew that if we stopped for long we wouldn't be able to walk again; our muscles would tighten up and refuse to move. We had to keep going!

The Aguaruna teenagers were taking us from the main river by trail to Chiangkus in 1960 to visit Alias and his year-old school. They kept encouraging us with, "It isn't far now." But they had been saying that for an hour, and the sun would soon be setting. We had left the river early that morning.

"It takes about five hours to Chiangkus," they had said. But we had already been hiking for more than eight! All day it seemed as if we would just struggle to the top of one mountain, only to find that the trail descended again. Continuous rain made each descent precarious. We slipped from tree to tree, grabbing handholds as we went. This worked fine—except when the trees had thorns! These thorn trees, with sharp spines protruding directly from their trunks, looked like holdovers from some medieval, armored forest. They were one exotic species I could have lived without. I often laughed when I saw them, thinking that Tarzan's famous shrieks were probably caused by an encounter with one of them.

As long as the trail was narrow enough to have trees on both sides, we managed to stay on our feet. But after a while, it seemed impossible. The people of Chiangkus had wanted to welcome us with a beautiful trail, so the week before they had widened much of it. Without treeholds we slipped and slid, and our muscles hurt more and more.

Going up each mountain was less precarious than going down, but more tiring. I would always run out of breath before we ran out of mountain. It seemed we had to ford a stream or inch our way across some chasm on a slippery log in each valley. Once we waded downstream for half an hour, sometimes waist deep in tumbling water, before we picked up the trail again.

Jeanne and I felt total relief when at last we saw Alias and his fellow teacher coming toward us on the trail. Chiangkus must be near!

The men showed us the house they had built for us. We gratefully accepted their help with stringing up our mosquito nets and inflating our air mattresses. I could never have gotten up enough wind for that! Alias sent someone for water; we washed up and put on dry clothes. How luxurious it felt to be warm and dry again—and to eat the steaming fish soup and flaky boiled manioc dished out to us.

As much as Alias and all the curious neighbors would have liked to talk all night, they could see we were exhausted. Each one left, saying the appropriate, "Go to sleep."

And sleep we did! We slept like rocks—and in the morning we felt just as immovable. I was sure I would never be able to walk again. Every tiny motion brought me pain. For three days we hobbled around, flexing sore muscles; every step was a rueful reminder of our hike. I determined to climb a hill every day thereafter, so that when the time came to return, I would be in condition.

We were delighted to see Alias again and to catch up on all his news. In the mornings we helped him in the school, and in the afternoons and evenings he helped me with translation or discussed medical cases with Jeanne. He also helped us to get acquainted with the rest of the villagers.

Alias recounted the events of his previous year at Chiangkus.

"I came here because they needed a school and they needed God's Word," he reminded us. "The village leaders here really took care of us. They built our house, the school, the church, the soccer field—and even prepared gardens for my family.

"These people are killers too," Alias continued. "Kuji is the strongest. So it was a risk for me to come. But once I had said, 'I'll go,' I kept my promise. I gathered all the people and told them why I had come. I said, 'Let's learn new things. Our ancestors were very wicked. Let's leave all that and learn about the good life, with no fighting. Let's teach the children to live well.'

"That's the way I talked to the old ones here. I said, 'If people die, we just kill. If anyone dies, we say, "It's *tunchi*," and we kill. But we don't really know. Maybe we have killed for nothing. This is very bad, this killing of innocent people. Let's leave off.' Like that I talked to the old ones.

"'Let's have the children learn to work paper,' I told them. 'Let's all be brothers. God is really alive. He exists. He created us all and all we see. God is in heaven and He made all. Let's obey Him.' Talking like that I began to tell them about Jesus Christ. All year long they listened. Only four truly believed last year. But this year more are believing. Chief Kuji almost believes."

We were fascinated as Alias continued.

"Chief Kuji has a reputation among all the Aguaruna. He is old now, but he has led many successful wars. When he heard me talk about God, he hadn't thought much about God before. He thought only about revenge and killing, about sickness and sorcery, about evil spirits and the power of the *ajutap* which had come to him when he drank *baikua* as a teenager. All his visions have come true. He has been a great chief and has killed many people. He has had four wives and has stolen many women. He is respected by all.

"But after hearing about God, Kuji thought, 'Can it be that what Alias says is true? Maybe killing *is* bad. Maybe God really did say, "Don't kill, don't lie, don't get angry, don't steal women, don't deceive, don't say untrue words about others." If God said all that, then surely I have displeased Him very much. And Alias said God must punish us for sin unless we commit ourselves to God's Son, Jesus, who came to earth and was killed to throw away our sins. Why would He do that? It must be true that God really loves us. He doesn't want to punish us. But I've sinned the most. Surely, He'll not forgive me!'"

Alias told us how week after week he continued to read God's Word and to teach the songs in the oval, thatched church Kuji had had the men build. Alias had asked to have it on top of a hill, away from the rest of the village. He often went up there by himself to read and to pray for the people.

During our stay at Chiangkus, Alias began to see the answer to his prayers. Late one afternoon, Kuji and his whole family (three wives and many grown sons—about twenty people in all) came to visit us as Alias and I were working on translation. Alias again read and explained the passage to them. They began talking about Jesus.

"I'm going to commit myself to Jesus. I'm going to do it now," Kuji suddenly said.

Everyone sat silent, impressed as the mighty chief began talking to God. His was no simple prayer; it was an oration! Loudly, rhythmically, he prayed, punctuating his words with "*ma, ma*" hesitation markers and occasional emphatic spitting. He would give himself to Jesus!

And Kuji did just what he said he would do. He committed himself to Jesus Christ. He thanked Him for His death, and for God being willing to forgive his sins. At his urging, each one of his family prayed and asked for God's forgiveness, including his three wives. They all did what Kuji expected of them; the purpose of their visit was fulfilled.

The whole community took notice. Word quickly spread to all the Aguaruna that mighty Kuji had become a Christian. One after another the people of Chiangkus followed Kuji's example. Many afternoons as Alias and I were working, we were interrupted by callers. Would Alias pray with them so they too could give themselves to Jesus?

Jeanne and I returned to the Marañon River, rejoicing as we continued our visits to other schools. Only weeks later did we learn of the testing of this new commitment for the believers at Chiangkus.

As word of Kuji's conversion spread, people from other villages started coming to hear Alias' teaching about God. One day a group from Kingkis started eagerly for Chiangkus to hear Alias. But a certain Aguaruna, appointed by the Spanish speakers of the mestizo community of Nieva to have authority over the Kingkis area, stopped them. He was against this new religion that Alias was preaching! Besides stopping the group, he arrested them. He cut off the hair of all the men, a terrible disgrace for them. Then he put them in a hole so deep they couldn't get out. He and his sympathizers dropped branches covered with tiny, stinging "fire" ants on top of the captives. The agony was almost more than the men could stand; they tried desperately to get out.

After further torture, the captives were set free. But instead of going home to Kingkis or on to hear Alias, they went on upriver to see Kaikat, the newly appointed Lieutenant Governor for the Aguaruna. Surely he would defend them.

"You go and capture the man who is causing trouble, and bring him here," Kaikat told them. "I'll punish him myself." He also wrote a note to Alias, asking him to help in the capture.

Alias and the men he rallied captured the leader from Kingkis who had made the people suffer so much. As they were taking him upriver, several canoeloads of men from Nieva followed them. They caught up with Alias and his prisoner. The mestizo party outnumbered them, and easily won back the captive. They beat up many of the people of Chiangkus and took their canoes and guns, as well as two hostages.

One of those captured was Kuji's son. Alias felt a great responsibility for this. He sent a letter to Nieva.

"Let these two men go or we'll come and get them—and we'll kill to do it," he wrote. But the answer came back, "We won't do it."

So Kuji and Alias conferred. Kuji got all the people together.

"Let's go and kill all of them," he urged. "The old ones, the children, the women—all of them!"

"Okay, let's do it," Alias agreed.

But then Alias thought, "Again we are going into wickedness." He turned back to Kuji and the others.

"No. Wait," he said. "First let's get all the people together, including the women and children, to pray. While we wait for the others we have invited to help us wipe out Nieva, let's pray."

Everyone trudged up the path to the church on the hill. As they prayed together, Alias pleaded, "God, keep us from this sin. Send our people back."

As the people prayed and waited for the other groups to arrive, the two men who had been taken captive walked in. Kuji's anger melted away when he saw his son. They decided not to kill. Once again Alias saw God answer his urgent prayer for deliverance from killing.

As Alias reflected on this, he thought, "God has given me victory over the desire to kill. For seven years I have not killed. Now I want to go further and tell His Word. Many of my relatives do not know. This year I told God's Word to all who live in Chiangkus. There is not one who is not committed to God, except one who is a killer. All are following Christ. This next year I want to go to my other relatives, where Agustin and Cristobal are teaching. They are young, and never having killed, are not respected. The others won't listen to them. So I must go to tell them about God's Word. I have been one who sinned. Now I very much want to tell them so that they who have also sinned may know and be as I am."

In 1961 Alias had another serious crisis to face. We were worried when he didn't arrive until the very last day of the teachers' conference. He had two good excuses, we found out: the national census and a charge for murder.

Rumors of a killing in revenge for sorcery were flying. The murderer was reported to have said, "I am Alias," and now many people were saying, "Alias is the killer."

Deeply disturbed, Alias told his plight to his fellow teachers.

"I couldn't possibly have done it," he argued. "I was busy in Chiangkus working on the census at the time that happened."

After much discussion, it was agreed that an imposter from Uut probably was the killer. And so a new rumor up-staged the old one.

Alias' other crisis revolved around the census. Each teacher of the area had been summoned to Nieva on a certain day to pick up census books for his community. But the letter saying to come to Nieva on the seventh did not reach Alias and his five fellow teachers at Chiangkus until the tenth. Since it was impossible to be there on the seventh, they didn't go at all.

The man in charge of the census was furious at the supposed insubordination of these six teachers who failed to turn in their census reports. But Alias, meanwhile, had made careful lists of all the people in the areas where he and the five teachers worked. An excellent typist as a result of working on translation, he typed the lists up neatly and made the trip to Nieva. He took them to the census office to turn in, but the offical insisted they couldn't be correct, since they were typed.

"The Americans must have just made this all up and have given it to you to get you out of trouble," he taunted. "After all, Indians living in the jungle don't type." And he refused to accept Alias' lists. Alias had no choice but to take them back home.

The next time Alias visited Nieva, he found out that the matter wasn't settled.

"You are under arrest," the town officials told him. "You get twenty-four hours in jail for failing to turn in the census."

"Okay," Alias agreed, "but first give me ten minutes. I'll be right back." He went straight to the priest in charge of the mission, an unlikely ally in such a conflict.

"They are putting me in jail," he told him.

"What have you done?" the priest asked.

"Nothing. I've done nothing," Alias replied. "I don't have time to go to jail. I have work to do. I must get back to my school."

Then recognizing him as a bilingual teacher, the priest changed the topic.

"Why don't you become a Catholic so you can drink fermented manioc drink? As an Evangelical, you can't drink."

Alias' reply took him totally by surprise.

"I can drink if I want to. Mark 7 says it's not what goes into a man's body that defiles him, but what comes out of his heart." He then gave the priest a sermon on the sins of Mark 7. When he finished, the astonished priest asked, "Who are you, anyway?"

"I am Alias," he answered.

The priest, won over by Alias' poise and intelligence, and what he had heard of his changed life, got up and went with him to the officials. Playing on their old fears of Aguaruna ferocity, he ordered the justice of the peace to let Alias go.

"Do you really want Kuji and his men to come and kill us all?" the priest demanded. "You know that Alias' friends will avenge him if you put him in jail."

13

Can the Truth Be Known?

"We'll kill off all the *kistian*," the Aguaruna threatened often during 1961, a year of increasing unrest. We heard many loud discussions about land rights, the incoming road, and the problems of outsiders. We heard long tales about the previous generation killing off every outsider who came. "We can do it too," they boasted.

"And what about Millie and me?" Jeanne ventured once as the men sat talking.

"Oh, no. We won't kill you. You work with the teachers."

Though it was reassuring to know we weren't considered to be like other outsiders, we nevertheless felt the tensions of the Aguaruna. The stress they felt over the problems of a changing culture and the outside world pushing in on them led to an upsurge of revenge killings; we heard more reports of suicides.

Even the toughest leaders found it difficult to have a foot in each of two worlds. Dantuchu took the co-op goods to market and sold 81,000 *soles* worth of hides and rubber (equivalent to $3,240). When we arrived at Chicais on our supervision trip, Jeanne audited the books and found the co-op well in the black. The co-op was now the owner of a boat—and of a motor besides! In spite of this remarkable success, Dantuchu didn't want to continue due to his constant worry about the co-op as well as his personal problems. Even his return trip had been depressing. He had been sick, and then was stuck for eight days on the downriver side of the fearful Manseriche gorge. He was tired of the responsibility; he was depressed and his spiritual life had declined.

Following the custom of his ancestors, Dantuchu had taken a young girl as a second wife, a common practice for men of prestige. Had he totally followed the Aguaruna way, this would have created minimal problems. But in wanting to emulate the larger Peruvian culture, he had gone against his own culture and had thrown out his first wife, the mother of his many children.[20] This behavior had resulted in a long series of problems. Several other teachers, accustomed to following his example, also took second wives. Three suicides resulted, as the spurned wives sought revenge or tried to escape the shame they felt. All this weighed heavily on Dantuchu.

As appointees of the government to supervise the schools, Jeanne and I were responsible to oversee the teachers' involvement in community affairs. We were supposed to "find out the truth" regarding any problems. Yet we never could be sure which side was relating the facts. As more and more of our time was taken up with community affairs, we discovered that "truth" was considered secondary to family loyalty. A witness had to be evaluated by his family connections. Finally, we also concluded, "The truth cannot be known," a favorite saying of the Aguaruna.

Yet we were supposed to listen and to offer solutions for the problems. Often days passed with no visible progress toward solutions. We just heard one tale after another: problems, problems, problems! Teacher was against teacher, or teacher against community, or community against community. We found that our role as arbitrator was impossible when the truth was never evident.

Jeanne and I were also frustrated in our desire to be peacemakers. We had come to bring the gospel of peace, and yet we saw so little evidence that peace had come. True, the old pattern of revenge killing was changing, but it seemed it was only being replaced by a new pattern of revenge: denouncing one another to the *kistian* authorities. Opponents raced to see who could get in his denouncement first; the relationship of the content of the denouncement to the truth did not matter.

We wearied of the stories. Yet we were responsible to the Peruvian coordinator of bilingual education and were expected to report to him about the teachers under our supervision.

Besides the renewed conflict among the Aguaruna themselves, serious confrontations were occurring with the outside world. Strong competition between the bilingual schools and the monolingual Spanish schools was cropping up, a conflict best understood from a historical perspective. Because the Spaniards who first came to the new world considered that the native cultures were pagan, they endeavored to "Christianize" or "civilize" the people by imposing the Spanish language and culture and the Catholic religion upon them. By trying to stamp out all facets of life that reinforced the supposed "paganism" of the native peoples, they created great hostility and seriously reduced the morale and self-esteem of many groups. Numerous groups have continued to lose their languages and cultural identity as a result of the Spanish cultural conquest, even though any armed conquest ceased long ago. Thus, the pride and morale of the Aguaruna and other groups is strongly tied to the issue of education in their own language.

Jeanne and I, along with the Peruvian Ministry of Education, encouraged the formation of more and more bilingual schools. These schools offered indigenous groups primary education in their own languages, along with the learning of Spanish as a second language. But at the same time, the Spanish mission at Nieva began opening Spanish schools in or near the same villages which had bilingual schools. They insisted that the only way the Aguaruna could learn Spanish was to go to a school where no Aguaruna was spoken. In spite of this, the Aguaruna themselves wanted bilingual schools.

More and more reports reached Jeanne and me of this conflict over the schools. One community built itself a school, and while the people were waiting for the bilingual teacher to arrive, a Spanish teacher came. Since he insisted on teaching, the people burned down the school they had just built.

"It's ours," they said. "We built it. If we don't want a Spanish teacher, we can destroy it. We built it in order to have a bilingual school."

Day after day as Jeanne's and my time was taken up with listening and trying to encourage peaceful coexistence, my frustration grew. As we spent hours and days discussing things about which it seemed we could do little, I longed to be working on the language analysis and translation. It was hard to believe that God was going to use all these conflicts and delays for good. Was all of this part of His mixing clay with ash?

14

Rafael Killed the Devil

The Aguaruna were learning to mix with each other and the outside world in new ways, particularly through the development of the school system. The bilingual teachers conference, held in July during the mid-year school vacation, became an annual event, a key time for sharing problems and solutions. I marveled as I saw God's hand in this, bringing unity and cohesion to men and groups who so recently were distrustful or hostile to each other. I thought again of Mamai working and melding her clay before she shaped her pots.

Besides the teachers, many delegations from various headwaters in the mountains came to these meetings to present requests.

Each conference was rich and colorful in more ways than one! All the visiting men dressed in their festive best—fresh skirts, clustered strands of beads criss-crossed on their bare chests, and shiny beetle-wing earrings and colorful crowns. Everyone talked at once, loudly, anxious to have his say before this respected assembly of teachers. The topics of discussion ranged from the solemn to the hilarious, sometimes going far afield from the classroom. They exemplified in a touching way the enormity of introducing both literacy and the role of teacher into a culture for the very first time. Identifying and defining the role of teacher was no easy task when they had no precedents to follow and when leadership was beginning to shift from the power of killing to the power of cooperation.

During the meetings, the teachers would sit on logs around the walls inside a large house, leaning comfortably against the palm slats. Dantuchu, very much in charge, would put another log in the middle of the dirt floor. One delegation at a time was invited to sit there, center stage. As Dantuchu questioned them, the session secretary took careful notes in Aguaruna. Most delegations were intent on getting a teacher for their community. Dantuchu asked key questions.

"Where is your community? How many adults will work for the community? Have you built a house for the teacher? Have you built the school yet? Have you cleared a soccer field and planted a garden for the teacher? How many students might come?"

Each member of each delegation insisted on giving a speech, Aguaruna style. If there were eight men in a delegation, their request was repeated eight times—in a loud oration, punctuated appropriately with spitting and foot stomping.

The teachers considered each request. Some communities they pronounced ready for a teacher. The delegates for those returned home, happy to know that the next April they would have a school if a teacher became available. Those who were turned down heard the reasons why: not enough students, lack of preparation, not enough community cooperation. They determined to come back better prepared the next year.

After the visiting delegations left, the teachers quickly dispensed with mundane affairs, passing school statistics on to the secretary. Then they would settle back to share problems and to swap adventures. Each one was eager to tell what had happened since they had been together in March at Yarinacocha. Jeanne and I would listen, fascinated, to what seemed a "can-you-top-this" show. No Aguaruna ever had stage fright. Hour after hour the men loudly shared their problems and boasted of their accomplishments. This interchange was far more than social convention. It reflected the increasing complexities of the teachers' lives, thrust upon them by their new leadership roles.

One young man had waited ten days for the rain to abate and the creeks to go down so he could hike the two days over the mountains to his school.

A new teacher had been embarrassed because he had no medicines and couldn't help the people. Since he hadn't received a salary yet, he couldn't buy medicines—but the people in his village didn't understand.

Another told how the community at Kingkis had split because of sorcery. The fathers were afraid to let their children go to school, lest they be placed under a curse and die.

Antonio suffered, trying to handle five levels of instruction, with thirty-three children.

Alias reported that he had no ink. How could he work on his registers with no ink? He also had discovered a new disease, which he called "boa's urine." One person had died of this. A woman from Chiangkus had been kidnapped. How could he help to get her back?

The biggest problem in Cesar's community was his own wife! She wouldn't work. He brought her chickens; she let them die. She let his pet birds get lost. He wanted to invite people in to eat, but she cooked no food. If he beat her or scolded her, she immediately told her family and they sided against him. His position was intolerable and fearful. What if she committed suicide? Her family would kill him. Could he be sent to a different community next year?

The big problem in Wawaim, according to Andres, was the waterhole. Some type of worm or leech was in it, which might kill the two cows he was raising for sale. And what could he do about the ticks and the horseflies that stung his cows? Bathing them with soap didn't help. These animals were important to his prestige; he had to keep them healthy.

"Bathing the cows in creosol should keep the flies and ticks away," Kunyach suggested.

Ukash had bought two large gardens with his own money so there would be food for the boarding students.

Shajian reported that in his village the two men trained at Yarinacocha in agriculture were fighting a losing battle with the mice. The mice ate the rice, the peanuts, the manioc, even digging it up for themselves. They snipped off the young cacao trees as soon as they grew above the ground. Did anyone have any suggestions?

Pablo had lost all his books when his raft upset.

"Ah," Miguel said, "Now I know whose books I have. Some of my students from Wawik found a box of notebooks going round and round in the whirlpool at Jangkichak and rescued them. If you stop by on your way home from conference, I'll give them back to you."

Kunyach was unable to celebrate Independence Day because his students were sick with measles and colds, but he was eager to announce that he was teaching them from the newly published Gospel of John.

Chujai told how the highway from the coast had arrived at his village, causing many problems. The soldiers bothered them continually, wanting food and women. The men had to stay home from fishing and hunting to guard their gardens and their women.

Senepiu had been assigned to teach in Imasa, but his relatives there had killed someone in that village, so he couldn't go there. Anyone in his clan was fair game for revenge; he didn't want it to be him! He went to Tuntungkus instead. He taught in his own house while the men built the school. But even in his home village, there were problems. The shaman had given one of his students, a seven-year-old girl, as a wife to a man who lived in another community. The girl's father was very angry and demanded, "Senepiu, you get her back. You're the teacher, aren't you?" He hadn't yet succeeded in returning the child to the parents and the school.

As if these problems weren't enough, Rafael had killed the devil. He had gotten excited over some shadows in the night. He shot at them, thinking it was the devil. He had actually killed a large rodent, on its way to the waterhole. The people teased him mercilessly; his fellow teachers were only too happy to join in!

The conference gave David the opportunity to emerge as an excellent leader. As the men reported, discussed and arrived at solutions hour after hour, he helped them change their focus from their personal situations to the broader aspects of their roles. For instance, since the schools had been open for several years, teachers had students at many different levels. This made it impossible for them to do their best teaching. David suggested they build central schools at strategic locations, where the advanced grades could be taught. Students in the early grades would remain in their own villages. He suggested that each teacher give part of his salary to help build these central schools. They would need gardens, dormitories, classrooms. He even suggested they offer scholarships for deserving students who had no family to help them.

This particular suggestion of David's met with disagreement. Few of the other teachers had the vision he had. They didn't like the idea of taxation. Their salaries belonged to them—even if they did use much of the money to buy medicines, clothing and food for their communities. Why invest in something they wouldn't be personally involved in? No, they would rather continue to teach four or five levels. Only a few years later, however, David's colleagues were ready to accept his idea, and central schools for advanced students were established.

The teachers did agree on other matters. They decided not to allow a student to transfer from one school to another without a letter of good conduct from the teacher. They didn't like students just taking off when they got unhappy and then becoming a problem to another teacher. They agreed students should not drink fermented manioc beverage. If a married man wanted to come to school, he should first work enough to buy his wife a machete and other tools for her work in their garden.

Another problem was the shortage of Scripture books. The 500 copies of James, just off the press before the teachers had left Yarinacocha, were insufficient. Several students cried because they didn't get a copy. In another school, a boy had actually stolen a copy from another student—an unheard of action. When his misdeed was found out, he was so upset he drank poison *barbasco* root to cover his embarrassment. Fortunately, he didn't die, for which the teacher was thankful. And fortunately also, Jeanne and I had brought another 200 copies with us. We gave these out, wishing all the problems had such immediate solutions.

During the evenings of conference week, the teachers sang and studied the various portions of Scripture we had translated. They prayed together about the problems presented during the business sessions—a dramatic shift to interdependence for men long accustomed to fierce independence. Staying up all the last night to distribute the school books, supplies and medicines that the plane brought for each village seemed a fitting culmination for such cooperation.

15

A Wounded Leg—A Healed Heart

For the wounded or ill Aguaruna help was often far away, where it would take days or weeks to be reached. Some fortunate villages had a more hopeful resource—the small short-wave radios used by our linguists and some of the bilingual teachers. These could summon help for serious problems. Pilot Bernie May answered one such call en route to another village. He stopped off to check on a patient reported to be in serious condition.

When Bernie set the plane down on the water, the villagers eagerly awaited him. They led him to the house of Aneng, the injured man, who was stretched out on his sleeping mat. But they were not at all eager for him to examine Aneng's wounded leg. Everyone protested.

"Don't touch it! Don't touch it!" they warned.

Bernie, thinking their fears were irrational, was determined to check the wound. After all, the doctor had said to examine the patient to see if he really needed to be brought in to Yarinacocha for treatment.

"I ought to at least clean it up and take a good look at it," he thought as he surveyed the mess of filthy, blood-soaked rags tied with a vine.

Bernie opened his emergency kit and unpacked the few gauze squares he always carried. As he began unwrapping the leg, everyone, including the teacher, became frantic.

"No! It will bleed! He'll die!" they pleaded. But Bernie continued unwrapping the wound. Suddenly he was covered with blood.

"My God!" Bernie prayed. "The artery is severed!" He slapped the gauze squares over the wound. The blood shot right through them. He grabbed at anything he could get his hands on and pressed the wound as tight as he could.

"Oh, why didn't I listen to them? Will I ever get this man to the clinic alive?" he wondered frantically.

Finally Bernie managed to stop the bleeding. But as he reached the river to gas up and check the the plane for the four-hour flight back, the teacher called after him.

"He's dying! His leg is all black!"

"Oh, no! I've got it too tight," Bernie thought. But he answered, "Bring him to the plane—quickly!" Several men carried Aneng down the steep bank to the airplane.

Bernie loosened the bandage a bit, only to have more blood spurt out. But whenever he tightened it, the leg throbbed and was very painful. He tightened and loosened it, tightened and loosened it. Finally, when he thought he had it adjusted just right, he took off with his patient. But at each stop he loosened the bandage for a minute, and then tightened it up again.

An hour away from Yarinacocha, Bernie radioed me to meet the plane with a vehicle to take Aneng to the clinic. He also radioed the doctor to be ready.

Many gentle hands moved Aneng from the airplane to the jeep. As we rushed up the hill to the clinic, I kept wondering, "Why must things like this happen when Jeanne is gone?" Jeanne was in Lima caring for an Aguaruna teacher who had needed surgery for a broken arm. The week after she had left, another teacher was brought in with hepatitis, and I was having to look after him. Now this! Alias had taken the year off from teaching so that we could translate, but it seemed we could get nothing done!

I tried to shake off my mood of self-pity. "Poor Aneng," I thought, "This jeep frightens him as much as the plane did—and all this with a severed artery."

As the doctor began unwrapping his leg, Aneng panicked. He grabbed my hand in fear and desperation.

"Make the doctor stop," he begged. "I'll die, I'll die," he wailed.

"He says the blood will really come out if you unwrap it, doctor," I said in English. But to Aneng I said assuringly in Aguaruna, "He has to look at it if he is going to fix it. It's all right. You won't die."

Then suddenly the doctor, the pillow under the leg, the floor—everything—was bright red with blood. I couldn't look again. I knew I must keep Aneng's attention away from the blood, and keep myself from fainting.

The doctor tried to clamp off the artery; the nurses started transfusions. They made many attempts to stop the bleeding; they gave more transfusions. There was more bleeding, more attempts, more transfusions. Because Aneng's wound was already two weeks old, it was difficult to secure the artery.

By the third day, Aneng was frantic. He ordered me to get a plane immediately; he wanted to see his mother before he died. He wanted to die at home.

After yet one more transfusion, which included blood donated by Alias, Aneng felt better, but his wound continued to ooze. Then what we all feared came true; gangrene set in. The doctor told me Aneng must have surgery.

"I think it's too late to save the leg," he said sadly. "But the hospital will not amputate without the patient's permission. You'll have to talk to him about it."

"Oh, God," I prayed, "how can I tell him this? Aneng has never been outside of his home in the mountains before. Everything is strange and fearful. What can he do in the jungle where the dexterity of feet and hands is all important? What can he do without a leg? He is still a young man." I tried to imagine what it would be like to be told, as a youth of twenty-five, that I could choose between losing my leg or dying.

As always, Alias proved to be the strong one. I told him what had to be done. In the morning, we sat with Aneng, and Alias explained the need for surgery. Aneng burst into tears. He cried and cried, so that I thought he'd never stop.

"What about my wife and children? I won't be able to take care of them. My wife will probably desert me. Maybe it would be better to die—but I would rather die at home." Aneng wept—and I sat and wept with him.

Aneng had no way of knowing what was involved in surgery such as an amputation or of living in a hospital for an extended time. But finally he stopped sobbing and told Alias he would go to the hospital.

The doctor took us to talk to the surgeon and to make arrangements at the small hospital nearby. I welcomed the comfort and help of nurse Patsy Adams, a dear friend working with the Culina. She offered to go with me and to stay in town with me as long as necessary.

After the surgeon examined Aneng's leg and studied the x-rays, he said he would try to save his leg by cutting away the gangrene. Only as a last resort would he amputate. I felt a surge of hope!

The surgeon invited Patsy and me to stay with Aneng during surgery. I said I'd stay only until Aneng was unconscious. Once he was asleep, I left. The surgeon and his nurse would do their best. Patsy held the flashlight for them as they worked, since there was no electric light.

For a week Patsy and I lived in the only hotel in the small river town of Pucallpa, on the sticky red banks of the snake-like Ucayali River. We trudged back and forth through the muddy roads to the hospital constantly, to be there for every visit of the doctor, every injection, and all the daily routine. Since Aneng understood no Spanish and his glossy hair was still uncut and hung far down his back, he aroused great curiosity among the patients and nurses. We tried to buffer the shock he felt by being with him. Alias faithfully came every afternoon to give us a break for supper and a rest.

We were all very grateful that the surgeon had not amputated. Eagerly we waited to be sure Aneng's leg would be well. Once the crisis was past, we returned with Aneng to Yarinacocha. Alias took over most of his care, giving out his prescribed medicines and bringing him food.

"What an incredible change," I thought. "Aneng is from a family with whom Alias and his relatives have been feuding for many years. Now Alias, instead of shedding blood, has given his own blood for Aneng, and cares for him. This is another historic act in the history of the Aguaruna. Alias has made another daring change!"

Aneng was soon up on crutches and often came to my house to sit. He wove cloth belts as he listened to Alias and me translate. Day by day, Alias explained the Word of God to him and cared for him with tenderness and genuine love.

"Only Christ can bring such a change," I thought. "Only He can heal such animosities; only He can heal hearts like this."

16

Ten Years of Mixing

"Sister, have we Aguaruna made any progress?"

David was at Yarinacocha in the summer of 1964, teaching in the training course. One day in March he asked me that very thought-provoking question.

"Of course, David," I replied. But then I started thinking. This year marked ten years of our work with the Aguaruna. I would soon be going on furlough again. It *was* time to evaluate those years.

The word *progress* was being used repeatedly in the teachers' class in community development that year. The Aguaruna were becoming increasingly aware of cultural differences and in the changes taking place in their own society.

David's question led us into a long discussion. We looked back over ten years, and talked about the many changes we had seen: schools, government involvement, literacy, letter writing, marriage customs, prestige and status, hygiene and medicine, new economic independence, the coming of the road and more outsiders—and yes, even a communication gap between the old and the young. All of these reflected enormous changes in just ten years.

David recalled how ten years before, very few Aguaruna even knew they lived in Peru. Now they knew they were part of a larger society with a president, a flag, a national language and culture, and clearly fixed borders.

I chuckled, remembering a group of Aguaruna who had gone to visit Lima for the first time. One of them had told me, "They said to us, 'Let's go see the president.' As we were going, I was thinking, What will the president be like? What will it be? How will I see it?' Then we arrived. I saw him clearly. He was the owner of a body. He was short. He wasn't sad. He was not something to be feared. He was just a person."

David observed that many Aguaruna now felt proud to be Peruvians. The annual *veintiocho* or Independence Day (July 28) celebrations held in the schools and the daily singing of the national anthem reminded them of their country.

"People don't even live where they used to," David pointed out. "The whole population seems to have moved down to the main river. Now it's easier to travel and to have contact with the outside. Villages have sprung up near the schools. For the first time, Aguaruna have begun to live in groups of more than two or three households."

We talked about the changes in leadership, too. A new social and political organization, based on elections and government appointments, had replaced the old ways. The Aguaruna system had always been built on the ability to talk and to persuade and on spiritual power. Now, this was not so true.

Certainly a new era of communication had arrived. Learning to write had become popular; letter writing had become a major activity. No longer did the Aguaruna have to remember all the oral messages for relatives and friends when they traveled. Now, instead, they were postmen! Invitations to interschool soccer games, tales of sickness and death, threats of hate and revenge, denouncements to local authorities, and simple, friendly greetings all went by letter.

We gave particular attention to how writing had affected marriage customs. Traditionally, parents might promise a daughter at birth to a prospective son-in-law. Or a young man wanting a wife would visit her father and offer to work for him. He might send his father or uncle, or another carefully chosen intermediary to engage in lengthy negotiations for him.

But with the advent of letter writing, the system of getting a wife was changing drastically. Older teenagers began sending notes to desirable girls—hard workers who knew how to care for gardens and domestic animals. Some girls, instead of being constantly protected from male attention by working only at home or in the gardens with their mothers, were now attending school with boys and young men. It was hard for both sexes to handle this unprecedented exposure to each other. Now an intermediary for marriage, instead of being a mature man, was often a good friend of the young man, perhaps a fellow student, who would sneak a letter to the girl. Elopements had increased, as young people ran off together, wanting to emulate what they had heard was "civilized" — to make their own decisions without consulting their parents.

Many times these young people chose partners outside the accepted pattern of cross-cousin marriage. They broke marriage taboos and aroused indignation in their communities. Such marriages seldom lasted, David reflected. The family would insist that the young man also marry the girl he was supposed to marry as a second wife. But often the first wife would run away or commit suicide. The stability of marriage had indeed been upset. We didn't see how we could call that progress.

David talked about how new means of getting prestige and power were also changing the patterns of Aguaruna culture. He remembered when prestige was synonymous with killing. The most powerful leader was the one who killed. He knew the history of the old days, when in times past the men's fiestas to celebrate their shrunken head trophies were of utmost importance. The ability to persuade by eloquent oratory had set apart the man of power. His many visions and dreams and contact with the *ajutap* spirit added to his power.

But all this was changing. The ability to speak Spanish now brought a man more prestige than did the ability to speak forcefully in Aguaruna. The man who could communicate with the outside world of the *kistian* was now considered to be powerful. A radio, a sewing machine, or even a cow, were new symbols of prestige. Did these changes represent progress?

The focus of life for the Aguaruna now was changing too. A young man used to aspire to be a good hunter, to own many productive gardens tended by his hardworking wife so that he could feed many guests, to kill many enemies, or perhaps to become a famous shaman. He longed to communicate with the powerful spirits who could give him soul power and make him invincible; he devoted much time and effort to his search.

The new young man seemed to think mostly of education—and the diversions that went with it, such as soccer. He dreamed of becoming a teacher with a good salary, or maybe a mechanic or a carpenter. He thirsted for more and more education. Having a taste of the wealth of knowledge found in books and in the outside world, he longed to have more and more contact with the outside

—an outside that often cared little about the impact of its values or goods on the Aguaruna life.

Yes, ten years of bilingual education, the coming of the road and increased contact with the outside world through soldiers, work crews, settlers and traders had revolutionized the younger generation. But a huge gap was now separating them and their fathers. Our efforts in adult education and agricultural training for the older men seemed only a weak bridge between them. Progress? Yes, we agreed—but with a price.

We moved on to other topics.

"People don't die as much as they used to," David observed next. "What a difference medicine has made. Measles, flu, malaria, serious infections, worms and amoeba are all being cured with the medicines given by Jeanne, the teachers, and the health promoters trained at Yarinacocha."

The bilingual teachers, by teaching hygiene and giving basic remedies, saved many lives. The power of penicillin was awesome; a few de-worming pills changed a weak, listless child into a vigorous, healthy one. The shaman's role changed too; now he was consulted for a new reason: he must tell whether the patient needed medicine or if he were indeed the victim of *tunchi* and needed incantations and visions for healing. Surely this was progress—but again, with a price.

The admiration for medicine caused problems as well as solving them. Treatment seemed so simple—penicillin and a syringe. The Aguaruna could buy these from any trader along the river or in the mestizo towns. Untrained amateurs offered their services in many communities. The injection was considered a cure-all; pills were second rate, but it was good to have a bottle of sulfa around because a couple of pills helped a tummy ache. Traders who moved up and down the rivers sold medicines to anyone asking for them. Every man was his own doctor. The people wasted much medicine because of incomplete dosages and hit-and-miss treatments. Jeanne stopped emphasizing the usefulness of medicine and began to emphasize the harmfulness and danger of misuse.

But the medicine and hygiene weren't the only new remedies. Many teachers prayed effectively for their patients too. When measles hit one village, the two teachers assured their students of help.

"If you stay right here, we will give you medicine and you will all get well. Don't run off into the jungle." They all agreed to stay, and everything went well until a boy of fourteen became critically ill. At about two in the morning, the crisis came.

"He's dead, he's dead!" everyone wailed. But the teachers were sure that God had promised to heal all of their students. So they started praying, and continued through the night. At dawn the boy opened his eyes, completely well. He didn't have to go through the slow recuperation the others went through.

It was true; the health of the people was noticeably improved. The trained men were doing an excellent job. This was progress.

Things had changed in the economy too, we agreed.

"A new day has arrived," David said. "We don't barter any more or trade a jaguar skin for a box of shotgun shells. We don't trade a huge ball of rubber for a piece of cloth."

Money had become the basis of the new economy. Most men had paid off their debts to traders and were now debt free, thanks to the cooperative. Basic arithmetic, the use of money, and the correct value of material items which the Aguaruna learned in school served them well. A few enterprising young men had even set up stores in their villages. Their efforts and the sales of the traders brought more and more manufactured goods into the area: aluminum pots, plastic buckets, axes, radios, soap, cloth, pants and shirts, flashlights and batteries, and on and on. All of these things made life easier or fuller—but again with a price. The leadership moved from the mature men with years of experience in the old culture to the young men struggling to find their way in the new.

New material wealth had upset the balance in other ways also. The old society was based on generosity. The number one offense was stinginess. When the people had little besides food to share, this system had worked well. But now with the new wealth, the people found it hard to share. If a man were generous, he soon had nothing left of his new possessions, as his relatives asked him for this and that. His only recourse, if he wanted to keep "his" things, was to go against his culture and find an excuse not to share. Some Aguaruna, wanting their own possessions, became misers, yet they didn't fully enjoy their new goods because of feeling guilty.

The main topics of conversation had changed too. War and revenge no longer consumed the people; now they talked more of matters relating to contact with the outside world. David summed it up.

"'What can we do to keep the *kistian* off our land?' the people are always asking. 'It's our land, so why must we ask for it? How can we sell the crops we are raising to get money? Where can we get birth certificates for our children so they can go to high school? How much pasture does one cow need? What breed of chickens is the best? Why are so many people committing suicide? If Jesus is coming back, why doesn't He come?' "

That last question reminded us of what I regarded as the most valuable change. Many people had less fear now both of evil spirits and of the old pattern of killing. God was becoming real to them. Hymn singing, prayer and listening to God's Word were now a normal part of community life in most villages. The people were eager to hear the new teaching, to know about Jesus and His love for them.

Later I thought through our discussion again. Yes, there had been much progress in ten years—in linguistic work, in translation, in education, in health, in community development, in evangelism, and in the teaching of Scripture. A new man was emerging, aware of his identity as an Aguaruna, yet also shaped by the Peruvian Spanish culture. But everything seemed mixed; even the new trust in God and belief in Jesus Christ was often overlaying the old, deeply entrenched fears held for generations.

I thought about myself too. I certainly was not the same person I had been ten years earlier. God had been reworking me, just as He was the Aguaruna. I had learned to cope in, and even to enjoy, a vastly different culture and language. I had become a lover of and a defender of the Aguaruna. I was not afraid of these headhunters; rather Jeanne and I were part of the same clay, standing with them against the outside world pushing in upon them. I was proud of the true progress they had made, and I was pleased with my part in bringing positive change. But I resented other groups who were working in the area, who didn't do things "right." They weren't really "helping" the Aguaruna according to my view of things. I neglected to see that they might be part of the adversity God would use to strengthen the Aguaruna.

I felt that I had accomplished what I had come to do. I was pleased that I had been able to do the work God had given me. I did not know then that God had yet to teach me some hard lessons in the following years. I had to learn about my spiritual impotence and be reminded again and again that He is the potter, and I am only one lump of His clay.

Like other Jivaroan groups in the Amazon basin, the Aguaruna tradition and history is rich in wars, raids, revenge killings, head hunting and sometimes head shrinking (as shown here), all based on their beliefs relating to the supernatural. For the Aguaruna, no aspect of life is unrelated to the spirit world.

Blowguns, like the one this ten-year-old boy is holding, are made of strips of hard palm wood, split open and grooved. The halves are then tied together with vines and coated with resin. The darts are made of bamboo slivers and tipped with a paralytic poison. The Aguaruna are accurate with the blowguns, often ten feet long, at thirty to forty yards.

Left: A shaman sucking out *tunchi* in order to prevent sickness or death.
Right: Aneng recuperates from his leg operation under Alias' care.
Below: An Aguaruna village with its thatched-roof oval houses.

PART II

Molding the Clay Pots

Does the pot argue with its maker?
Does the clay dispute
   with him who forms it saying,
   "Stop, you're doing it wrong!"
   or the pot exclaim,
   "How clumsy can you be!"?
   Isaiah 45:9

17

It's Better to Be Hungry

When I returned from furlough in 1965, I was shocked by what I found. There were new sounds at Nazaret—dynamite and bulldozers. The road from the coast had crossed the Andes Mountains and arrived across the river from the village. The beautiful, lush mountain visible from our front door had been defaced. A bulldozer was digging up gravel on the island where we had planted a garden in previous years.

Motor boats also ruptured the once quiet foothill air. The river was busy with motor traffic, replacing the quiet canoes and balsa rafts of the recent past. Almost daily soldiers, tourists, government officials, anthropologists, or prospective colonists wandered into the village. So-called civilization was arriving; life for the Aguaruna would never be the same.

The women were wearing cotton dresses. Gone were the finely woven skirts of the men; they wore pants now. Many had also cut their long hair. All the material changes in the Aguaruna life were shockingly obvious to me, including the litter of beer bottles and cigarette butts.

I found that a whole new set of temptations had overtaken the Aguaruna too—the desire for wealth, a new kind of status-seeking, the formerly unheard of temptation to steal, and the temptation to be stingy in a society where generosity was a prime virtue. Many of the leaders were tempted to pessimism and discouragement. I could easily identify with that! It seemed most men talked incessantly of raising cattle and pigs, or marketing the rice, and of the other new problems they faced.

One of Alias' cousins was the first to come and tell me his tale of woe. The soldiers working on the road had dug up his manioc for their own food, and now they were digging up Alias' garden. Alias had protested.

"Why are you complaining?" the officer in charge had asked him. "Aren't we building a road for you so you can have all the wonderful benefits of civilization? We're not charging you a thing. You should be happy to pay us with a bit of manioc root."

"But with the gardens gone, Millie," Alias' cousin pleaded, "with what will Alias' wife feed her family of ten?"

I heard more of Alias' complaints from him directly.

"Our chickens and ducks just disappear," he said. "The road is going right through my pasture. They say, 'If you don't get your cows out of here, so that bull of yours quits charging the tractors, we'll kill your cattle.' But I don't have any other pasture to take them to."

The problems didn't end with the food supply, I could see. As the road progressed, family after family of Spanish-speaking colonists from the harsh Andes Mountains moved down into the jungle-draped foothills, seeking land and an easier life. Soon the land belonging to the Nazaret community was swarming with newcomers. David, Alias, and the other leaders all protested to the army officers in charge of the area. They presented their village land papers, only to have the army officer show them that the army had a title to the same land.

Competition raged even on the river. One day an army boat ran into Alias' canoe, in port at Nazaret, splitting it in half. But in rare instances, the Aguaruna were the victors. Another day as Dantuchu's son and his friends were coming downriver, soldiers in an army speedboat going upriver decided to give the boys a scare. Coming in close, they sideswiped the canoe. But to their surprise, the speedboat rather than the canoe flipped over. The soldiers swam for their lives, while the boys in Dantuchu's canoe laughed and laughed.

The coming of the road had brought big problems for the schools. David, director of the bilingual school at Nazaret, was the most depressed of all the leaders. His students were running away to the new school being built at Chiriaco, where the road crossed the river before continuing down into the jungle. Taking advantage of the road, the Spanish mission had brought in truckloads of aluminum and other building materials, playground equipment, factory-made desks, food, clothing, and medicines for their school.

The glamour that once surrounded the simply constructed bilingual schools was extinguished by the brilliance of this new kind of school.

"Why should we work, building schoolhouses and planting gardens for the school here at Nazaret?" the parents reasoned. "We can send the children to Chiriaco. It's free—even the clothes, the food, and the medicines. The bilingual teachers don't give us all these things."

David struggled with it all. "The fancy buildings, the polished desks, the teeter-totters, the swings and slides, the new clothing and the interesting food have all attracted the students," he told me. "But the parents forget that material benefits do not equal education; they forget that their children learn best in their own language through the bilingual method. I know that all this is true. But what chance does my knowledge of educational theory have against the tangible objects of civilization being offered by the monolingual Spanish school?" He became more and more depressed. His frustration and depression led him into self-doubt; he began to feel ashamed of their simple schools. He spilled out his feelings in a community meeting.

"We have no food, no good playground, no clothes for the students," he said. "I am ashamed. You are saying we don't teach anything here in Nazaret. Maybe we don't. We don't have aluminum roofs. We teach in old thatch-roofed houses. Our students wear their tattered, worn-out shorts. We just eat manioc and fish. Maybe what you are saying about our school is true."

Later that day, we talked a long time. I tried to help David see the real issues. I encouraged him to keep going and not to spend so much energy fighting the competition.

Two weeks later, two fifteen-year-old boys who had run away from the Nazaret school to study at Chiriaco came to visit us. I was surprised to see them; students were not normally allowed to go home on weekends. This was the first time they had returned in two months.

"Please," they begged, "can we come back to school in Nazaret?"

"What is the problem?" I asked. "Don't they teach you well?"

"It's not that, Mother Millie," they said. And to my total astonishment, they began to weep. "It's that we aren't allowed to read our Aguaruna Scripture books or sing from our songbooks. We're supposed to confess our sins to the priest, and then to cut grass to pay for them. It's better to be hungry, and to be able to read God's Word in our own language."

I was deeply moved.

Several weeks later, as I stayed alone at Nazaret, I needed those words of encouragement. God had led my SIL colleague, Martha Jakway, to leave her teaching assignment at Yarinacocha to join Jeanne and me in the work in 1964. Martha had taken over the supervision of teachers and other areas related to the schools. She had gone upriver to visit the school at Shushung, leaving me alone in the village. I was preoccupied, especially with David's struggle over problems caused by conflicting values: material gain versus spiritual values. The believers seemed weak; many had spent the previous night drinking and fighting. Translation was going very slowly. I felt defeated and discouraged. A blanket of darkness seemed to cover Nazaret.

One windy afternoon I walked out in front of our house to the edge of the cliff. Dark clouds hung on the mountains across the valley. The chill of the afternoon accentuated the chill in my heart. The wind tore at my dress, and I shivered.

"Is it worth it?" I thought. "Am I wasting my life on people who don't care anyway? Does God even care? Does He care that David wants to give up, that many of the believers are indifferent to His Word, that translation is going at a snail's pace?"

I stood on the cliff, all alone. I couldn't hold back my tears.

"Lord," I prayed, "don't you see what a mess everything is? Don't you care? If you do care, why don't you do something to change things?" I bitterly complained to God. "At least I have been honest," I comforted myself.

I stood there, looking out across the valley where the great Mara ñon River runs north and south and the Chiriaco joins it from the southeast. In my mind, I followed the rivers far up to the many small streams which rush down from the mountains to join the Marañon, before it flows on down to the mighty Amazon. I thought of the hundreds and thousands of Aguaruna living along the banks of those many streams in scattered houses and tiny villages.

Suddenly my bitterness melted. I was overcome with great concern and love for the Aguaruna. Then I prayed. In my mind, I followed each stream up again and then traveled all the way down the main river. I claimed for each village and household the victory

I suddenly knew was going to come. God, in that instant, handed me the gift of faith to believe that in His time the Aguaruna would truly turn to Him. They would come to love His Word and to know His power. I couldn't make any of that happen, but He would. I could praise Him for what I knew He was going to do. I could trust Him, the Master Potter, to mold the Aguaruna according to His plan in spite of the wheel of change that seemed to be spinning out of control.

The days, the weeks, and the months that followed were not much different from the ones that had gone before. But I was different. The darkness of doubt and hopelessness had lifted. I never again could doubt that the outcome was going to be victorious. No matter how dark the day, how fierce the attack of the enemy, or how discouraging the facts of the moment, the assurance that God gave me that lonely afternoon at Nazaret remained with me.

But I still didn't realize yet that God would have to change me too. He would have to give me a new attitude toward Spanish priests, army officers, and other non-Aguaruna. I had not learned to love these people whom I regarded to be enemies of the Aguaruna. I would have to learn to accept these "intruders" as instruments God would use to mold me, and the Aguaruna, into the image of His Son.

18

Roman's Revolution

While David struggled with the encroachment of the outside world at Nazaret, another Aguaruna struggled with social injustices at the University of Trujillo, out on the dry coastal desert. The first Aguaruna to finish high school, Roman was in his second year at the University.

As a ten year old, Roman had taken over much of the teaching of the younger students while his father, Shajian, concentrated on the older ones. He drilled them with flashcards and helped in other ways that kept him from boredom. When he quickly mastered all that the bilingual school could offer, his father eagerly sought more education for him. He spent most of his teaching salary boarding Roman in the home of a Peruvian pastor out on the coast so he could attend high school.

Even though Roman was the first to graduate from high school, he wasn't satisfied; he wanted to continue to study. He wanted to become a physician, in fact. When Dr. Eichenberger heard of his interest in medicine, he invited him to come to Yarinacocha to work with him. At the same time, Roman's mother, Sakejat, came to attend the health promoter course.

Roman was delighted with this new opportunity to learn, and we were delighted to see him. Jeanne and I had last seen him when he was a boy, helping to care for the sick during a measles epidemic. Now he was a handsome nineteen year old and very polished because of his years on the coast. Yet Roman was so typically Aguaruna—boisterous, quick to laugh, quick to cry, quick to get angry, and slow to forget.

Roman spent his mornings in the clinic working with Dr. Eichenberger. In the afternoons he helped me work on an Aguaruna-Spanish dictionary for the schools. The evenings he used to get reacquainted with the fifty-five Aguaruna teachers who were at Yarinacocha, many of them his relatives.

While at Yarinacocha, Roman celebrated his twentieth birthday. He felt very much at home with the others by then. They had played soccer together, had sung and prayed together, and had talked for hours on end. He was thrilled that the teachers held a party for him. After several noisy games, they gave him presents—a comb, handkerchiefs, a book, cash, and, best of all, a Parker pen from David. It was so exciting being with his own people again! Tears rolled down his cheeks as he tried to thank them.

Roman told of his years on the coast as he struggled to learn Spanish.

"I didn't learn much history and geography in those first years," he said. "My struggle to learn the Spanish language was all absorbing. I often was lonely for my parents and my brothers. I missed our close family. I was hungry for my mother's cooking, for fish and manioc. But I kept at it. It was a struggle, but I finished high school. And now," Roman went on in tears, "I find that you brothers are proud of me, that you pray for me, that you want to help me. It is overwhelming.

"These three months have been the happiest I have ever known. I have had many difficult, lonely years studying far from my family. It will never be so hard again, because I know that you, my brothers, will be praying for me!"

When the teachers returned to their schools, Roman returned to Trujillo to begin his studies at the University. But soon the pressures of new ideologies squeezed in upon him. The foundations on which his life rested were profoundly shaken.

Letters Roman wrote to me only hinted at his struggle. In August, 1965, he wrote, "Pray for me. Life at the university is hard. I am having trouble studying because of all the politics. Why do the students spend so much time on politics? I want to help my family. If we Aguaruna had money we could all be well educated. We're not donkeys. Someday an Aguaruna will be president."

As an Aguaruna boy at home, and throughout his years in high school, Roman had been taught that the Bible was truth. Now it seemed that no one around him believed it. "It's a book of myths," some people said. "Religion is the opiate of the people." His fellow students ridiculed him constantly for his belief in God. On his desk often during those days lay his Spanish Bible and, alongside of it, a book on Marxism. He struggled to believe. Was the Bible right? He had been offered money, a car, and even study abroad if he would renounce the Bible and join in with those who accepted Marxist philosophy.

Roman knew from bitter experience of the inequality between men. He knew firsthand of social injustices. He was one of the poor, the minority, the downtrodden.

"The Bible talks of love and promises freedom—but where are these practiced?" Roman found himself wondering. "Maybe there is a better way of life after all. At the University I am already a leader. I will someday lead my people. Which way is the way to equality and freedom? I am not choosing just for myself; I am choosing for the Aguaruna also."

For days Roman battled, his Bible in one hand and his atheistic books in the other.

"God, if you really exist, I must know," he prayed. But then he remembered he had to accept by *faith*.

Roman finally told the pastor with whom he had lived about his dilemma.

"Read Amos and you will learn the truth about it," he told him. So Roman poured over the writings of the prophet Amos. He saw God's sovereignty in the rise and fall of the nations. He saw that God cares for the poor and defends the downtrodden.

As Roman read and reread Amos, his faith grew stronger. Yes, God would overrule social injustice. He would bring ultimate justice. "Only God is greater than man-made philosophies," he thought. "It is all true. God lives! God cares about the poor. God cares about me!"

Roman's resurgence of faith had a powerful outcome. He poured his energies into working with the young people in his local church and in the University. He was elected president of the association of evangelical young people of the city of Trujillo.

When Roman returned to Yarinacocha in March of 1966, he was still seeking revolution—but one with the Scripture as its banner. He spent long hours convincing the teachers that only Christ could heal the ills of society. He even taught the teachers a song he had written about this:

All of you Aguaruna, really think.
Let's all work together to make our land progress.
By completely obeying God's Word,
Let's all go to heaven.

Let's all work hard,
Let's all work hard,
Let's all work hard,
That our land progress.

Our God, loving us, helps us here on earth.
He gives us mutual love and good life.
If we have problems, Jesus will help us.
He is our Savior.

On both Sundays of his two-week visit, Roman spoke to the assembled teachers. They sat on the edge of their benches, captivated. Several recommitted their lives to Christ. One of these was Cristobal, who told me one night, "I hunger to hear Roman talk." The Spirit was indeed working through him. But I felt a vague alarm somewhere deep inside me. The men took everything Roman said as the final word.

19

David's Plot

Roman came home from the University during the midterm break to attend the teachers' conference. David, on the other hand, informed me that he was not going.

"Why do you want to skip the conference, David?" I asked.

"I'm going to cut cane and sell it to earn some money," he said. But I knew he was hedging.

"I'm sorry, David, but it's not voluntary," I told him. "This is not part of your vacation. The government is paying you for these three days of conference. You can't earn enough by cutting cane in three days to pay back the government for not working. Every teacher is obliged to attend unless he's ill."

David's father, Kunyach, was elected president of the conference that year and presided over the seventy-four teachers present. He listened carefully as teacher after teacher told about students switching to the Spanish mission schools because of the free food and clothing. Finally Kunyach stopped the reports with a shocking disclosure.

"I want you all to know that I was offered the directorship of these Spanish schools," he said. My mouth dropped open. We had been living right there at Nazaret near Kunyach and hadn't heard a word about this!

"I didn't say yes," Kunyach continued. "I thought, 'How does this man know I would make a good director? There must be some other reason. He must be deceiving me.' And so I said, 'No, I don't want to be director of your schools. I will continue teaching my

114

students here at Nazaret!'" Kunyach waited for the buzzing to cease.

"I know that right now the director from Chiriaco has gone to talk to the people at Nazaret," he added. "He is asking them if they want to change and have an all-Spanish school, rather than a bilingual school. If they all say yes, then beginning next March there will be no more bilingual school at Nazaret."

David was stunned by his father's words. His expression said, "Oh, no, Father! Why did you have to tell?" He turned to me and said, "I've got to go to Nazaret right away."

"Oh, no, you don't," I thought, but I said, "Oh, I'm sure the people won't say yes."

"But they will," David confessed. "I told them to say yes."

Alias jumped to his feet.

"I heard this was going to happen! I went around and talked to all the people. I told them, 'If you do this, I won't live here at Nazaret any more. There will be no one to teach God's Word. Millie, Jeanne and Martha won't live here any more because they work with the bilingual schools. It is just the beginning of a plan to destroy the bilingual schools!'"

Alias continued speaking forcefully for fifteen minutes, arguing on behalf of the bilingual schools. Then his cousin, Tomas, who also taught at Nazaret, spoke up.

"Everyone has been talking about the problem of food for students. David says he wouldn't have done this except that he saw the students suffering because they have no food. Why are we talking about the government giving us free food, free clothing, free medicines, free aluminum to roof our schools? Why are we always begging? I don't want my children to grow up to be lazy. They can work to have food and clothes.

"And what's more, I have a boy at my house now who ran away from the school at Chiriaco and came to Nazaret. He said, 'They give us food, but it's not our food, and so the boys go out at night and steal bananas because they are so hungry for their own food!' Do you want our children to steal? All we need to do is plan, and get organized, and plant gardens ahead of time so there will be plenty of manioc and bananas for the students."

Roman had been sitting silently, taking in all the discussion. But after this speech he rose.

"I like what this man has said. He is a man who thinks well,"

Roman said quietly. Then he told the teachers what the government does and does not provide. He urged them not to live off the state. He discussed the importance of having freedom to read the Word of God. "Don't fight; don't be angry. Just quietly do your best and you can't lose," he told them.

"Why do you think they have tried to get David to work for them?" Roman continued, wanting to win David back with the truth. "Why do they want Kunyach for a director? It's because they don't have any teacher as good as David and no man that would be as good a director as our president. The bilingual teachers are the best; that's why they want them. If we've got the best already, what are we worrying about?" The conference burst into applause.

From that moment on, a new unity permeated the conference. Roman talked to me privately about the situation and then spent time with David. By the time David gave the Nazaret report on the last day of conference, his dark scowl was gone.

"Sister," he told me, "I have been thinking badly." Then the whole plot tumbled out. "They offered me an incredibly large amount of money if I would turn the school at Nazaret over to the Spanish mission, so I could build a new central school there under their direction. They asked me to build it during January through March, when all the teachers will be at Yarinacocha.

"Desiring to be the director of a modern, well-equipped school, I thought badly. I see now that I was wrong. I have not made a formal agreement with them. I only agreed in my mind. Now I will not do it."

Roman, too, made a change in plans as a result of the conference. When I asked about his plans, he told me that he was not going to study medicine, after all.

"I have changed to education," he said. "There is nothing else I really want to do. I'm only truly happy when I'm here in the jungle, and I see no greater thing that I can do than to serve the bilingual schools."

After conference, we returned to Nazaret. David was beaming when we arrived.

"The community said no!—one hundred percent—to the plan to change schools, even though I had told them to say yes!"

20

Problems, Problems, Problems

"Oh, no! Another letter!" I groaned as I ripped open the letter, hand-delivered to me from the teacher downriver. "My sister, I know you are too busy to have time to talk to me, so I'll write you a letter," it said.

"Martha, do you realize I've gotten 100 letters since we came out here two months ago? I guess I shouldn't complain. It probably takes less time than if the people came in person like they used to. But I can't put off answering these letters like I do my English mail. The postman just sits here and waits. After all, he was sent to bring back an answer!"

"There *has* to be a better way," I kept thinking. "Problems, problems, problems! And all I do is scratch off a hasty reply. Someone ought to be looking into all these problems and doing something to solve them. I don't want to stop translation to run from community to community again. Many of the schools are back off the main river now. Supervision trips take time and energy. Yet letters from the teachers tell only one side of the story; it's difficult to find out the truth without being there in person.

"How can I know why the students burned down the school at Yumigkus? How can I know why the teachers at Duship were fighting or why the community development promoter has been forced to leave Yama Yakat? Why were we accused of charging the teachers for books paid for by the government? How should I know what to do for the 'singing sickness' hitting many teenagers? Why do they act like they have epilepsy and sing shaman songs which they have never learned? How could I know whether the people at

Sukutin should or should not have a new school next year?" My questions were as plentiful as the problems!

That afternoon, Dantuchu came over to talk about plans for the first Community Development Promoters' Conference to take place in early August. By now, forty men had been trained in the occupational courses or clinic at Yarinacocha and were busy in some aspect of community development.

"I've just come back from the Cenepa River. Everything is chaos there," Dantuchu told me.

"Yes, I know," I sighed. "I have received a letter about teacher Pancho's attempted suicide, another about the *kistian* building a school in the middle of teacher Augusto's garden, and another about teacher Felipe beating up the priest. Teacher Alfonso has written about being in jail for being too sassy to an army officer, and teacher Mariano complains about Miguel's sick child. But what can I do about all this?"

"I could have tried to settle some things," Dantuchu said, "but I have no authority. We must have someone with authority, who can *act.*"

"Yes, here is the answer!" I thought. "It's as clear as if someone had said it aloud. Dantuchu is the man! He can do it! All he needs is the authority!"

For several years Dantuchu had not been teaching, in order to give full time to the cooperative. But now people were not interested in rubber and hides any more. The supplies they wanted from the outside now came in easily on the road; Aguaruna-run stores were springing up in the communities. So Dantuchu had dropped the cooperative and was raising cattle instead.

"If Dantuchu could be reinstated as a bilingual teacher and then freed to supervise, that would be perfect," I thought. "He's not a man for academics, pedagogy, registers, and all that. But he is perfect for handling problems with the *kistian*, problems between teachers, and problems between teacher and community. He would be great for investigating the need for new schools and for getting in supplies for the schools. He could make trips to Lima to report to the coordinator and pick up materials. He could also supervise the Community Development Promoters. He is respected by all the Aguaruna more than any other man. Over half of the teachers have been his students."

I shared my thoughts with Martha and Dantuchu, and we prayed together about the idea.

"Yes, this is the answer," we all agreed.

Dantuchu was more than willing; he was excited at the prospects. But he had one problem.

"I want to teach the Word also as I go to communities, like I used to. But can I do that? Since I took a second wife, perhaps I can never preach again. I know that I was wrong in throwing out my first wife."

We had a long talk on God's forgiveness. Dantuchu wept as we talked. I assured him of God's forgiveness; I encouraged him to study the Word more and to continue to share with others what he learned from it. As Dantuchu prayed, he rededicated himself to God and to His work.

At the mid-year teachers' conference, the idea of Dantuchu as supervisor became one of the main topics of discussion. The teachers decided to request Dantuchu's reinstatement as a bilingual teacher and his appointment as administrative director of Aguaruna schools. After much enthusiastic discussion, everyone voted yes —standing and waving their hands for emphasis.

The conference officially closed at eleven o'clock Wednesday night. Then the delegates prayed earnestly about the problems at Nazaret and about Dantuchu's appointment. As Roman led them in his song, "Let's all work hard, let's all work hard, that our land progress," the lusty singing made the thatched roof quake.

Then Roman drafted, in Spanish, the request for Dantuchu's appointment. By midnight the last of the signatures was on the petition, but no one went to bed. Everyone chattered and packed until three. Then boats began leaving the port and loud farewells filled the predawn air.

At 7:30 the next morning, Dantuchu blew his whistle and called to order the first Conference of Community Development Promoters. In the places where the teachers had sat were forty farmers, mechanics, carpenters, health promoters and storekeepers.

Dantuchu's opening remarks were instructive.

"Tell about the progress you have made and about your failures," he urged the men. "We are here to help each other, to share the things we have learned, and to help each other overcome our difficulties. If you have made a discovery, or have seeds or plants to share, tell us about it. If you have only problems, maybe we can help you. What we do here is very important. We are the ones who guard the land. If no one works the land, we will lose it all to the *kistian*. So we must work hard, and urge our families to work hard."

Dantuchu had prepared visual aids of all sorts: the branch of an orange tree with a withered fruit, a stunted pineapple, a cocoa shell covered with fungus. The men discussed each problem; some suggested remedies. I could see at once they desperately needed agricultural help. I was the daughter of a farmer, but I certainly knew nothing of tropical agriculture.

Dantuchu's conclusion to this talk amazed me. "Two things that do well in the jungle are rice and popcorn," he told the men. That was good news to me, a lover of popcorn.

Each man gave a report. What the accounts lacked in organization they made up for in variety or humor. Those who had done little were amazed at the progress of others; they went home with new ideas and enthusiasm.

Julio had done something unique. While at Yarinacocha he had collected two sacks of used clothing, paying only five dollars for all of them. Back at home, he gathered the people and explained how they could work together as a community.

"I said to my people, 'I know it will be a while before we can sell our crops,'" Julio told the assembled promoters. "'So I bought some used clothes for you to use while we are working, until you have money to buy new ones.'

"The next day a man complained that the shirt I gave him had a hole in it," Julio continued. "So I just said to him, 'How much did you pay for it?'"

Egkashna's crop report was not quite so optimistic. "I planted rice across the river, but after my canoe floated away, I couldn't get across the river. My rice all died. My corn didn't sprout, but my beans have done well. I've been working with my brother-in-law; we've planted eight gardens, and have cleared the soccer field for the school. I have forty-nine chickens, thirty-nine turkeys, and twenty citrus trees. The people of the community, including the teachers, have pooled their money to buy aluminum roofing for the school. We are getting civilized in our village now," he concluded proudly.

Petsayit spoke up next. "I also planted rice, but the birds ate it," he said.

"If you plant the rice at the right time of the year, you won't have to defend it from the birds," Dantuchu told him. "But if you plant it so it gets ripe just when the birds come, of course it will be a problem."

Biji's story fascinated me the most. "One of my three turkeys got sick," he told us, "so I operated on its craw. I took out the bad food, washed out the craw, put in an aspirin, and sewed the bird up. And it lived!" he beamed.

All day long the men talked, on and on. As I listened to their seemingly endless stories, I reflected on the significance of this time for them. "It's not their successes or failures that are so important," I thought. "It's the togetherness that has developed. Each man no longer feels alone in his struggle against weather, wild animals, jungle mold, floods and disease. Now he has hope. He is not alone in trying to cope with nature and with the outside world."

Each evening during the four days, an Aguaruna pastor taught the men songs and read from the New Testament. His teaching centered on the second coming of Christ.

At the end of the conference, Dantuchu stood up to close.

"Long ago, Pastor Wynans and I prayed together for this very hour," he reminded the men. "We prayed for the time when we would be hearing sermons preached in our own language, by our own people. We should all be grateful. God has answered our prayer!"

21

Drinking Water With a Fork

During the time that Alias had patiently cared for his former enemy Aneng, his spiritual growth was also evidenced by his eagerness to know more and more of the Word of God. His prayers as we began each day of translation had been a challenge to me.

"Father, there are many kinds of good work, but writing your Word is the very best," he prayed one day. "God, I want to do this work because I want very much to know your Word. Doing this work I am learning your Word.

"This is difficult for me, but there is nothing difficult for you. Make this easy. Help my sister tell me so that I can easily do it, so that we can write your Word."

In August of that year Alias had begun praying for someone to evangelize all of his people. He was especially concerned about those who had never heard the Word. Then he announced to me one morning in September, when we were putting the finishing touches on 1 John, "I'm not going to teach any more."

"What are you going to do then?" I asked.

"Just what we are doing now," he said. "I'll translate until it is all finished."

"That's good, Alias," I told him. "But next year I'm going to my country for more than a year. You could teach another year, and when I get back we can work together again."

"No, sister," he said, "during that year I'll preach what we've written. I'll go where they haven't heard it yet and tell them of Jesus." Thus, Alias had become the answer to his own prayer for his people.

Later, in 1966, Alias continued his leave of absence from teaching to help translate the Book of Acts. During January he attended a conference of Christian workers in Lima. We hoped this would give him a broader view of how Christians of different cultures and places could work together. But the conference was in Spanish; he came back somewhat dismayed.

"Trying to understand Spanish is like trying to drink water with a fork," he told us. "I am more convinced than ever that we must get on with the Aguaruna translation!"

Martha and I arrived back at Nazaret from Yarinacocha on a Wednesday afternoon. The next morning at seven sharp Alias appeared, eager to get to work.

"Oh, my brother, I am sorry. I'm not ready yet. I need one day to get the house clean and to put things in order," I begged him.

The next morning, Alias appeared again at seven sharp. But he was frustrated that I couldn't start until after our 7:15 radio communication with Yarinacocha. The school started at seven; he wanted to keep the same schedule, seven to twelve each morning. So I changed our radio time to 6:45.

This turned out to be a good plan. I was happy to be able to work so many hours on translation. Because of Alias' willing help and Martha's assignment to the educational work, I at last had the time I had so longed to have. All the children and teachers were in school, the women were in their gardens, and the men were out hunting or fishing this time of day. Fortunately, people no longer came just out of curiosity. Since we had traveled all over their area and had lived with the Aguaruna for so long, they now accepted us as part of the family. If people wanted medicines, we sent them to the village health promoter. Thus, our mornings were full but productive as we worked hour after hour, going through Acts. For what seemed like the first time, we had few interruptions.

But one interruption spurred us on in our translation efforts. We heard shouting from the gardens down on the island. "Japa has been bitten by a snake!"[21] everyone yelled. Then members of Japa's family rushed by our house and down the steep river bank to help. Other people came running from all directions, as word of the mishap quickly spread. Martha and I shared the people's alarm. Few Aguaruna live long enough to have gray hair, yet Japa's hair was almost white. He was the oldest man in Nazaret and had been our friend from our first day, twelve years before. He was respected; two of his sons taught at Nazaret, and Alias was his nephew.

By the time the men brought Japa up the hill, his leg had begun to swell. Then he began to bleed from his eyes, his ears, and his mouth. We knew he would be bleeding internally, too, and would soon have bloody diarrhea. His sons quickly prepared their time-tested remedy, a drink made of three drops of the bile of agouti[22], a large rodent, mixed into a half cup of tepid water.

By the third day, Japa was much better. When Martha and I went downriver to visit another school, it looked as though he would survive. But then someone insisted he have an enema, with ginger root ground up in water. The irritation caused the internal bleeding and diarrhea to start again. In desperation, his relatives decided to take him to an army doctor several hours upriver.

A believer for many years, Japa told Alias what to do if he died.

"I don't want everyone to wail," he said. "I want them to sing instead. And also I don't want to be kept on a platform and have food brought for my spirit. Bury me in the ground. My spirit will not be there. I will be with Jesus."

Japa did not survive the difficult trip. He died shortly after arriving at the army post. With much wailing, they brought his body back to Nazaret. A number of men sat with his body during the night. As they were praying together, an elongated, oval light suddenly descended from the sky and hovered in the palm trees near the house for a few minutes. Everyone saw it. Then it went back into the sky.

Martha and I received word of Japa's death just as we were getting ready to return to Nazaret. We arrived back while the people were burying him. Our sadness over his death was suddenly tempered with our joy; the people were singing the Aguaruna words of "Amazing Grace!"

Alias told us what had happened the night before.

"The light was shining like the fluorescent lights in the Aguaruna study hall at Yarinacocha, only much brighter. We know that my uncle's spirit is not here. He told us his spirit would go to heaven to be with Jesus. It really did. We saw it go. So we don't need to bring food and keep a fire going. We just buried him in the ground like he told us to do."

Comforted in his uncle's death and elated by the power of God's Word in such a crisis, Alias and I continued translating with even greater zeal.

As we continued through Acts, Alias was thrilled with the adventures of Peter and Paul. When we returned to Yarinacocha to put the finishing touches on our work, Alias couldn't wait to share it with the Aguaruna in the occupational training course. One Sunday he told them about Paul.

"Paul had really sinned," he told them. "He was God's enemy. But God forgave him and had him preach His Word. Even if I am a terrible sinner, and have killed five people, God wants to use me to tell His Word.

"I want to go to all the places where the Aguaruna have never heard about Jesus," Alias said. "But I will need a more powerful motor. So I am praying about this. If God wants me to have it, He will make it possible."

I still do not know how Alias' need became known, but God answered his prayer. A man in the United States, a friend of someone at Yarinacocha, sent half the money to pay for the motor, suggesting that Alias pay the other half. Alias had just enough money. When he returned home in September, after finishing Acts, he had his new motor with him. He was ready to start on his own missionary journey. I think he secretly hoped to be thrown in jail so he could sing in the middle of the night and watch God open the doors, as He had done for Peter. His faith was not in vain; on this trip, God used Alias to bring hundreds to know Himself.

"He certainly isn't giving out water with a fork," I thought. "He is truly offering living water from an overflowing cup—God's Word in Aguaruna words.

22

Roman in Conflict

Roman's letter to me shortly before the next mid-year conference startled and worried me.

> Millie, I am an Aguaruna, and I shall die an Aguaruna. Because of that some people reject me. I am dark. Here in this world the dark people are despised. What do you think about that? Why did God make us suffer like that by making us dark? After I am dead, maybe I'll find out.
>
> Didn't God say to love one another, to love all people? Why do Christians not love us? There is no love. We are only Aguaruna. There are others who love us more than some Christians do. I have stopped going to church. I will work with those who love me.
>
> I will see you at conference. I want to talk to you.

I was glad to hear that Roman would be coming, but I was also very apprehensive. I prayed often for him.

"Who will lead the evening fellowship time?" I wondered. "What influence will Roman have on the teachers this time? Will he turn them away from Christ? What in the world has happened to cause this change in Roman?"

Roman came to conference, and as it got underway, some of my apprehension lifted. I could see that God had prepared Alias to be the spiritual leader for the week. He was like a giant among his fellow teachers. His teaching was powerful and practical.

"God's Word is like a gun," he said the first night. "When you walk in the jungle you are not afraid of animals or your enemy if you have a gun. God's Word is like that. It gives you assurance of victory over demons and sin. It makes you feel secure."

That first night, Roman listened in silence as Alias taught. I was thankful he had come to the meeting. Afterwards, as the chattering teachers took off for the various houses where they were to sleep, Roman walked to our house with me. He wanted to talk.

"What's wrong, Roman? What has happened?" I asked, seeing that he was very troubled. Then I just listened as all his bitterness over injustices and unkindnesses spilled out.

"The final blow came, Millie, when the pastor with whom I had been staying was transferred to a different city. For a long time, seven of us Aguaruna young men studying in Trujillo had been sleeping on the floor in the back of the church. In the daytime, we rolled up our blankets and put them away in a closet. When a new pastor came, he did not like having people sleep on the floor of the church. He told me I must move all these young men out of the church, and find places for them elsewhere. I begged for time to look for another place, but the new pastor was impatient. I lost my temper. We argued. I left and never again returned to the church."

"Oh, Roman, I am so sorry," I told him. "We know that it was wrong for him to do that. But I don't want to see you bitter and resentful. Let's look at what God says about times like this."

I opened my New Testament to 1 Peter 2: "It is when you do right but have to suffer for it, and yet take it patiently, it is then that you have God's approval. In this way Christ, too, suffered for you and left you an example, that you should follow in his steps. He was reviled but did not retort in kind. He suffered but did not threaten vengeance. Rather he turned the matter over to Him who judges justly."

We continued to talk about the problems and Roman's feelings. Then I remembered Alias' sermon, about God's Word. Maybe that was part of the problem. Perhaps Roman had stopped studying the Word.

"Roman, do you still read God's Word every day?" I asked.

"No, Millie," he admitted. "I stopped reading the Bible and praying a long time ago."

We continued talking late into the night. At last Roman decided he wanted to pray. We bowed our heads, but there was only silence. Then Roman began to weep, and I wept with him. Finally, with much difficulty, he prayed. He repented of his bitterness and resentment, asking Jesus to forgive him and restore him.

Later in the conference, Roman led a discussion on social problems due to cultural change. His concluding statement, after an hour of excellent discussion, set my heart aglow.

"The answer to these problems is the Word of God," he affirmed. *"God* is the only one who can help us."

23

The Far Corners

A nd God, help the Aguaruna, because there are so many of them," an Amuesha teacher prayed one night during the teacher training course the next January.

When Martha Duff, linguist and translator for the Amuesha told me about it later, I thought, "Thank you for that prayer. That's exactly our problem—there are so many of them. How will we ever get the Word to them all?"

We were vaguely aware that hundreds of Aguaruna lived far downriver in the low jungle. They had little contact with the rest of their people because of the difficulty of traveling up through the gorge, where the river crashed through from the foothills to the lower jungle, and fell swiftly in a series of treacherous rapids. Even though more than fifty communities above the gorge already had teachers, many villages still lacked them; thus we had let thoughts of the downriver Aguaruna rest in the far corners of our minds.

But Dantuchu had other ideas. In his new position as supervisor, he wanted to see that every Aguaruna child had a school available to him. He set off on a long trip, with a motor on his canoe, to see where new schools were needed. He descended through the violent rapids, where the river burst out of the mountains into the flat lowland, and on down the Marañon River. Then he turned up a winding tributary, and slowly, day after day, continued upriver until he contacted the Aguaruna at Potro. As he visited each isolated house, Dantuchu brought news of the families' relatives. He shared God's Word with his people. He told them about the schools and the help they were to the others.

After visiting and listening to Dantuchu's talk about schools, all the people agreed.

"Yes, surely, a teacher should come here too," they told Dantuchu.

When Dantuchu returned home, he reported the need in the Potro area.

"Who could we send to teach them?" he asked the others.

Alias was quick to volunteer. "They need to hear God's Word," he said. "I'll go."

But later, Alias changed his mind, thinking of the dangers of being with Aguaruna who still thought in the old ways.

"How can I go? I have a big family. I have no relatives down there. They might kill me. I really don't want to go. I'll tell Dantuchu to find someone else."

But Alias was not at peace with his decision. He kept thinking about it.

"This is not my work I am talking about," he thought. "It's God's work. If God wants me to go, I'll go."

Alias told Yanang, his younger wife, about the need at Potro. Would she be willing to go?

"Okay, I'll go with you," Yanang said. And so Alias told Dantuchu, "Yes, my brother, I'll go to Potro."

At the end of March in 1968, a pilot from Yarinacocha landed at Nazaret. He loaded Alias, Yanang, their three children, dogs, chickens, parrots, pots, baskets, clothing and other possessions in the plane and took off for Potro. As they flew across 150 miles of Aguaruna area, Alias watched village after village pass beneath them. He thought of his fellow teachers, each an hour or more by canoe from the next one. He knew he would see none of them until a plane flew him out months later.

"But God is sending me," Alias thought. "Paul went far from his own people too, to tell the Gospel. He was even beaten, and put in prison."

As the small float plane flew up the Potro River, Alias and the pilot watched for signs of a village. But they saw only a thatched roof here and there. The river was winding and narrow; it seemed doubtful they would find a stretch on which to land.

"We had better go back to the main river to ask at the army post whether anyone knows where you are to go, Alias," the pilot finally said.

A soldier who knew the area volunteered to go back upriver with them, to show Alias where a school was being built. Returning, they flew over a long, straight stretch of river, with a big house on one bank and two smaller ones on the other.

"This is it," said the guide, and so the pilot settled the plane down onto the murky brown river.

They could see immediately that the two buildings were new. One, with only half walls, must be the school. The other house, with walls reaching to the thatch, must be the teacher's house. But where were the people? Not even one person appeared to greet them.

Alias said goodbye to the pilot. Then he and Yanang lugged their baggage up the bank and across the clearing to the house, with the children and dogs trailing behind.

Suddenly, Alias realized he was truly alone—alone in a strange land.

"It feels hot down in this low jungle, out of the foothills," he thought. "And there are so many bugs! Where can we find clear water? Surely no one drinks out of that dirty stream! Oh, why have we come? Has God really sent me?"

Finally Alias and Yanang heard people coming. After shouting the usual lengthy greetings, Alias explained that he was the new teacher.

"But we thought our cousin Santos was coming," the men told him. "He is our relative. We don't know you."

"I'm sorry," Alias told them, "but they sent me." Gradually the tension eased away. The more the people visited, the more they liked Alias.

"Okay, you can stay and teach our children," they finally decided.

"I'll stay," Alias agreed. "But you must move in closer to the school. Build your houses here. Let's make a village."

Just a few days later Alias faced another challenge. The *patron*, or trader, who lived in the big house across the river came over to investigate.

"What are you doing here?" he shouted at Alias. "These people are working for me! You can't tell them what to do. You pay me for every hour they have worked for you. Pay me for the time they spent building your house and that school."

"I didn't come here to sell things like you do," Alias said. "They aren't working for me. They are working for themselves. The school isn't mine. The teacher's house isn't mine. It's theirs. When

I leave, I won't take the house or the school with me. So why should I pay for them? If they were mine, I would pay. If I were always to live here, I would pay. But I'll leave, and another teacher will come. I've only come to help them. The house and school are theirs."

On Sunday, Alias called the people together to worship and to study the Scriptures. This too infuriated the *patron*.

"They have to work for me today!" he insisted, threatening Alias.

"You can kill me if you want to," Alias told him, "but I am going to preach the Word of God."

"I'll report you to the lieutenant governor!"[23] the *patron* threatened, hoping to intimidate Alias.

"Even if you put me in jail, I'll still preach the Word of God," Alias told him. And so he continued to teach.

A few days later, Alias got a summons from the lieutenant governor at San Lorenzo, on the main river. He went down to see him.

"What are you doing up the Potro?" the official asked him. "They say you are deceiving the people."

"I am a bilingual schoolteacher, sent by the government to teach the Aguaruna children of the area," Alias told him. Then he discussed with the governor the problems the *patron* was causing. Finally the man told him, "Okay, go on back to work."

The *patron* decided to try another tactic, this time aimed at the people themselves. He refused to give them any cloth or shotgun shells or machetes. He would no longer do business with them.

"If you need anything, ask your teacher for it," he taunted. This caused a hardship, because Alias had brought nothing to sell. He had only brought medicines to care for the sick.

Alias decided he could win this round with the *patron* too. He went down to the main river again and contacted a trader there. On credit, he collected the merchandise the people needed, promising to pay soon.

Back in the village with the goods, Alias got the men together.

"Look," he said, "I haven't paid for these things yet. We must all work rice very hard to pay for them. Let's work and earn enough so you will be free from this *patron*. Let's pay all your debts."

After the harvest of community rice, Alias paid the trader downriver with the proceeds. Then he went to visit the *patron* across the river.

"How much does so-and-so owe you?" he asked. The *patron* named a figure.

"How much does so-and-so, and so-and-so owe?" Alias continued. The man named more figures. Alias kept all these in his head and went home and wrote them down. He took the money left from the rice, and his own salary, and went back and paid the debts.

"Now these people are free," he told the *patron*. "They will not have to work for you any more."

But the *patron* was furious. He had no records of what the Aguaruna actually owed. He had just given figures at random, not anticipating Alias' plan. He had made a good living for years by exploiting the people; now his livelihood was gone!

Besides teaching the children, directing the community, resisting the *patron*, and treating the sick, Alias found time to teach the Word of God to this group who had never heard it.

"Your spiritual need is your greatest need," he told them.

"No, we don't believe that," they argued. "When our cousin Santos visited us two years ago, he didn't tell us that."

"But Santos wasn't following Jesus then," Alias said. "He only started following Him this year, just three months ago. If he were here, he would say, 'Follow Jesus!'" But the people listened, without making any commitment.

Then one of the men had a dream, in which Jesus appeared to him.

"I'm coming back," Jesus said to him. "Prepare yourselves." In the usual way, the man immediately woke up everyone to tell his dream. From that day on, everyone listened intently whenever Alias explained the Scriptures in their language.

The plane shuttled Alias and his family out from Potro just in time for him to attend the teachers' conference. He was excited to see his relatives and friends again. His conference report lasted two hours. During the free hours at noon and in the evenings, he continued to tell his adventures. His listeners were fascinated and asked many questions. And as Alias shared the Word in the evening sessions, they responded just as eagerly.

After the teachers' meeting, Jeanne and Martha went on to the annual conference of community development promoters. I returned with Alias and Yanang to Potro. I was thrilled! Alias had agreed to check the Gospel of Luke, which I had been working on with other Aguaruna. With the printing of Luke, half the New Testament would be published for the Aguaruna!

What I found at Potro filled me with joy. I found many believers, among people I had never seen. I found a thriving church, born through Alias' faithful witness and teaching. That night I could see Alias' joy too. He sang lustily as he taught new hymns. The others followed, a couple of syllables behind him, happily oblivious to the strange harmony this produced.

Alias' sermon was one big dialogue. He talked above the voices of his listeners, who asked questions, made comments, or simply punctuated his lesson with, "That's right!" Enthusiasm was high. The people were actually living in daily expectation of Jesus Christ's return. Their faith challenged me!

Alias taught school in the mornings and checked translation in the afternoons. I was curious to visit his classroom to see how his students were doing, especially since he had been teaching without books, blackboards, or notebooks. Somehow in his flight to Potro, these supplies had been left behind. Now, four months later, we brought them in. The students were excited as they put up the Peruvian flag and their shiny new blackboards for the first time.

I wondered what the children had learned in four months without even the essential classroom tools. But Alias was not easily stumped. He had put up three broken canoe boards to use as chalkboards. He drilled the children on the syllables and words written on the boards. When he took out the new flash cards, the children easily recognized their friends, the syllables, on the cards. He put the syllables together into words; the children read them. When he handed out the new primers, they found the familiar words first and were soon speeding through the book.

I found that all the children had learned to count to twenty. Alias also had taught them many Spanish phrases, which the children repeated fearlessly. But writing—that was a problem. Even Alias hadn't figured out a way to teach writing without pencils or notebooks. Now they were eager to begin. I knew it wouldn't be too long before I would be getting letters from Potro, too.

24

To Get the Dirty Shirt Clean

Dantuchu's appointment as school supervisor was approved in 1967. His leadership proved to be very valuable; he helped to solve many problems, but his responsibilities did not include class-room aid to the teachers. We could all see that each teacher needed help with teaching methods and keeping school records and documents. In her responsibility for the schools, Martha could no more stretch to cover fifty communities at once than I could.

We presented this need to the bilingual school authorities in Lima.

"Perhaps several Aguaruna teachers need to be freed from the classroom to give full time to supervision," we suggested. But the answer was negative.

"It's not possible to have supervisors who are no better prepared than those under them. How can an Aguaruna supervise other Aguaruna?"

But when a new coordinator of bilingual education was in office, we tried again. The new man was sympathetic to the problem, and in 1968 he arranged for four teachers to be freed for supervisory roles. David, Fermin, Agustin, and Jeremias took on these duties, as "auxiliary supervisors."

Martha's job changed radically. Instead of traveling from school to school, she now concentrated on training these four men. When we met for conference during the mid-year break, David expressed his appreciation for her efforts.

"The month of orientation Martha gave us at the beginning of the school year was excellent," he said. "And the two weeks of on-the-spot training with each of us supervisors in our own area was very helpful. But even with only twenty–five teachers to look after, I don't have time to solve all the problems!

"How can I get the dirty shirt clean when I don't have time to wash it?" David concluded. We sympathized completely. It was exactly those same feelings that had prompted Jeanne and me to talk originally about the need for school supervisors.

Supervisor Jeremias began his conference report by telling about a *kistian* who had come to one of his communities.

"This man overheard me talking to one of the students in Aguaruna. 'Why do you speak Aguaruna to the children?' he quizzed me. 'You should talk only Spanish,' he said. But I told him, 'We Aguaruna are intelligent people. We can learn two languages! How many languages do you know?' But, of course, I do think we should teach Spanish to our students. After all, we are Peruvians.

"But mostly, I want us to discuss this question: For what are we educating our students? As I have traveled around and talked to many older students, I have found many with only one goal in life—to become a teacher. But where will all these fellows teach? We don't need that many more teachers. I'm saying this to you, my fellow teachers, because I have heard you in your classrooms. You say, 'Study hard, and you too can become a teacher.' This is false. This is giving the students a false motivation. Don't say this. What are we educating them for? Many are finishing their primary education. What will they do next? I see this as a critical problem. What shall I tell these students? What shall I tell their parents? What should you teachers be telling them? Are we teaching in vain?"

Jeremias had indeed uncovered a critical problem, one which Jeanne, Martha and I had seen developing also. Each year more young men were finishing primary education. What was next for them? Some had gone to Yarinacocha to take the occupational training courses. They came back to work in their villages as storekeepers, mechanics, carpenters or agriculturists. But these were only a handful. Some had gone on to high school on the coast. But for what? Would they be willing to return to hunt, fish, and plant? No, it seemed they all wanted to be teachers; they wanted salaries. Had the education we had so eagerly given and the Aguaruna had so eagerly received become a dead end? Were the young people no longer content to live with slash-and-burn agriculture, hunting, and fishing?

Bilingual education representatives in the new government had foreseen this problem too. They now insisted that each school have a garden—surely a step in the right direction. Most of the teachers had complied and had started school gardens to help students learn more about crops.

But then the parents protested. "I didn't send my child to school to learn how to cut with a machete. I sent him to learn to read paper and to talk Spanish. If he is to work in a garden, he can come home and work in mine," they said.

David took up the discussion where Jeremias left off.

"Tell them that by tending school gardens the children will learn how to plant new things, how to work together, how to solve problems, how to sell the foods they grow, and how to eat new foods," he told them.

The teachers all agreed that including physical labor in the school program seemed like a good way to show the children that other jobs besides those in the classroom had value and could be learned at school.

The supervisors discovered that their work had only begun. In 1969 Martha taught them another intensive orientation course, followed by regional pedagogy conferences. Each supervisor gathered with the twenty-five or so teachers under him at a central school. With the students of this school forming demonstration classes, Martha trained the supervisor in good teaching principles. He, in turn, trained his teachers, again in demonstration classes. After two weeks the men returned to their own classrooms, eager to practice what they had learned. The supervisor began to visit each village, to check the teachers individually. As Martha moved from supervisor to supervisor, training him in his own area, she could see our dream was coming true: the Aguaruna would some day be completely in charge of their own education.

By the 1969 conference, Jeanne, Martha and I were all noticing that the supervisors were feeling acutely the frustration we had felt: they were turning into policemen—the last thing they wanted to be. "I just walk among the thorns," one of them said.

"I like the work of traveling from school to school," David reported. "I'm proud of you teachers. You are now better prepared than ever for your work. You are doing well. I'm grateful to the linguists. Without them it would be formidable. This year Martha taught us much. She has given us the road; we know how to walk.

"But I don't like the talk against the teachers. I hear it constantly from the adults in the communities. I don't even want to listen anymore. If I listen to the people, you teachers estrange yourselves from me. I want to leave all that to other authorities. I just want to be your friend and to help you teach better."

Agustin, the downriver supervisor, was even more disturbed that people expected him to be an arbitrator.

"So many people come to me all the time with stories about you teachers. I don't know if what they say is true. I'm tired of listening to them. But if I don't listen, they get angry. If I do listen, you get angry, and then I can't help you be better teachers. Next year, I'll just teach in the classroom again."

"Is it really necessary to have supervisors?" David threw in, challenging them. "Should we continue?" The others reacted strongly to his questions.

"Of course, we need supervisors. My supervisor helped me very much," one teacher responded.

"The people also deceive us teachers," another said. "It really helps me when our supervisor comes and talks to the old ones, and finds out the truth."

"Our supervisor takes his job seriously. We must accept his leadership and not be critical."

"We need them," said a third. "We forget, but they help us remember. I can't do my school reports right without them."

Jorge brought up a related problem the teachers were also facing. "I helped to punish someone in my community for adultery," he said, "but the family turned against me and left the community. Should a teacher help to punish those who do wrong?" he asked.

"If we see someone doing wrong, we can grab him and take him to the Spanish authorities. But if we don't see it with our own eyes, we had better stay out of it," Miguel advised.

"If we try to solve the problems of the people in the community," Sabino countered, "we will receive payment only in headaches, many tears, and nights without sleep."

Dantuchu told the teachers about the kinds of authority and punishment in the outside world. But he didn't see how this could help them solve their problems.

"As teachers," he concluded, "we had better not get involved. We must tell the people that that's not our work. If you say, 'I'm here just to teach the children,' then you can remain a friend to your students and help them.

"Remember," he told them, "we started this to help the linguists, who couldn't be fifty places at once. Supervision can't solve all these problems. But should we stop trying to? None of us wants to be a policeman. But we need to give our help."

But the many unresolved problems continued to pressure both the teachers and the supervisors.

25

Teaching Them To Do It

While the Hong Kong flu ravaged Lima and other major cities taking many lives, it created havoc for the Aguaruna too. We discovered that our friends were still gripped, vice-like, by the fear of sickness and death.

Instructions sent to the teachers to tell them how to care for anyone who might come down with the flu led to the rapid spread of rumors about the disease. The fear these rumors engendered disrupted the schools and caused many people to flee again to the higher jungle, away from the villages. But by July, the flu had not come, and the people began to sheepishly joke about their over-reaction. This was another topic of concern at the teachers' conference.

"We must always read very carefully," David reminded his fellow teachers. "This paper was sent only to help us care for patients with flu, since it isn't included in the health manual. It wasn't meant to alarm us. We must be careful about these things. We don't want people to be afraid for no reason."

This panic pointed up another need. Aguaruna adults needed to be included more fully in the educational process. They needed to "know paper" and arithmetic too. Our working philosophy was "teach people to help themselves." Our goal was to give the tools for self-help, and then to withdraw, leaving the Aguaruna to work things out for themselves, in their own way. Thus we were delighted at any of the people's requests for help—for new tools to help them cope with all the pressures they were experiencing.

Nazaret had been the first village to ask for classes for adults. Off and on, David and the other teachers there had taught the adults after school, but motivation was low. Now the adults had a reason to learn; many Spanish speakers were moving into their area. The villagers wanted to be able to speak Spanish with them and to learn arithmetic to help in selling their crops at a fair price. The women also wanted to sell eggs, chickens, and garden produce to the stores in Chiriaco. But they were afraid. They couldn't speak Spanish, and they knew nothing about money. Thus, they had asked Martha to help; she trained two men as teachers for adults in Nazaret in 1965. Three men and nineteen women came to their class.

Everything went well for awhile. Then some of the teenagers began saying, "You can't learn anything in afternoon classes. Adults can't learn anyway." Some of the adults became discouraged by this negative talk and quit. But the ones who stuck with the classes learned. By the next year they were already studying subtraction.

As other communities expressed a desire for adult education, Martha took it to heart. In 1969 she held the first official training course for teachers of adults. Four men attended, two of whom already had experience. Kuja had been teaching two years, and his students were beginning to read the translated portions of Scripture. Abrang's students were doing well too, and could already count money. As the Aguaruna supervisors took over more of Martha's work in supervision, she could give more time to the education of adults, especially to training teachers for them.

Abrang, a storekeeper trained at Yarinacocha, reminded Martha how he had become interested in teaching the adults of his community.

"My customers would stand watching me line up the wares on the split cane shelves of my store," he said. "They were eager to buy. The first day the store opened, my uncle stepped up and asked for a pair of pants.

" They cost 150 *soles*,' I told him. So my uncle dug around in his palm-fiber shoulder bag and came up with a roll of tattered bills, tied with a vine. He put the whole roll on the table in front of me. I carefully untied it and began to unfold and count the well-worn bills. He had only 95 *soles*.

" 'It's not enough,' I told him. 'You can't buy pants. What will you buy?'

'Could I buy a shirt?'

'Yes, but you can buy more than that. A shirt is only 75 *soles*'.

'What else can I buy?' I named the prices of other items, but I might as well not have bothered. My uncle had no idea what the numbers meant; he didn't know the value of money. It was just too complicated for him; he had never been to school. Finally he said, 'I don't know. Just give me what I can buy.'

"So I laid out a shirt, a bar of soap, and two flashlight batteries. 'You can buy all that,' I told him.

"But as the days went by, I felt frustrated. I could see why my relatives were so easily cheated by *patrones* and traders. I could have easily taken twice the price of items from them, and they would never have known they had been cheated. I decided I must teach them arithmetic, so they could understand money and add up prices. But how could I do it? At Yarinacocha, I had watched the reading classes for the men in the occupational course; some of them had learned to read.

"So at the next community meeting, I asked my people, 'Would you like to have classes to learn to count and to use money? If I have classes every day to teach counting and reading, will you come?' 'Yes!' they said enthusiastically. They were just as frustrated as I was that they couldn't count or understand prices.

"So, Martha, you also saw the need. You helped me have an adult literacy class with lots of arithmetic."

Martha had been delighted to help Abrang. She had gotten books for him, had outlined his course of study, and had helped him in pedagogy. For three years he held classes for eighteen adults until they could read, write, count their own money, and add up their own expenditures. And now he was in this official course, to improve his teaching.

When the storekeeper in the village near Abrang's saw the success of Abrang's classes, he asked Martha to help him get started in teaching the adults in his village too. He too came to the course. Kuja, the pastor at Wawik, had different reasons for wanting to teach adults.

"There are so many new believers in our village now," he told Martha. "They want to hear God's Word. They are always asking me to read it to them. But how can I do that? I want to travel and preach in other places too. Maybe I could teach them to read for themselves. Then I would be free."

Kuja's twenty students were all eager to read the Word. With this kind of motivation, Martha was sure, they would learn quickly. They came five hours a day, for reading, writing, singing, and study of the Scriptures in Aguaruna. With the help of Martha, the area supervisor, and the village teacher, Kuja learned how to teach, and his students learned how to read and write.

We had seen that in medical work too, the best approach was to teach the Aguaruna to help themselves. Through the years, medical work had occupied much of Jeanne's time. But now, more and more of her time was devoted to the training and supervision of Aguaruna health promoters. Teaching these men became her primary focus. Her first "on location" class for three young men, in 1970, lasted three months. She taught them anatomy, microbiology, first aid, nutrition, nursing arts and pharmacology in the mornings. In the afternoons the students treated patients from eight surrounding villages. In the evenings, Jeanne corrected tests and made lesson plans.

The microscope brought for the course proved to be great entertainment as well as being educational. But keeping the materials for study was a bit perplexing. To teach the circulatory system, Jeanne used a frog. She focused the foot under the lens of the microscope and told the students to take a look.

"It's just like a river!" the astonished students exclaimed as they watched the red blood cells coursing through the capillaries.

After all three had had a look, Jeanne asked them to save the frog over the noon hour so the patients who came could look at it too. But when she came back after lunch, the frog was gone. Somehow, it had just "gotten away." She asked the students to bring another one for the next day, but again, it had mysteriously disappeared by afternoon.

"But how can this be?" Jeanne quizzed them. "I had that frog so well tied down that only his nose showed!"

The students couldn't keep the secret any longer. They all laughed. One sheepishly admitted he had eaten the frog for lunch. No doubt the first frog had undergone the same fate.

As the students learned hygiene, they passed on their knowledge to the people of the village. The microscope was their most convincing visual aid. Each day there was something new for them to look at. They especially liked looking at head lice. At viewing time, the women lined up. Each looked in the hair of the woman ahead of her to see who could find the first louse. Once under the lens, the louse became a huge monster, whose inner functions were a source of astonishment. On some days, the women grabbed the naked little boys and searched their bodies for chiggers. They viewed these under the magical machine. The women would scream and clap their hands, while the men, in awed voices, would measure off a couple of feet to indicate the size of the monster they had just seen.

The students' lessons about water were also most effective. On the first day, they illustrated the adults' health lecture by showing a drop of water under the microscope. The next day each woman brought a gourd of water from her own water hole, carefully covered with a banana leaf. Each one hoped her water would be bug-free. For each gourd of water, the students made up a slide, and then asked the owner to take a look. But each one turned away sadly, saying, "Mine's dirty, too." Some of the people were convinced enough about the reality of microbes to begin boiling their drinking water. The health training thus began to make a difference in their daily lives.

Meanwhile, Dennis and Eleanor (Susie) Olson were helping the Aguaruna in community development. Dennis, an anthropologist, and Susie, a medical technologist, had joined us in 1968. Jeanne, Martha and I were most happy to have the Olsons join our team; it was especially nice to have a man to help in the community development projects.

One of Dennis' main jobs in 1969 was helping a community with a rice project. He told us about this when we got together.

"The people spent 1200 hours clearing and planting five acres, 1700 hours shooing away the birds, and another 1700 hours harvesting. With the foot thresher and a hand winnower I took out, they prepared the rice, and then sold it for $465—a reasonable earning of about ten cents an hour for their work.

"Now that they have gone through the whole growing and selling process, the people have more confidence to go ahead on their own. Already they are busy clearing more jungle, to grow more rice."

Even with Dennis and Susie on our team, however, we couldn't hope to help every Aguaruna community. Dennis focused on supervising projects which would serve as models for those Aguaruna who wanted to go ahead on their own.

When community leaders gathered for their second conference, in 1969, Dantuchu was again in charge. Dennis was on hand to give technical advice on development projects. Dantuchu, on the last night of the conference, concluded the week's discussion with wise advice.

"We must all remember that material things alone will not mean real progress in our communities. Only as we all put God first will we experience true happiness in our lives. Obey the Word. Follow Christ. Look to Him for help in your work. If there are disagreements in your community, settle them among yourselves. That's what God's Word says you should do. Don't run to the *kistian* to denounce your neighbor. That's not what God tells us to do."

Yes, we all reflected later, we had had a great year. Jeanne had trained men to treat the sick. Martha had supervised the schools and trained teachers for adults. The Olsons had helped with community development projects. And all their work had left me time to plug away at translation. Our goal of training the Aguaruna "to do it themselves" was being reached! Soon they would be able to carry on without us.

26

Stronger Than Medicine

During 1970 Alias pioneered in yet another new area, on the Kaupan River. The Spanish-speaking *patron* of the area was against him from the start. He lied about Alias and urged the people to kill Alias—even offering to pay them to do it.

But the *patron* forgot that he was talking to the Aguaruna—and that Alias was an Aguaruna. The people went straight to Alias.

"The *patron* wants us to kill you," they told him. "He says you will steal our women and our things, and will bring sickness. Are you like that?" they asked.

"No, I am not like that," Alias quickly assured them. "I have come to free you from slavery to the *patron*. I want to tell you about God and to teach your children to read and write."

As Alias and Yanang lived with the people, he presented the gospel to them. But they were slow to accept his new teaching. When one woman finally committed herself to Christ, the others laughed at her, doubting her motives.

"Maybe Evangelicals eat better food. Maybe it's because she is thinking, 'I will eat better,' that she has done that," they mocked.

Alias felt especially discouraged one Sunday in May after he had taught the Scriptures with no response. It seemed no one had listened.

"God, how can I help these people? How can I make them hear? Help me," he prayed. And then he waited. "What will God do?" he wondered.

God answered Alias' prayer much more dramatically than he had dared to hope. The ground suddenly began to shake. The earthquake filled the people with terror. So frightened were they that a woman in a community nearby killed herself by drinking poison.

After the quaking stopped and the earth was calm again, Alias called the people together.

"For nothing you are afraid of a little earthquake. It isn't fearful. I'm not afraid of it. Earthquakes are not to be feared; the demons don't cause them. They don't have the power for that. But God is to be feared. If God can make the earth move, He is the one you should fear. But you don't even listen to His Word. You don't commit yourselves to His Son who died for you. God will punish you for your sins. That will be worse than an earthquake! You had better repent and obey Him."

The people wasted no time in accepting Alias' words this time. Many people turned to Christ that Sunday afternoon. They began listening to Alias teach the New Testament. They begged to learn the Christian songs. They started praying in their homes.

As was usual whenever a teacher first went to a new place, Alias found that medical work took up much of his time. As the people's confidence in him grew, more and more came to Alias for treatment. But not all patients responded to medicine; some had problems which no medicine could cure.

For instance, one woman had never had children. Her first husband had thrown her out because of this, and now her second husband was planning to do the same. She asked Alias to give her medicine, so she could have children.

Alias admitted that he had no medicine for such a problem.

"But could it be that if you asked God, He would help me?" she pleaded. "Didn't you say that God heals us?"

"Yes, it's true. God is stronger than medicine." Alias told her. "Okay, we will pray to God. You come each morning, each noon, and each evening. We will pray to God, asking him to give you children."

The woman agreed to come. Each visit, Alias read from the Word and he and Yanang prayed with her. God heard their prayers; in just a few months she became pregnant. When Alias and Yanang left Kaupan three years later, she had two children.

When Alias later told me about this dramatic answer to prayer, he asked about my thoughts on it.

"What do you think, sister? Do you believe that when medicine can't heal, God heals? Have you seen Him do that? That's how it happened at Kaupan."

I thought about Alias' faith and God's faithfulness to him for a long time. No, I had to confess, I didn't have that kind of faith. Had anyone been miraculously healed because of my prayers? Alias simply took God at His Word and God never failed him. Why couldn't I do the same?

When the story of the woman's healing got around, a blind shaman came to see Alias.

"Like the woman was healed, perhaps I may also be healed," he said. "I also want you to pray with me. Perhaps God will heal me."

"It's true that when we pray to God, He heals," Alias assured him. "There is nothing difficult for Him. But if you want God to heal you, you will have to put aside all the things you use for sorcery. You must stop using *tunchi*. When you place a curse on people you are working with the devil. You must leave all this to follow Christ."

"I will do as you say," the shaman agreed. "I will leave it all. I will follow Christ. I will just pray and think about God."

Each day, three times a day, the wife or child of the shaman led him down the narrow, bumpy trail to Alias' house for prayer.

"Heal this one. Cause him to see," Alias prayed. "Then the others will really believe in You."

For a week Alias prayed this way. Then on the eighth day, the shaman walked over to Alias' house alone.

"I can see! I can walk about by myself!" he told Alias. "I can see well enough to walk by myself during the morning hours! I can see people also! But then I can't see for the rest of the day."

"Okay, let's just keep praying," Alias told him. "God will finish giving you your sight."

But because he could see partially, the shaman was eager to return to his home, several hours away. Sadly, he didn't come back to Alias for more prayer. Alias told me later, "If he had stayed, I know he could have been healed completely. But he went home. I don't know how he is now. Maybe he is blind again because he didn't obey.

"The shaman was only one of many who came, sister. There were many who were a little bit sick. But we prayed and they were made well. It's true that I am a sinner, but I know that if I ask God, He heals. When people believe God, He answers."

I found myself longing for Alias' kind of faith. It seemed I had been so conditioned to believe what God does and does not do in our modern age that I found it difficult to accept His promises at face value, even when I myself was translating them so that Alias and others might believe. "How humbling—and ironic—that their faith has now surpassed mine," I thought.

The following year, several teachers from the Marañon River joined Alias in the Kaupan area. They opened schools on the surrounding tributaries. Young, energetic Pancho was named by the government as supervisor of the Potro and Kaupan areas, with fourteen teachers under him. He ably handled the river travel, the pedagogy and school reports, and community problems. But Alias was his wise advisor, to whom he frequently looked for encouragment and consultation.

The teachers brought more than just education, the people discovered. In Kaupan the villagers marveled at the improvement in their general health.

"Why is it that before you teachers came there was so much more sickness?" one man asked Alias. "We were always sick. Now we're not sick very much."

"It's because we think about and talk about God here. Before, the demons made everyone sick. But since we talk about God much now, the demons have left. God's Word says, 'When the light comes, the darkness must go.' *That's* why everyone is so much better."

27

Who Cuts the Trees?

My first day of vacation! How refreshing was the November coolness of Lima after the heat of the jungle. I dug out my sweaters and warm clothes, and looked forward to lunch of steamy *sopa a la criolla* and crusty French rolls. I needed a week in a different world as a break from my Aguaruna work.

But at lunch time, Jim Wroughton, our Lima director, found me.

"You're just the one I've been wanting to see, Millie!" he said. "Are there any Aguaruna living north of Moyabamba?"

"Hey! I thought I came in here to get away from Aguaruna work!" I teased him. But his question made me curious. "We've heard a rumor that there are some in that area, Jim. Why do you ask?"

"Well, the army is trying to build a road through that area. But every time they get a stretch cleared, somebody fells trees across it. They think it's the Aguaruna. The soldiers are afraid, and the engineer himself is in town, too frightened to go back without some help. He asked me to contact you about getting an Aguaruna to go back with him to check out the area.

"Could you go with me to see the engineer this afternoon, Millie?" Jim continued.

"My first day of vacation?" I sighed. "I thought I was going to forget about what's going on in the jungle for a few days. I don't like the idea of them putting in a road there, but I sure don't want to see anyone get hurt. I'll go with you."

So I went with Jim to see the army engineers. They brought out all sorts of maps of the area.

"I know nothing about this new location," I told them. "But Dantuchu is the Aguaruna school supervisor in charge of surveying new areas. Perhaps he would be just the one to help. He and I have often wondered if there are any Aguaruna around Moyabamba, and if so, how many. He has wondered if they need schools in that area."

"If Dantuchu will go with us for a month, we'll pay him for his services," the army engineer offered.

We radioed Dantuchu and told him about the problem. He agreed to come to Lima to talk to the engineer. After discussing the proposal, Dantuchu left immediately with the engineer for the road building site. However, when they reached the area, the engineer was still too frightened to go all the way to the end of the trail.

"You go on, with this workman," the engineer instructed Dantuchu. "Don't tell them now that you are Aguaruna. Just listen and see if you can get the opinion of the people on the work we are trying to do."

Dantuchu and his companion continued on. Finally they came to some thatched roof houses of a style Dantuchu recognized.

"Surely these are my relatives,'" Dantuchu thought. But at the first house he doubted his conclusion. They found only a woman at home, washing clothes in the courtyard. Her sarong was tied around her waist rather than over her shoulder in the Aguaruna way.

"Our women don't sit around dressed like that," Dantuchu thought. "Maybe these people aren't Aguaruna after all." But he didn't dare ask.

In Spanish, Dantuchu asked where the men were, but the woman didn't answer. He decided to wait a little and see. So he and the workman remained outside in the clearing, waiting. Soon the man of the house came home.

"Who are these men?" he asked his wife in Aguaruna. "Workers for the road?"

"I don't know," she replied. "They just came. He's probably an engineer. He has a watch. Workmen don't wear watches."

Dantuchu greeted the man in Spanish, but said nothing else. Again the man and his wife talked together in Aguaruna.

"Shall I feed them?" she asked.

"What do you have?" her husband asked.

"We have nothing but eggs. Or we could kill a chicken."

"Let's wait until our son gets back; maybe he'll have game. Chickens are expensive."

The man didn't seem to know enough Spanish to converse, so Dantuchu sat and waited, hoping they would talk about the road. The son returned, and his mother prepared some food. Finally she served supper for her family and the two guests. After they had eaten, the daughter offered a bowl of fermented manioc drink to the workman, who drank it. When she offered it to Dantuchu, he said quietly in Aguaruna, "No thank you. I don't care for *nijamanch.*"

The girl went back to her father.

"The engineer speaks Aguaruna very well," she told him. Dantuchu's secret was out. Immediately, his host came over to begin the formal Aguaruna greeting process. Dantuchu and he exchanged names and the names of all their relatives.

"I am Tsamajain. My wife is Dase. Long ago our grandfathers came over the mountains from Chiriaco because of fighting there."

"Oh, then we are relatives," Dantuchu assured him, reciting the names of their common relations. After passing on the family news, Dantuchu brought up the problem of the road.

"I've come to find out whether any Aguaruna live in this area, and if they are the ones cutting the trees," he said frankly.

"We have been trying to stop the road because our *patron* has ordered it." Tsamajain said. "He says the road is bad. It will bring sickness and many people."

The men continued their discussion, and Dantuchu and the workman spent the night. The next day, Dantuchu thought out his strategy.

"Do you have anything to sell that the engineer working on the road might want to buy?" he asked Tsamajain.

"I have chickens and eggs," he said.

"Very well. Bring one chicken and some eggs. We will go back to visit the engineer today." So they hiked down the trail for several hours to reach the work camp.

The engineer was glad to see Dantuchu again. Dantuchu presented Tsamajain, Dase, and their son Chumpi to him. He told him they had brought eggs and a chicken to sell.

The engineer paid Tsamajain fifty *soles* for the chicken.

"But I don't want money," Tsamajain told Dantuchu. "Instead I would like to have shotgun shells." So the engineer took back the *soles*, and paid Tsamajain fifteen shells."

Tsamajain stared at the shells. Fifteen shells for a chicken! The *patron* never gave him more than three! This was fantastic!

Since Dantuchu and Tsamajain's family had walked so far and would have to spend the night, the engineer ordered a plate of rice and meat for each of them.

"How can this be?" Tsamajain asked Dantuchu. "The *patron* told us that these men are bad."

"No, they are not bad men," Dantuchu assured him. "Their boss in Lima has even sent medicines with the engineer to help the people of this area."

The next day Dantuchu and Tsamajain walked over to visit the local *patron*. But they found only his wife at home. She too mistook Dantuchu for an engineer and told him how she was helping the Aguaruna by having school for the children. She talked on and on about what she was teaching and the good that she was doing.

Of course, the *señora* had no idea that Dantuchu was a teacher; she had never even heard of a bilingual teacher. After she had boasted for a long time, Dantuchu took out his official card from the Ministry of Education.

"I was a teacher also," he told her. "Now I am a school supervisor, and I have come to check on the needs for schools in this area. Would you please call the children? I would like to test them."

There was no way the *señora* could get out of Dantuchu's request. Reluctantly, she called all the children together. But when Dantuchu asked them to sing the national anthem, none of them knew it. Then he put a simple addition problem on the chalkboard; they were stumped at this too. He asked them to write *mamá* and *papá* in Spanish. But none could even write an "a", much less *mamá* or *papá*.

"What have the children learned?" Dantuchu asked her. "It looks like they have learned nothing."

"They didn't learn because they were afraid of me," the *señora* answered.

"She did call the children a few days," Tsamajain told Dantuchu in Aguaruna. "But they didn't understand her Spanish. She soon gave up and went off to work in her gardens."

"Gracias, *señora*," Dantuchu told the woman. "I see that these children do need a school in their language." He turned to leave.

"Do you really want the children to learn to read and to speak

Spanish, my brother?" he asked Tsamajain. Then he explained to him at length about the bilingual schools along the Marañon River.

Dantuchu stayed in the area for a month, according to his agreement. He met with the leaders of several communities and discussed bilingual education with them. He promised to send teachers soon. He talked them out of a revenge killing they had been planning when he arrived. He treated the sick with the medicines from Lima, and he shared with them about Jesus. He not only accomplished his mission of making peace, but also much more. When he left, the people were cooperating with the road crew. They saw that they were paid much better by the engineer than by the *patron*.

Later Dantuchu revisited the area to make definite arrangements for schools to open. He arrived just as the *patron*, baggage in hand, was leaving for good. He could no longer make a living deceiving the Aguaruna.

Schools opened in all eight Aguaruna communities in this isolated area. As a result of Dantuchu's influence, eight bilingual teachers left their homes on the main river and accepted these distant teaching posts. When I visited the area for the first time in 1974, I was greeted by many men and women who had come to know Christ through their faithful witness.

28

Little Fish Testing Salt Water

While Dantuchu, Alias and others continued to open new Aguaruna areas to education and the gospel, Roman continued his studies. He graduated from the University of Trujillo with a degree in education.

The month after graduation, Roman returned to Yarinacocha to serve on the faculty of the teacher training course. During these weeks, we prayed together that he would find a job at the end of the summer. The final week of the course, we prayed specifically that when the government officials came for the closing program, God would open a position for Roman in bilingual education among the Aguaruna.

The morning after the closing program, Roman sat down to breakfast with our Lima director, Jim Wroughton. Soon they were joined by Dr. Picon, the head of primary education in Peru, who had come from Lima for the occasion.

"What will you be doing, now that you have graduated, Roman?" Dr. Picon asked him.

"I don't know," Roman answered. "I'm going to Lima this coming week to register as a teacher. I hope for a position some place."

"No, no! We need you in bilingual education!" Dr. Picon protested. "When you come to Lima, register your title and then come to my office."

Another significant event happened during the same program at Yarinacocha. The minister of education officially declared Peru to be a multilingual country. He said that all native languages would be recognized as official languages of the country. As a demonstration of this new position, the national anthem was sung in Shipibo and Aguaruna, as well as in Spanish.

In May and June, a special commission met in Lima to draw up plans for the National Bilingual Education Program. This commission proposed that all speakers of native languages be taught to read in their own language. They also encouraged all Peruvians who spoke only Spanish to learn at least one other Peruvian language.

Dr. Picon, true to his intention, helped Roman to get an appointment as a specialist in bilingual education. He was to work with the state director of Aguaruna schools in the city of Jaen. Both bilingual and Spanish monolingual schools alike were to be supervised from this office. Roman spent the year in his new position planning new ways to work with the Aguaruna schools on the Marañon River.

In November, Roman accompanied his supervisor and other education office personnel on a trip down the Marañon to visit Aguaruna schools. Dantuchu, David, Jeanne, Martha and Dennis traveled with them. Jeanne, Martha and Dennis watched with pleasure and pride as the three leaders oriented the government officials to the schools and the life of the Aguaruna. "Praise God for the supervisors," Jeanne commented later. "They are doing fantastic work!"

Roman's success in winning the confidence of these officials was remarkable for two reasons. First, as a native Peruvian from a class traditionally looked down upon by the mestizo class, his achievements in education and his ascent to a prestigious position had won him new respect. Second, during his involvement in student politics at the University, he had helped to oust a professor—the very man who was now his supervisor in the bilingual education office!

In December of that year, the vice minister of education called another special conference on bilingual education. All the regional directors of education in Peru, who would for the first time be responsible for bilingual schools, were included in the 150 assembled educators. The vice minister invited Roman, Dantuchu, David, and bilingual teachers from other indigenous groups to attend. He explained the goals of the meeting: decentralization of bilingual schools in the jungle and the establishment of norms for educational reform.

The vice minister's opening speech was something new in educational circles. Some months before, this man had given his life to Christ through a Catholic Bible study group in Lima. Now, as a dedicated Christian, he wanted everything he did to be Christ centered.

"With the permission of the bishop and other clergymen present, I want to say that I believe in Christ, and I believe in the member of the Holy Trinity who is called the Holy Spirit. By the holy power of God, He not only sanctifies us, but also illuminates and helps to direct us. He comes into our minds and illuminates our thinking so that we have more lucid ideas. He comes into our hearts and opens them to goodness and brotherhood.

"I ask this Lord, this Holy Spirit, at this moment to come and enter our minds and our hearts so that we will be able to make decisions for the good of this town, the good of the jungle, the good of Peru—perhaps even for all mankind. Through the Holy Spirit, men in all places may find answers to profound human problems and be made into new men. We in Peruvian education desire to help men become new."

The vice minister also invited Dantuchu to speak at the beginning of the conference.

"I heard there was a revolution here in Peru," Dantuchu remarked. "But I didn't understand; I didn't see any guns. Then I came here to this conference, and now I understand. We are in the middle of a revolution. It's not one being fought with guns, but a revolution being fought with ideas. It is happening right here, right now." Later, Dantuchu added, "Jesus revolutionized the world with a few fishermen. We Aguaruna are also just simple fishermen."

Participants in the conference had a wonderful week of planning and interaction—a specific answer to our prayers. The plan for decentralization was also a specific answer to our prayers. We had asked God to work it out so that Aguaruna schools could be more autonomous—both from the centralized educational control and our own involvement; we wanted them to function solely with Aguaruna leadership, within the national framework. Our goal was to complete our work among the Aguaruna by 1977. Now changes were coming at just the right time. Had they come sooner, the Aguaruna would not have been prepared; had they come later, we would not have met our goals. God, at the perfect time, caused the supervision of the schools to move from Lima to local educational offices. To have Roman himself assigned as coordinator of the Aguaruna bilingual schools was indeed a wonderful answer to prayer.

On the final day of the conference, the vice minister asked Dantuchu to speak again. Although the previous speeches had all been carefully prepared, Dantuchu chose to speak extemporaneously, from his heart.

"We Aguaruna are like a certain little fish I read about. It is born in the Amazon River. As it gets a little bigger, it goes and sticks its nose out into the ocean for a few minutes of salt water, but it quickly draws back. Then it goes out again later and sticks its nose in again, and draws back again. After several trials, it finally becomes accustomed to the ocean. Then it goes out into the ocean and swims without fear.

"We Aguaruna are like that. The first time I went to Iquitos, I looked around at all the people. I said, 'They don't even know that we exist.' I tried living there just a little bit, but I drew back to my own land. Then I went to Chiclayo to school. I tried it a bit and drew back. Then I went to Lima, and little by little I have become accustomed to the way you live. Now I am able to swim with the rest of you Peruvians in your civilization."

When Dantuchu concluded, the delegates gave him a standing ovation. His illustration had gone straight to their hearts; it proved to be unforgettable.

The vice minister closed the conference.

"Thank you, Dantuchu, for your example. Forgive us for not recognizing you Aguaruna as Peruvians. You are more Peruvian than we are," he said. "Please give me your hand."

Dantuchu's response to this expression of unity created quite a stir! It was not meant literally, but Dantuchu jumped to his feet, ran to the rostrum and extended his hand. The vice minister not only took his hand and shook it heartily, but he also embraced Dantuchu as the whole conference applauded loudly. Then he continued his speech.

"You of this town are protesting for water and sewage, while many villages which are just as Peruvian as yours are asking for more basic services such as education and medicine. God commands us to love one another. If we don't love our brother who is here with us, how can we love God, whom we don't see?"

I was ecstatic! I left the conference praising God for this Christian man who, led by God, was bringing about the answer to our prayers for bilingual education. As an official part of the government program, with the Aguaruna and other indigenous leaders themselves in key positions, the bilingual system of education would continue without jeopardy.

We determined afresh to implement our plans for withdrawal, so that by 1977 we would be able to leave Aguaruna education in Aguaruna hands, knowing we were not needed. In just the same way, we could look forward to leaving the Aguaruna themselves in God's hands, knowing He would complete the task of molding them to fit His own designs.

Left top: Dress and undress, formal lines in the middle of wild jungle, children and adults, all are mixed together at the start of another day at a bilingual school.

Left bottom: Learning to read and write their own highly complex language and then Spanish, their national language, enables the Aguaruna to function in their rapidly changing world more effectively.

Right top: In the translation of the New Testament, Millie Larson and Alias Dantuchu use reference books and card files to check and recheck their work.

Right bottom: Jeanne Grover, Millie's co-worker, brought the Aguaruna not only medicine and her skills as a nurse, but compassion and dedication as well.

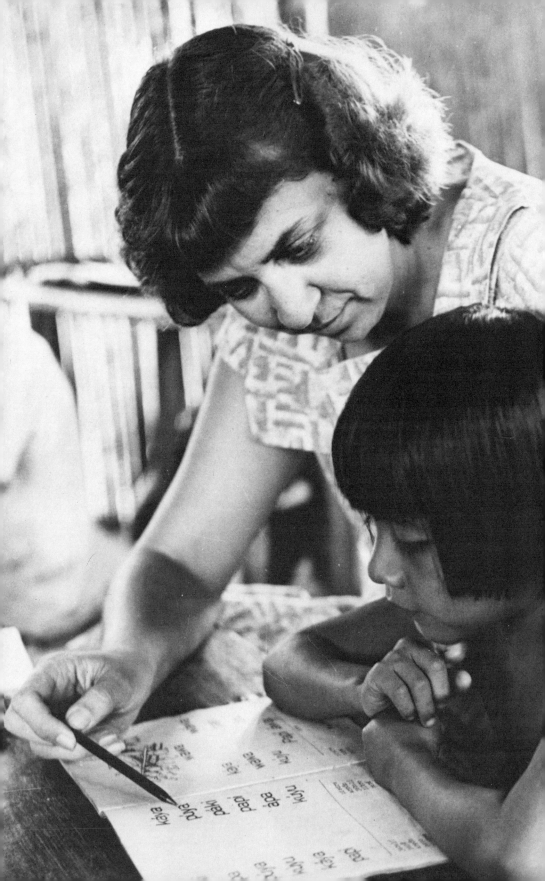

PART III

Firing the Clay Pots

You have purified us with fire, O Lord...
but in the end, you brought us into
wealth and great abundance.
Psalm 66:10-12

29

Nelson's Dark Side

L ord, you know I need someone to work with me on the translation. But who?" I prayed often when Alias decided to return to teaching again in order to continue to bring his people the Word of God.

Over and over, as I prayed, Nelson came to my mind. I remembered Nelson as a child in school, but I hardly knew him as an adult. I knew he had attended the Swiss Indian Mission Bible School, because the previous year, on his way home, he had stopped at Yarinacocha to wait for a plane. While he waited, I had asked him to help me for a couple of hours with some questions about the Aguaruna language. He caught on to what I needed very quickly, explaining word meanings very well and providing apt illustrations. I remembered this as I prayed for a cotranslator. I never dreamed how much a part of God's plan for translation Nelson was to become, or how through him the fires of strengthening would burn so hot.

When Jeanne and another nurse left Yarinacocha for an extensive measles vaccination trip among the Aguaruna, I thought maybe she could help me.

"Jeanne, would you see if you can find Nelson Pujupat for me and ask him if he would like to come in and work on translation?" I asked her.

Jeanne radioed back later that she hadn't been able to see Nelson. People said he had gone up the Santiago River to see a shaman about his bad eye.

"Oh, Lord, why do you want me to have him come if he has a

bad eye?" I groaned. "A man with poor vision is not exactly my idea of a potential translator."

But Jeanne left word with the teacher in Nelson's village that I was inviting Nelson to come to Yarinacocha. The teacher, who had a radio, listened each morning for announcements from Jeanne and Yarinacocha. On the day the plane was to go out to bring the nurses back, we announced that if Nelson was coming, he should meet the plane in Wawaim the next day. The teacher passed the message to Nelson, who met the plane on schedule.

I was eager to find out more about this new cotranslator, since he was such a definite answer to my prayers.

Nelson told me about the events of the last few years of his life, and why he too felt that God had directed his coming to Yarinacocha.

"A few years ago, Millie, I began meeting with the people of my village to teach them God's Word. Even though I was young, they listened eagerly. They said that I could make the message very clear and that I used good illustrations, which kept everyone's attention. My brother Esteban and I built a meeting house, and we encouraged others to move in closer so they could hear the Word more often. During the next three years, a small village formed, with Esteban and me as leaders even though we were still very young. We named the village Nueva Vida (New Life). During these years, I attended the Bible school of the Swiss Indian mission, and finished the course. Back home, I spent all my time on the church and the community.

"But then, about a year later, a man who lived nearby began to oppose me. He invited me to his house one evening. When I went to visit, he began to criticize me. There was much bad talk. I became very angry. Then I stood up to leave, but the man grabbed me, and we fought. I was very unhappy. We became enemies. I tried to make peace, but failed. So I stopped talking to him and his people.

"Later, someone heard about the fighting and confronted me with it. You are working with the devil,' he told me. You cannot preach the Word of God when you live like that.'

"This made me very angry, so I began to talk against this Christian. Also, even though I knew it was wrong, I stopped teaching the people. 'He says I'm working for the devil,' I told myself. Okay, I'll live like those who don't follow Christ. I'll destroy the house where we meet for church!'

"My mother begged me not to do it. Esteban pleaded with me. They both cried much as they talked about what I said I would do. But I went right on and tore down the church. I gave the song books and Scriptures to anybody who would take them. But inside, my heart was in turmoil; I was in agony. I thought of suicide.

"I became an enemy to my own life and to others. I posessed no happiness. Then suddenly, I was grabbed by sickness in my eye. I didn't sleep day or night. I faced the dawn sitting up. I had no money for travel and no money for a doctor.

"Some of my relatives wanted to take me to the shaman. I didn't want to go. For two days my brother and I resisted, praying to God about my sickness. I cried a lot, thinking that if I went to the shaman I would be lost forever. I was very frightened, but I couldn't win against my relatives. They said, 'If you don't go to the shaman, you will die. Let's go and ask him if you will get well. We will ask him what medicine you need to get well, and then we'll quickly look for the medicine.'

"Because of my great fear, I said, 'Okay.'

"'Let's see who has placed a curse on you,' the shaman said when we saw him. He drank *datem* and smoked tobacco. Because of his vision he knew that it was two of our own people who had done it. He caused me to sleep well, so I began to believe him.

"Since this shaman had helped me, I decided to go to an even stronger one. He lived far away up the Santiago River, but I went anyway. Drinking *datem*, he also saw visions of the two people who had made me sick. 'Please cure my eye,' I told him. 'I'll pay you whatever you ask. I want you to cause both of the people who have placed a curse on me to die. Cause them to die with pain.' I was sure I was lost after that. Surely God would never forgive me. I might as well become a killer too.

"My new friend assured me that he would put a curse on my enemies. But he warned me, 'If they are stronger than I am, then they will kill you also.' But I didn't care. I had forgotten God. I was happy obeying the devil. I did everything the shaman told me to do. I drank the drink he prepared. I entered into his ritual.

"While I was doing all this, I realized I was separating myself from Christ. 'My soul will be lost and I will suffer,' I thought. Then I begged God to forgive me, but even so I wasn't able to leave my involvement with the shaman.

"But even while I was involved in all this wickedness, God did not forget me, Millie. He helped me! At the very time I was up the

Santiago River, you called for me to come to Yarinacocha. I didn't know until I was going back upriver to my house that you wanted me to help translate God's Word. You didn't know about my infected eye, or that I was at the shaman's when you called me. When I heard of your call, I decided to come. Surely the doctor at Yarinacocha can cure me,' I thought."

At Yarinacocha, Dr. Douglas Swanson examined Nelson's eye. He was convinced he must go to Lima for treatment by a specialist. This wasn't my idea of getting translation done, but I got ready to accompany Nelson to Lima. This would be his first visit to a large city.

Since we arrived in Lima on Saturday, I called the opthamologist at his home. Dr.Cordero, a good friend who often helped many of the indigenous peoples free of charge, lived near our SIL guest home. He suggested we come right over. After a quick examination, he said we must go to his office for a more thorough check.

"I'm not sure we can save Nelson's eye, Señorita Larson," he told me later. "But get these medicines and I'll do all I can. He will never have sight in this eye again, but perhaps we can save the eye itself."

The medicines alleviated Nelson's pain, so that he felt well enough to work. On Monday we set up our desks in the library at the guest house and began working through a draft of Colossians. As I taught Nelson the principles of translation, he immediately applied them as we worked. He had a genius for finding the best way to express the concepts of Scripture that were new to the Aguaruna. I quickly got over my doubts about God's choice of a translator.

For Nelson's diversion, as well as efficiency, I started teaching him how to type. I insisted on "no peeking," so he would become a good typist. Between the frequent visits to the doctor, we worked away on Colossians and Nelson typed during his free hours.

Then, on Friday morning, Nelson awoke with severe pain. I could see that material was protruding and leaking out of the perforation at the front of his eye. We drove immediately over to Dr. Cordero's home, hoping to catch him before he left for the office. But we just missed him, as he had left for an early operation. When his wife called him, Dr. Cordero said, "Keep Nelson flat on his back until I can see him at five this afternoon. You can give him more medication for the pain, too."

At five, Dr. Cordero took one look at Nelson's eye.

"It's got to come out right away," he said. "If we don't remove the eye, he might lose the vision in his other eye as well and perhaps even his life."

Even though we had known this might happen, both Nelson and I were stunned. I felt like bursting into tears right there, but I managed to hold them back until I returned to my room.

After the initial shock, Nelson was marvelous. He expressed nothing but thanksgiving to God. He agreed to the operation, knowing that this was God's way of sparing his life.

"At home, I would surely have died, my sister," he said.

That night, Nelson wrote a song in Aguaruna:

> Now I have something to tell about,
> I will tell how Christ helped me,
> I will tell how He saved me.
> I am very content, I am very happy.
> Christ has given me never-ending joy.
> I am content, even if I should go to be with God.
> Where Christ lives, there is freedom.
> Let's all go there.
> Let's all live contentedly. Let's all stay contented.
> Let's stop being sad and let's live with Christ.

Nelson's faith and optimism touched me deeply. The next day, when I went to check on him in his room, I found these words scribbled on the back of a calendar: "Thank God for His eternal mercy and help. Suffering with this sickness, because of my pain, I cried to God. Miraculously Millie called me, without knowing that I was sick, because God spoke in her heart telling her to call me. I thank God for His salvation."

I saw Nelson's courage again as my colleague Bob Vance drove us to the hospital the next morning. Bob and Nelson sang most of the way—something I found hard to do.

Nelson quickly adjusted to the hospital room. The seemingly elaborate furnishings and equipment matched nothing in his jungle world, but he accepted them all. He especially liked the call button for summoning the nurse at any moment.

Even though Nelson was a bit drugged from the pre-op sedative, he managed one last joke as the orderlies wheeled up the bed to take him off to the operating room.

"Here comes my canoe!" he quipped to Bob.

Surgery lasted an hour. The eye was terribly infected, yet the operation itself went very well. But during the first three days of recovery, Nelson seemed withdrawn. The first day I chalked it up to the sedatives. But when he still didn't want to talk on the second day, I knew he was depressed.

"I was fine until the doctor cut the nerve to my eye, and all of a sudden the light was gone, Millie," he told me later. "There was nothing but darkness. Suddenly, I knew what it would mean to be blind, and I felt overwhelmed."

Nelson's depression over the surgery was complicated by the physical aspects of losing half his vision. Whenever the nurse got him up to walk, he bumped into things. This distressed him greatly. Dr. Cordero assured him that his other eye would soon adjust and make up for his loss of depth perception. Nevertheless, Nelson was oppressed with a terrible fear of not being able to walk right.

By the time Nelson left the hospital, his eye socket was healing well, but he still bumped into things. He felt embarrassed by that, and by the eye patch he wore. He didn't want to see anyone except Bob and motherly, bubbly Mrs. Cudney, manager of the SIL house. She supplied him with his favorite apples, brought him a radio, and showed him love in many other ways.

On the second day home, Nelson became dizzy and nauseated; he had chills and a terrible headache. I was frightened by this unexpected set-back. Dr. Cordero could find nothing wrong with his eye socket; there was no indication that this new problem was related to his surgery. When Dr. Eichenberger arrived that afternoon from Yarinacocha, I rushed up to tell him about Nelson.

"Ralph, I just don't understand what's happening to Nelson," I said. "He has nausea, headache, dizziness and chills."

"I don't think it's from the surgery, Millie," he assured me. "It sounds like malaria to me."

"Oh, of course! Why didn't I think of that! The change from the hot jungle to cold Lima has brought the malaria organism out into the blood stream."

"We can start him on the treatment for malaria right away," Dr. Eichenberger stated. Two days later, Nelson's symptoms were completely gone, and he was ready to resume work.

We began translating 1 Thessalonians, as best we could without Nelson using his eyes. Even though he was happy to be working, I was still concerned about his depression. He didn't want to leave his room, except to work in the library. I wanted him to go down-stairs to eat in the dining room, but he refused.

"I feel ashamed, Millie. I don't want people to see that my eye is missing," he said.

"We can fix up your dark glasses with black paper, Nelson, so no one can see," I told him. But even after we did this, he wouldn't leave the library during the day. Then he began to worry about having the stitches removed, about what it would be like to have an artificial eye, and all sorts of other questions.

Finally, Nelson decided to go to the dining room.

"I'll sit with you, on your dark side," I told him.

"Okay," he agreed. "I'll sit with Bob too." But when Bob had other guests that night, Nelson was very upset. When he got back to his room, he burst into tears and cried for half an hour.

"Bob doesn't love me any more," he sobbed, but I could see that the days of stress were taking their toll. Nelson had been control-ling his emotions by sheer determination; now suddenly they broke loose. I began to weep also, and then I realized that I too needed the therapy of tears.

After we had a good cry together, Nelson was finally able to verbalize his fears.

"Millie, I am afraid of what might be on my dark side, where I can't see. Maybe I will make a fool of myself by bumping into things. Or maybe someone will attack me there. People will stare at me. They won't accept me as a normal person anymore."

"Let's pray together about this, Nelson," I said. At last he seemed to relax and from sheer exhaustion he fell sound asleep. I continued to pray that God would take away his fears.

The Lord answered our prayers in an unexpected way. The next day, Dr. Donald Adams, the dentist from Yarinacocha, arrived in Lima.

"How is Nelson doing, Millie?" he asked.

"Oh, Don, he has terrible fears, even though he's healing well," I said. "He's worried about so many things, such as what it will be like to have an artificial eye."

"You know, I have a plastic eye myself, Millie," Dr. Adams con-tinued. "Let me talk to him and show him how his eye will work. I even made my own eye in my dental office."

"Really, Don?" I asked, astonished. "I certainly didn't know that!"

Dr. Adams' visit was perfect therapy for Nelson. Don shared

with him how he had lost his eye in an accident. He showed him how he could take his eye out and put it back in again easily. Nelson's fears melted away. He had never dreamed that Dr. Adams had a plastic eye. Now he looked forward to his own; in three more weeks he would have his new eye! He began going down to meals, although he still wanted only me to sit on his dark side.

A few days later, Nelson wrote to a friend:

> Please pray for me. Because God has helped me I want to work for Him again. I lost one eye and through this experience God has taught me to thank Him, because He has saved my soul. I don't worry about my eye because I know that what really matters is what I have in heaven. There I will receive everything God has for me. I am very happy, because through Christ, God has saved me. I want to obey Him. This is all I am able to say now. It is enough.

The next three weeks went by quickly. We translated and Nelson practiced typing, played his guitar, and wrote songs. Our visits to Dr. Cordero were encouraging.

"You're ready for your plastic eye now," he told us finally, giving us the address of a dentist who would make the eye. Both Nelson and I would have been shocked at that idea had not Dr. Adams already told us that he made artificial eyes.

The dentist carefully studied Nelson's eye. He made notes about coloring, the size of the iris, and many other details. Then he took an impression of his empty socket, made a mold from this, and poured the liquid plastic into it to form a prosthesis perfect for Nelson.

"Come back in three days," he said. "I'll have it all painted and ready to wear."

Nelson was excited; he could hardly wait. At last the day arrived. As we stepped off the bus and headed for the doctor's office, I walked on Nelson's dark side so he wouldn't bump into people on the crowded sidewalk.

Nelson's eye was ready—and it was a perfect match. The doctor put it in and then handed Nelson a mirror.

"Could you make me another one with a Peruvian flag on it for holidays?" Nelson quipped. We all laughed. Then the doctor gave

Nelson careful instructions on how to put in the eye, how to take it out, how to wash it, etc.

"Here, take this medicine," he said, "and use it if there is any sign of irritation during the first days."

Back out on the sidewalk again, Nelson was jubilant.

"I feel like the man cured by Peter and John, Millie! I just want to jump and run and praise the Lord." He was even more elated, and cured of his worst fear, when we got back to the guest house. Mrs. Cudney greeted him with a big hug. Then she stood back and took a good look at him.

"Which one is it, Nelson?" she asked in all seriousness. Nelson grinned. When his best friend couldn't tell, it must be a good match!

Nelson's spiritual vision continued to make a great comeback in spite of his loss of physical vision. We returned to Yarinacocha and continued on translation. Each evening Nelson taught the Word to a number of Aguaruna in the occupational training course. When I had to leave for Mexico for three months to prepare a training manual for translators, Nelson stayed at the center. During this time he helped the students, recorded on tape what we had translated together, and translated some Old Testament stories on his own.

I had been training Nelson in translation principles as we worked day by day. I wanted to test how he would do on his own; the Old Testament stories would be relatively easy. He could write them as stories, rather than as actual translations. I felt sure he could handle it while I was away.

When I checked Nelson's stories later I was enormously pleased. His work was excellent. The stories were just what would challenge beginning readers: easy, interesting reading, and very accurate.

Later I found out some amusing news about how Nelson had accomplished such accurate work. Several of my fellow translators, working in other languages, told me that whenever Nelson wasn't sure what something meant, he would call on the telephone and ask one of them for help. I had assumed he would save the questions for my return, but he didn't have the patience for that. He wanted to know right then! He wanted to get it right and to go on to the next part of the story. I praised God for my longsuffering fellow workers. And for Nelson's diligence and enthusiasm.

Later when the Old Testament stories were printed, many

Aguaruna read them eagerly. One man read the entire book about Moses, seventy-five pages, without stopping—surely a feat for a newly literate person. The story of Samson became a great favorite; with his long hair, he might have been an Aguaruna! Whenever the people came to the account of Delilah, they exclaimed, "That's just the way women are—always deceiving you!"

Nelson's ability as a translator was becoming more and more evident. God had sent him to help finish the New Testament, I felt sure. I believe it was for this very reason that Satan began to tempt him in extraordinary ways. But the flames he meant to consume Nelson, God used to strengthen him. Our next four years of translation were turbulent years, which tested the faith of both of us far beyond our expectations. Nelson had another dark side, I discovered—one much more difficult to overcome.

30

In Other Words

God gave Nelson a unique vision and unique experiences to prepare him to fulfill that vision. Uppermost in his mind was his desire to found a Bible school at Nueva Vida. Attending the Swiss Indian Bible School, near Yarinacocha, had helped to prepare him for this task. But since this was a new school, made up of students who knew very little Spanish, it gave him only limited training. Nelson wanted more. He decided on a four-year school where he could gain further education and also earn a diploma. He chose the Christian and Missionary Alliance Bible School in Huanuco, in the mountains.

Another key stage of preparation for Nelson was his work as my cotranslator. Working through books of the New Testament word by word, line by line, thought by thought, was about the most thorough kind of Bible study a person could do. During Nelson's first summer off from his studies in Huanuco, he returned to Yarinacocha to work with me on the final revision of the book of Luke and other portions of the New Testament. Keenly perceptive, Nelson picked up many small details which needed clarification for an Aguaruna reader. As we began going through Luke 1, he asked, "Who was Zacharias' other wife?"

"What do you mean?" I asked. "He had only one wife."

"Then why does it say 'your wife Elizabeth' if he had no other? We have already said in verse five that Zacharias' wife's name is Elizabeth. If we say 'your wife Elizabeth' again, it will mean he also had another wife by some other name. We should just say 'your wife' here in verse eleven. We know her name already." We made the correction and continued on through the passage.

After a minute, Nelson again stopped writing. He thought for a minute.

"I know why people translate literally, Millie," he said. "It's because they don't know what something means. When I truly know what a passage means, then I can say it like we Aguaruna say it. But if I don't, all I can do is put down words. I must know what it really means in order to translate well."

"How true," I thought. Over and over as we had done the preliminary translation of Luke, we had hit problems. Only if I understood and could explain exactly what Luke meant could we get a clear translation that expressed his meaning in Aguaruna terms. I had thought that Luke would be easy in comparison to the epistles we had been working on, but right from the beginning we were continually faced with the question "What does it truly mean?"

For instance, in verse one the text says, "The things which have been accomplished among us." But "things" in Aguaruna are only physical objects. If we translated literally, it would mean something like "those objects which some of us made." Luke, of course, is writing about what Jesus had taught and done, about His life as He lived among the Jewish people. We translated this thought to read, "how Jesus taught and lived here with us."

"Most excellent Theophilus," in verse three, was another problem. In Aguaruna speech, vocatives come only at the beginning or the end of the idea. So to have a name here sounded like Luke was starting some new idea right in the middle of his discussion. We placed the greeting at the very beginning of the book and joined the ideas of verses one and three. Then it sounded right in Aguaruna. "Theophilus" served as a greeting and signalled the introduction of the idea.

"The division of Abijah," in verse five, also needed explanation. I described for Nelson how the priests were divided into groups and took turns with the work and responsibilities in the temple. But Nelson wasn't happy with this idea. The Aguaruna do not think of dividing to work, but rather of uniting into groups with a leader.

"We must translate it this way, Millie," he said. "Zacharias worked with those who united to work with Abijah.' "

Luke traced Elizabeth's line by describing her as "a wife of the daughters of Aaron." But if we translated this literally, the Aguaruna would get the idea that Elizabeth's actual father was named Aaron. We had to express this relationship by saying, "his wife was from priest Aaron's lineage." Luke knew that Theophilus would understand who Aaron was—their ancestor Moses' brother, the first of the priestly line. Luke's meaning is implicit—that Elizabeth was also of the priestly line. In translating clearly for the Aguaruna, who had no background in Jewish history, we had to make this meaning explicit.

Luke 5:10, a favorite passage for us in English, also created a problem for the Aguaruna. Jesus, in speaking to the disciples about their role in bringing about His kingdom, says, "Henceforth you will be catching men." He compares catching fish to catching men. But for the Aguaruna, fish are not *caught*, they are *killed*. To carry the analogy across literally would be to say the disciples are to be *killers of men*. Even to say "catching men" would not work. It would be unnatural and would still lead to wrong meaning because "to catch men" means "to put them in jail." At best, this would make Peter out to be a policeman. To use Jesus' play on words in Greek was out of the question when expressed in Aguaruna words. We had to express Jesus' essential meaning—that Peter would become one who would tell God's Word in order for people to be brought into the kingdom of God—in a clear way. We finally solved this problem by translating it "Beginning now, leaving off killing fish, you will tell God's Word in order that people become those belonging to God."

The responsibility for seeing that Nelson understood each passage fell to me. I spent a full month, all day every day, studying through Hebrews before we started to work on it together. Then we spent two full days discussing and writing a description of the tabernacle and the Jewish sacrificial system. We worked out all the vocabulary before starting our verse-by-verse translation. This background was essential for Nelson in order to make our work accurate as well as idiomatic. We enjoyed doing Hebrews. It communicates as clearly as any book we translated. I had told Nelson before we started that Hebrews would be difficult, but when we finished he said, "This wasn't so hard. I thought you said it was difficult."

"Oh, Nelson," I laughed, "the hard part was *my* job, before we started to work together."

The translation process truly fascinated me. I was excited about finding solutions to difficult problems in communicating the Word, but an even greater thrill for me was seeing the effect of the translated Word. Many times it seemed like we worked on a passage that was exactly right for a problem in our lives at that moment.

One day in February, Nelson seemed preoccupied; he was unable to concentrate. I knew something was bothering him. In the afternoon, when I had to be away at a meeting, I left him to retype some of the material we had been working on. When I got home he was gone. He had left a note:

> My sister, I'm returning to my house. If I want to, I'll come back tonight. However, if I don't want to, I'll come tomorrow. If I do, I'll see you. Now at 4 P.M. I am leaving to go to my house to think. Don't worry about it. This is my personal business. I want to think by myself. Forgive me for being like this.

I tried to think of any reason Nelson might have for being upset with me. The only difficult discussion we had had recently was about his salary. He had met a man in town who asked him how much he was paid. When he told him, the man said, "You should get twice that much. A bilingual translator is worth much more than that." The man was referring to an English-Spanish translator on the Lima pay scale. This scale did not apply to wages in the jungle for an Aguaruna-Spanish bilingual. Nelson received the standard wage for such work in the jungle. We had discussed this and I had thought that Nelson wasn't taking the man's advice too seriously. But maybe he was, I now reflected.

Then I looked at the passage I had asked Nelson to retype. It was Luke 17, including verse 13: "You cannot serve both God and money." I found that this was precisely Nelson's struggle. God was dealing with him about this, and he wanted to go home to work through his conflict.

Nelson often wrote in his diary whenever he was under special pressure. Later he showed me his notes for that day:

> I knew that even before I was born God chose me to translate His Word. I am content even when there are problems. When others get more money, I think, 'Surely in this work I should get a lot more money, equal to others.' But I also know that in this thought of mine there is much to be feared. If I love money more, and leave God to the

side, money may become my god. So I'll not concern myself more about money. I'll just be concerned about having
the things I need most, without worrying about it.

The next day, Nelson was back at work, translating again. He
never again mentioned the matter of salary. He had found his answer in the very words, in the Word, he was translating.

31

Nelson's Other Dark Side

During the time Nelson worked with me on Luke, the sixteenth teacher training course was underway. It looked like we were in for a tremendous summer. Ninety-six Aguaruna were at Yarinacocha. Some were in the teachers' course; many were attending high school in Pucallpa, in special sessions designed to help the bilingual teachers finish their own secondary education.

Roman was on the faculty of the teacher training course, teaching history and arithmetic. David was teaching pedagogy and supervising practice teaching sessions, working closely with Martha. He had finished high school the previous summer. Alias was attending high school, trying to make up for the summers he missed while helping me translate. Martha, Jeanne, Dennis and Susie were all at Yarinacocha to help. I had high hopes of getting much translation done during those summer months.

Day after day, Nelson and I continued to translate together. In the evenings, he led a devotional time with the teachers. He also took the responsibility to lead two meetings for them on Sundays.

Everything seemed to go well for a few weeks, but then one Sunday in February Nelson didn't show up to lead the evening meeting. Roman took over for him, leading the singing, and speaking.

"What could have happened to Nelson?" I wondered, feeling troubled at his sudden absence. Then I found out he had gone to visit in a neighboring village because of a girl he had seen there. Later he told me about it.

"Beginning in February, I didn't feel like I could live well any more. At first I had done my work well. But I began thinking of my problem of not having a wife and of wanting to be married. I became angry at God. I wasn't able to do my work anymore. I thought, 'I'll just leave and go home and suffer in my own house and do my work. I'll tell my sister Millie, "Work with somebody else. Work with somebody that really knows. I don't know enough."' "

Nelson sensed the true source of his battle. He wrote in his diary:

> I think the devil doesn't like the work we are doing. He is planning how he can cause the teaching of God's Word to stop so that the teachers will not follow God well. I think about that and I really want God's power to enter into me. But I have no power.

Nelson's struggle continued, evident in his work as well as his other activities. One day he would be in a good mood, and our work would move ahead. The next day, he would be dark and stormy, and we would accomplish little. It seemed as if nothing I said helped him.

I too felt weak and powerless before the enemy who was so obviously tormenting Nelson. Nelson continued to feel powerless. Yet his deep desire to obey God never left him. In late February he wrote to a friend:

> God's Word tells us that He says, "My followers, you should not worry about what you will eat or what you will wear. I am your Father and I will never die." I was thinking about that and thinking about my own father who had died a long time ago. I thought, "It's true that my earthly father is gone. But it is really God who gives people life, not anyone else. I can say to everyone, 'God is my Father.' Also, like a person obeys his own father by listening to him, I should obey my heavenly Father and then I will live well.
>
> I have done God's work for seven years now. Pray for me. I want to tell God's Words to those who haven't heard yet.

As Nelson continued to lead the teachers, his messages often centered in his own struggles. I longed that he might find the answer for his spiritual impotence and be able to share answers more than problems. Then one day in March he opened his heart to them with touching honesty.

"I want very much to follow God, but I am separating myself from God," he said. "But that won't happen if we just do what God has told us to do. It's not obeying him, it's doing what we want, which separates us, my brothers.

"I am really suffering because I've been getting into trouble with women. I'm very wicked and the others are gossiping about me. Sometimes I am tempted to stop doing God's work and just do some other work. Then I wouldn't feel embarrassed and ashamed. I could just forget that I am supposed to obey God's Word.

"But in my heart, I don't despise God. The desire to obey God is there, but I just cannot do it. I long to live like others who live well. They pray for me. They say, 'God help him, free him, change his heart so that he will not separate himself from You, so that he will again live with You.' I thank those who pray like that for me. They love me. But I don't know what to do. Really, only God knows my problems. I live for nothing. People listen to me and respect me. But before God I am completely useless. What I am doing is so empty. But God knows that.

"God's Word says, 'I can do all things through Christ who gives me strength.' The devil has deceived me. Pray to God and read God's Word so the devil will not deceive you."

The teachers listened empathetically to Nelson as he shared. But no one seemed to have an answer for his dilemma. I could quote all kinds of Scripture for him, yet I knew that my own life was just as weak as his. I was just as powerless. My temptations were different ones, but the weakness I felt was the same.

A week later, Nelson wrote this note:

> Today I have been even more wicked. I'm not living at all well. I bother other people by always talking about how bad I am. I don't want to read God's Word because it also reminds me of how bad I am. When others pray I feel ashamed. I am afraid that if I die feeling like this, I won't go to heaven. But then, bad people like me can't go to heaven anyway, so I am sure I won't be able to go. I will be lost because of my evil desires. God, I want to live a good life, I want to be free, I want to be happy. But I am not able to live the way I would like to live. God, help me.

The next day as we were again translating, Nelson's spiritual battle became even more evident. He turned the radio up loud, as it blared out a wild song about sensual love, to show his indifference to God. But at the same time, he was checking Luke 18—the parable of the Pharisee and the publican praying in the temple.

"Lord, if only Nelson would cry out to you," I prayed silently. "I know that's what he really wants to do." I could scarcely hold back my tears as I felt the struggle of darkness against Nelson's soul. "Oh, God, please win this battle," I prayed. I wish that I had known then that I need not beg God to win, that His victory over our enemy was already won. But I was so ignorant of spiritual warfare that I did not know then that I need only claim what He had already accomplished.

Next, Nelson took time out to play with a razor. He wanted to do anything except to read the next verse. Then his eyes filled with tears.

"To me the Bible is like any other book," he said, weeping. "I'll keep on working, but as though it's just like any other work, not like it is really the inspired Word of God. Everyone knows what a sinner I am. Even my friends say, 'You're acting like a worldling.' How can I pray? I don't feel able to pray. I don't believe."

Nelson gave way to a flood of tears. We wept together, and eventually he was able to pray.

Three days afterwards, he again wrote in his diary:

> Today hasn't been like the other days. I was able to do more. I thank God because I feel he is helping me. We can't say that God doesn't help us when we sin. God has helped me very much. I want to complete His work. If God helps me, I'll tell His Word.

Considering Nelson's depression, it seemed best that he return home rather than return for another year of studies. Once he had settled the question of marriage, he would probably be much happier; that would be easier to do at home.

Nelson returned home by way of Lima to see Mrs. Cudney and then went on up the Peruvian coast by bus. He took a truck over the Andes to Nazaret and from there caught a boat to Nueva Vida.

I wasn't able to return to Nueva Vida until the end of June. In early July the teachers held their yearly conference. When I arrived, Alias, Tomas and Nelson were planning the evening meetings for the conference together. I felt grateful to see Nelson back in fellowship with God and his fellow pastors. "Perhaps we will get a lot of translation done in these next few months," I thought, never dreaming of the struggles that were yet to come.

32

So This Is Julia

"Julia has arrived! Julia has arrived!" One after another, Nelson' relatives dropped by my house at Nueva Vida with this news.

His relatives had realized that if they didn't act soon, Nelson would go on trying to get a wife his own way. His mother and her brothers decided it was time for his marriage to his cousin Julia. Julia's mother had run away from her husband, Jempeket, before Julia was born and had lived downriver near Nieva ever since. Julia, however, was still considered to be her father's property to give away when she was ready for marriage. So, he had gone downriver to bring back the prospective bride.

Nelson came over to my house when it was time for us to begin translating.

"I suppose you've heard that Julia has arrived," he said casually, trying to suppress his excitement.

"Have you seen her?" I asked.

"No," he said, "she's at her father's house. He's going to bring her over here this morning so we can meet her." I could sense Nelson's high spirits. "We won't get much done on Romans today," I thought. "At last, he is going to meet this cousin he is supposed to marry."

The moment arrived when Nelson would see the much-talked about Julia! We heard a rise in the volume of chatter at the house of Tiginkas, Nelson's mother, and knew that her brother Jempeket and Julia had come. Soon everyone moved over to our house. Jempeket and Julia came in and sat down on a bench by the wall.

"Buenos dias, Señorita," Julia greeted me. I was surprised that she knew Spanish.

"So this is Julia," I thought. "Why, she's just a gangly teenager, probably not more than fifteen." Julia had big, expressive eyes and a pretty oval face. But it was hard to know what she actually looked like beyond that. She was smudged all over with *suwa* dye. Obviously she had been dying her hair with the seeds the Aguaruna use to make it blacker and more shiny. But she had managed to get it all over her face and hands as well. She wore an old, tattered dress, also splotched with *suwa*. It was much shorter than those usually worn by Aguaruna women. Later I would understand why her appearance on such an important day seemed so careless. She told me several weeks later that when her father told her he was taking her to see her future husband, she decided to make herself as repulsive as possible so he wouldn't want her. But her ruse didn't work.

"My sister, I must go and work now," Jempeket said to me after a while. "I will leave Julia here today."

I let go of my last thoughts of getting any translation done. I pulled out the latest *Life* magazine, filled with pictures of men walking on the moon, and some other books I had around. We all looked at them together. Both Julia and Nelson wanted to get acquainted, but they were not acting like themselves at all; they felt awkward and self-conscious, knowing everyone's attention was focused on them.

When Jempeket returned in the afternoon, he was encouraged by what he found.

"I will bring Julia back tomorrow," he said.

It was soon obvious that Nelson and Julia liked each other. At noon on the second day, Nelson said he would like to have the afternoon off work to talk with Julia. Since I knew no one objected to their being together, I agreed. They must have had a good talk, because it took them only an hour to agree that the plan of their aunts and uncles was good.

That evening, Jempeket went home alone, leaving Julia with Nelson. After knowing each other for only two days, they were married thus, according to Aguaruna custom. They were more fortunate than most Aguaruna youth in this regard. Usually the girl had no prior knowledge of her marriage and no voice in the matter.

"This is just like Isaac and Rebecca," Nelson beamed. "It's really marvelous! I asked God for a wife, but I was busy looking for one myself. Now He's given me one without my looking, and she's the only one who is just the kind of girl I wanted. I wanted someone who speaks Spanish, is friendly, likes people, and is full of fun and jokes. Julia is just like this!"

"I know God gave you to me," Nelson told Julia, "so I'll never throw you out."

"But if you beat me, I'll run away," she countered. Both would remember those prophetic words many times in the tumultuous years ahead.

33

New Life in Nueva Vida?

With Nelson's need for a wife settled, it seemed that Satan began to attack in new ways, to keep us from progressing in translation of the Scriptures.

A youth from the village of Kayamas, across the river, was caught having an affair with a girl in Nueva Vida. The people of Nueva Vida punished the boy and sent him home, which angered the people of Kayamas. Tempers flared and words flew, fueled by past grievances between the villages. Nelson was the most outspoken about it at Nueva Vida. He said much which he later regretted. Earlier, the people of Kayamas had killed his brother-in-law. His peaceful brother, Esteban, now the teacher at Nueva Vida, had witnessed the killing. It was hard to forget, and Nelson's anger over the current incident was wrapped up with this old grievance.

By September, the feuding had cooled down, and Nelson and Julia returned with me to Yarinacocha. On the last Sunday before leaving, Nelson urged his people to follow Christ and not to fight with the enemy.

"May our town's name not just be a name," he told them. "May there truly be "new life" here.

"During January and February, I plan to travel with Alias and Tomas to evangelize new areas," he continued. "Will you pray for us, and for the completion of the translation of the New Testament by 1972? We need your prayers for this work."

Esteban stood to pray before the people went home. "God, please forgive us for not loving our enemies, as your Word tells us to do. Help us to live in peace. Help Nelson and Alias and Tomas as they take Your Word to our brothers who don't know it yet."

As we were flying to Yarinacocha, I felt a strong desire to stop off at Potro to see how Alias and the people there were doing. I could see right away that my desire to stop had been prompted by the Holy Spirit.

We found an epidemic of malaria among the people; many were ill with the typical high fevers and racking chills. Though Alias had taken a large store of medicine with him in April, it was all gone now. He didn't even have one aspirin to give his five-year-old son, who sat by the fire shaking with chills, crying because of his aching head and bones. The pilot gave him what little he could from his emergency medical kit.

A woman had also been bitten recently by a snake; her wound wasn't healing well at all. She too needed attention. How glad I was that we had stopped.

In spite of these crises, and the fact that we had just arrived in Potro at about four o'clock, Alias called a meeting at five. He asked Nelson to teach. Alias began the meeting.

"Yesterday, we prayed together that God would send the plane so we could get medicine," Alias reminded his people. "And the plane came! Now we must thank God together."

Nelson taught about the second coming of Christ. Most of the people were already believers because of Alias' faithful teaching, but fourteen committed themselves to Christ for the first time that afternoon. I was even more convinced that God had brought us there!

Alias and Nelson sat up late into the night, planning their evangelistic trip. Alias also made out an order for more medicines.

A few days later, when Nelson, Julia, and I arrived at Yarinacocha, I was greeted with an urgent radio call from Jeanne, still in Nueva Vida.

"There has been a battle between Nueva Vida and Kayamas, Millie. Many were wounded, including Esteban. He's wounded badly, but I'm taking care of him. I think he's going to be okay."

When I shared the news with Nelson, he wanted to return immediately. Desire for revenge burned within him, lessened only slightly by Jeanne's assurance that Esteban was going to be all right. He agreed to stay on at Yarinacocha, but he couldn't resist sending a couple of letters to his enemies:

Timias, how are you? Why do you just keep on fighting?

Now you've beaten up my brother. Now listen well, you who kill my relatives. If you want to live longer, take off to the high mountains and live with the bears. Learn how the bears fight and fight with them. Do you think when you killed my brother-in-law you killed a man with no family? I am his family. When you killed him you didn't kill me. If you want to kill me, kill me quickly, and then you can kill the rest of my family.

About the same time, Nelson wrote to Alias a totally different letter, revealing his inner struggle between God's way and the Aguaruna custom of revenge.

Big Alias, I'm writing this letter to you. May God help you to tell His Word with power. I'm thinking a lot about the trip we are going to take to preach God's Word. Tell the brothers there with you to continue obeying Christ.

I watched Nelson's struggle, sympathetic to the conflict he felt. "What would I do if someone killed or injured my family?" I thought. "I'd tell the police, and then the police would put him in jail or send him to the electric chair. I'd probably go and testify if I had seen it happen. I would feel I had done my duty. My society takes care of revenge for me. It punishes my enemies. But what if I were in a society without a police force? And what if I did report the murder, and no one listened? Would I sit calmly by and say, 'It's all right. I forgive him.'? In our society, from earliest childhood on, we are taught to love, to forgive, and not to fight. Yet I get angry if a neighbor slights me. What would I do if all my life I had been taught to revenge? If failing to revenge was synonymous with being a coward, would I be willing to be a coward? If it would be interpreted as not loving my family would I still not take revenge? Jesus said, 'He who hates his brother is a murderer.' Maybe Nelson's sin of wanting revenge isn't so much greater than mine; perhaps it is just more obvious."

I prayed for Nelson in his struggle, knowing his weakness and my own. Gradually he turned his attention back to other things.

While at Yarinacocha, Nelson and Julia were officially married, according to Peruvian law, by the justice of the peace nearby. Nelson also asked a Spanish pastor from the Swiss Bible school to perform a religious marriage for them.

"This really ought to last," I thought. "They are thrice married now!"

The hot tempers cooled down in Nueva Vida and Kayamas. When we returned there the first of December, life was quiet—on the surface at least. But when Nelson saw Esteban's swollen face, he felt another surge of hatred toward the people of Kayamas. But he smothered his feelings and again turned back to translation.

Nelson had seen pictures and a demonstration of the Christmas story. He was determined to have an original Christmas program, to demonstrate Aguaruna-style how Christ came into the world. He got the community together to explain his plan for the drama, and then invited many families from neighboring villages to come to see it.

Of course, no Aguaruna had ever seen a wise man, or a shepherd, or even a sheep. But Nelson assured them that Millie and Martha would know what a wise man looked like, and that we could work out the characters. So Martha made crowns for the wise men, with jewels cut from the colorful wrappers of hand soap. I hunted up props and costumes for dressing sheep and shepherds, Mary and Joseph, and the kings and soldiers. Two of our dishpans made effective shields for King Herod's soldiers. An old canteen made a fine box for myrrh; a cookie box served for the frankincense. Gold was a bit harder to come by, but we found some yellowish paper to cover a small box. We cut sheep ears out of paper and pinned them to flour-sack dish towels tied under the chins of the three wiggly, would-be sheep.

Nelson and the men got busy manufacturing beards. They decided palm fiber would work for the shepherds, wise men, and Joseph. But King Herod deserved something more elaborate; a three-year-old lost his beautiful, long hair to make King Herod's the best beard of all. Hector was pleased; he made an appropriately fearsome King Herod. Since Esteban and his wife had the newest baby in the village, the people chose them to be Mary and Joseph.

When the day of the performance arrived, Nelson was master of ceremonies. He announced the scenes one by one.

"You will now see Mary and Joseph and the baby Jesus," he intoned. As the players appeared for each scene, Nelson read the Christmas story, translated into Aguaruna. When the shepherds came "on stage," they were followed by three little sheep, crawling on all fours. They waited patiently for the reading. But when the scene was over, the three little sheep got up abruptly on their hind legs and ran off the stage, white dish towels flapping behind them. For children who had never seen sheep, it was a beautiful performance. No one laughed at all, except Martha and me.

After all the scenes had been acted out, Nelson again read the whole story and explained more about Jesus coming to earth because of His love for man. We were thrilled then as four men from far up in the mountains committed themselves to Jesus.

"We want to follow Jesus, too," they said, "and to have him as our owner."

Afterwards, we had a big community dinner, with wild pork and banana soup and baskets full of manioc and roasted green bananas, served out on huge, clean banana leaves.

Martha and I had pinned up our Christmas cards on the cane half-walls of our house. Nobody had paid much attention to them before the Christmas program, but afterwards, the cards suddenly came alive. Everyone looked and pointed. All afternoon we heard, "There is Mary!" "There is Jesus!" "Look! The wise men!" "Look at the sheep." We were very grateful for Nelson's imagination and drive, which had captured the Aguaruna's hearts and minds so graphically.

Before Martha and I returned again to Yarinacocha, in early January of 1970, Alias arrived at Nueva Vida. He and Nelson made final plans for their evangelism trip. They packed books and medicines. They had money for gas in hand, and a boat ready to go. When we left, they lacked only one thing: a mechanic was to stop by to fix Alias' outboard motor, and then their missionary journey would be underway.

34

The Flood

Eager to be on their way, Alias and Nelson were very disappointed when the mechanic found serious problems with the motor; they would have to wait for parts. On January 9, Alias decided to return upriver to Nazaret to wait for Nelson there and to buy the gas supply for their trip.

Late that day, Nelson began to realize that something was amiss. The river came up quickly; it was no ordinary rise. Fed by heavy rains in the mountains above, and unable to push its way through the gorge below Kayamas, the river backed up, forming a huge lake. It quickly became the worst flooding of the Marañon River in decades, covering Kayamas, Nueva Vida, and Wawaim.

At Nueva Vida, the water rose so abruptly that the people had little warning of disaster. It quickly flooded the first row of houses above the river bank. Nelson's uncle jumped into his canoe, and calling for help, began throwing everything into the boat. He could feel the ground giving way beneath his feet. Escaping just in time, he watched his huge house crash into the rushing water.

The people worked together furiously, fighting the ferocious enemy. At each house, they quickly piled all belongings into canoes and moved up to the second row of houses. The homes of Nelson, Esteban, and all their close relatives, as well as the house that Martha and I used whenever we were there, were safe on this higher land.

But then the water rushed higher, filling the small valley separating the first and second rows of houses. With another deafening crash, Zacarias' house tumbled into the current. Nelson's grandmother's house was next; in just a short time the whole first row of houses was gone. Horrified, the people watched them disappear into the whirlpools below them.

But there was little time for watching. Water was already swishing through the second row of houses too. They must abandon them at once!

A huge balsa raft provided their only hope of saving their possessions. Frantically they pulled it up to the houses, one by one, as the river continued to rise, and began to pile everything on the raft. Since we had excess baggage on our flight out, Martha and I had left our radio, with our other things, in our house. The pilot was to pick it up a couple of weeks later. Considerate of our things even in our absence, the men grabbed the radio and battery, our small cupboard with dishes, pots and pans, a suitcase in which I had left papers and books, and my old duffle of clothes. They piled these on the raft, leaving the antenna dangling from the roof in the darkness. They hastily threw on their own pots, baskets, and animals, as well the boxes of books and medicines that the plane had just brought out for Nelson's and Alias' trip.

By now, the storm itself had overtaken them directly. The rain continued to pour down; the river continued to rush up. The abandoned houses filled with water.

The homeless people, drenched and cold, tried to keep track of crying, frightened children and whimpering dogs as they maneuvered the raft up the mountainside in the dark. With machetes, they hacked a passageway for the raft; it often snagged on the trees and slowed them down. By midnight the water reached is peak; the people were by then at least a half mile from the site of the village.

Finally they reached the one house that was not flooded. Tying up the canoes and the raft, they gathered in the house. Eleven families, soaked and exhausted, all slept in that one small house. All their possessions sat out in the rain, getting wetter and wetter. As the women all wept, Nelson commented, "If Millie were here, she'd be crying too."

The next day, in spite of the incessant rain, the men cut saplings and leaves and built temporary shelters in the jungle. The women searched for food. All their gardens were still under water, but they managed to find palm heart in the jungle and the few bananas they had thrown on the raft as they left their flooding homes.

Two days later, the water had receded enough that Nelson could take the radio and battery back down to our house. The second row of houses, including ours, was still standing. Wading in, he managed to find a high place to put the radio and battery; he was happy to find the antenna still dangling in its place. Standing in water up to his chest, he radioed us at Yarinacocha to report the flood.

"It's impossible to think of going ahead with the evangelistic trip now, Millie," he said. "I can't think of leaving my family. Many houses have to be built; we have to plant our gardens again and search for food. By the time the water recedes, the manioc and banana plants will all be rotten.

"But, Millie, we saved all your things. Someone even found your cat sitting high up in a balsa tree, where it had been all three days."

"We'll do what we can to help you, Nelson," I assured him, feeling very grateful that our radio, having been left behind, was now such a vital link to help.

We found out that other villages had suffered the same fate. At Kayamas, seven houses had disappeared into the raging river during the night. Napuruk, below the gorge, suffered most from the disaster. Numerous homes were flooded, and all up and down the river the gardens were destroyed, wiping out several months' food supply.

Dennis immediately went to Lima to make arrangements for relief food. He wasn't able to secure food the Aguaruna were accustomed to, but at least he got food that would keep them from starvation until the gardens grew again. In desperation, Nelson took some of the money planned for the evangelistic trip and went downriver to buy food after the flood passed. He used most of the gas they had purchased for their trip to go for food and to help Dennis distribute the food he brought from Lima.

We all wondered why God would allow such a delay in taking His Word to new areas. Yet it seemed that having the money and gas in hand for the evangelism trip was God's way of providing for the people during this crisis. I was thankful that Nelson and Alias had not left before the flood. It would have been so much worse for them, and for their families, if they had been gone during that disastrous time. Their own lives might also have been in jeopardy had they been traveling downriver then. We were all grateful that God spared these two special servants of His, knowing that His work with them was not complete.

35

I Can't Stop Myself

Before I had left Nelson and Julia in January, I had arranged for them to come to Yarinacocha at the end of March so we could work on translation for a month before Nelson began his second year at Bible school in Huanuco. Since I would be leaving to train new linguists at our summer school, held at the University of Oklahoma, it was important for us to have this time together.

When the plane from Yarinacocha went out, Nelson met it alone, without Julia. He flew with the pilot as far as another airstrip, where they spent the night. But the next morning, the pilot called to say that Nelson wanted to talk to me.

"I'm going back to Nueva Vida, Millie," he said. "I'm not coming. My brother is sick, and my mother is going to have a baby. I need to be here to help build her shelter for giving birth and to help with the work afterwards when she is weak."

"I'm sorry you can't come. I did so hope you and Julia could come. Perhaps it will still work out somehow," I suggested. Nelson's excuses just didn't make sense to me. He had known all that before he had gotten on the plane. He wasn't giving me the real reasons. But I knew it would be impossible to get to the bottom of the problem by radio, so Nelson returned home on a shuttle flight for other passengers.

On March 30, the plane returned, with a letter from Nelson. It gave me no concrete help in seeing why he had turned back. I could see that he was thwarted in what he really wanted to do, but he wasn't telling me the whole truth. His anger and depression troubled me greatly.

My dear sister Millie,

I wanted to do God's work just as you want to do it, but now I've lost all desire for that. I'm not well. My head aches every day. Sometimes I wonder if I'll ever feel good again. I really did want to help other people and especially to go on the evangelistic trip. But because we didn't have a motor we weren't able to go. I've tried everything in order to go but it hasn't worked out, so I think I'll just stay home and suffer like everyone else.

I'm also giving up my plan to have an Aguaruna Bible school because I don't have any money to use for it. I'm just nobody and people laugh at my ideas. They make fun of my plans, so I've decided to forget it all. There are other pastors who know a lot more than I do. I haven't learned well. I think about this a lot and wonder what I should do. I said that I would evangelize and have a Bible school but now I don't think I will. If I had a motor, I could travel with my brother Esteban and sell Scripture. I feel like I haven't really done anything worthwhile. I have sinned a lot. I haven't treated you well either and you have suffered much because of me and the bad things I've done. I'm not trying to hide my sin because God knows all about it.

Why am I thinking like this? I said goodbye to all my family. Also I told my wife, "I'm going to school," and I came here to meet the airplane. But here there is no food and no place to sleep. Here I have no friends. I have no food and I am hungry. So I'll just go home.

What shall I do now? Perhaps I will work for the priest. Sister, I wonder if I should quit working with you. You should have someone else who knows more work for you. I used to say, "With God's help I will leave something that will be remembered." I said that about the translation I wanted to complete. But now I say, "I don't help. I just destroy." I'm very unhappy.

You will be saved. But I don't know yet; perhaps I will not go to heaven. I am most concerned about that.

I am very grateful to those who helped me study. Tell them that I appreciate their help very much. But I haven't used it to accomplish anything worthwhile. I'm ashamed that I didn't learn to live well. Therefore I'm going to stay at home. I'll never come back to your house because I'm ashamed of what I have done. But don't be concerned when you hear this. Just keep thinking good thoughts. I tell people about the good you do. Please forgive me for writing this letter.

Julia loves you most of all, and now she will never see you again. My mother loves you very much also, and she will also feel our separation. I too will always love you, but now we part. We part and I am completely sad.

Give my greeting to Grandmother Cudney. She will not be happy when she hears. Give my greetings to all who know me there at Yarinacocha. That's all for now. I'm not going to build the bookstore. Also the house we were going to build for you—we will probably not build it. Rather I wonder where we should send your things. They are all ruined by the flood. I will not do any of the things we planned to do. That's all there is to say. I just go around in misery. Perhaps I will die. May God help you. Nelson.

I had just finished reading Nelson's letter and was wondering what to do, when the director came to see me. That was unusual. Usually if he needed me he called me to his office.

"Millie," Rolland said gently, "I have some difficult news for you. Your father has passed away in Minnesota."

"Oh! When did he die?" I asked. "I've been expecting it." Then we talked about my father's death and I told him of his long illness. Rolland prayed and read Psalm 116:15 (THE LIVING BIBLE) to me: "His loved ones are very precious to him and he does not lightly let them die."

"Yes," I thought, "surely this is a comfort. My father, at eighty-three, is now free from suffering. It is easy to commit him to God. My real burden is for Nelson."

"But Millie, don't you see," God seemed to whisper back to me, "this verse applies beautifully to Nelson too. I love him also. He is very precious to me. I do not lightly let anything happen to any of my children. I am still in control."

There was no way I could discuss Nelson's depression or his problem with him immediately. I was occupied with our branch executive committee meetings, branch conference, and then some translation seminars. But I prayed daily that Nelson would still somehow return to Bible school in May. I didn't foresee that God would use me to encourage Nelson directly.

Then Lorrie Anderson, linguist with the Candoshi, located to the west of the Aguaruna, came o see me.

"Do you have anything you want sent out, Millie?" she asked. "I'm paying for an emergency medical flight, but the plane is going out empty. You might as well use the weight."

Jeanne and Martha got busy right away getting cargo ready. I began to feel God wanted me to go out on the flight too. I couldn't escape the idea, so I called Jerry Elder, my supervisor.

"Jerry," I said, "you know about the problems Nelson's been having, and about the flood. Lorrie's sending a flight out today. What would you think if I..."

"I think you should go," Jerry interrupted without hesitation.

Thus I packed quickly, not knowing whether I was going for two days or two weeks. It turned out that I stayed three weeks.

When I arrived at Nueva Vida, Nelson had gone upriver again for food. So I knew I must stay until the next flight scheduled to bring Jeanne and Martha out. Lorrie told me later that the patient she sent the plane for didn't come to Yarinacocha after all. They had already taken him downriver when the plane arrived. So it seemed as though Lorrie's flight was meant to get me to Nelson's village.

I was impressed with what the people had done in the four months since the flood. Every family now had a new house—some of them large—back up in the hills, away from the river. They had cleared a great deal of land and had planted as best they could. Since the flooding, the trees and underbrush had not yet dried out enough for them to burn them, as was their custom in slash-and-burn style gardening. That left little space for planting.

There were still no manioc, plantain, or other staple foods. A few bananas or a manioc root had become a great treat. The river was too high for fishing and many of the small animals had drowned. The people finally butchered their one pig, but with eleven families to feed, it didn't last long. If Dennis hadn't taken out relief food, the people would have faced starvation or severe malnutrition. For the three weeks I was there, we continued to live off government relief foods—flour, milk, and oil. But even these were rationed. I found some soda in the supplies I had left at Nueva Vida in January. I made soda biscuits and taught Julia how to make them too. Biscuits were a bit more appetizing than plain fried flour and water. I shared my few packages of dried soup too, but they didn't last long with so many hungry people. (I took my own evidence of the disaster back to Yarinacocha with me; I lost thirteen pounds in three weeks!)

During the four days I waited for Nelson's return, I lived with Julia and we cooked and ate together.

"Millie, Nelson dreamed that you were coming here on the plane," she told me. "When he left, he told us you were coming, so we weren't surprised to see you." I could only marvel again that someone's dream had come true.

When Nelson returned, he still seemed depressed.

"I went to look for other work, Millie," he said. "I've decided to teach in the Spanish primary school."

I said little to Nelson in reply. There was nothing to say. I just wanted to listen to him, to pray, and to try to find his real problem. I was sure I hadn't heard it yet. Finally I decided to be forthright.

"Why didn't you come to Yarinacocha in March, Nelson?" I asked.

"Because when I asked if I could come in the small plane, rather than in the big Catalina, you said, 'That's very difficult.' That made me mad."

This was only an excuse, I knew, so I continued to wait. Our first day together was strained. Nelson's usual relaxed friendliness didn't emerge until I told him about my father's death. Then he melted completely. He knew my father had been sick. He had prayed for him when we were at Nueva Vida in December.

"Millie, do you mean that instead of going right to the States, you stayed in Peru so you could come out to see us first? You really care that much about us?"

"Yes, Nelson, it was important to me to come to see you and Julia," I said. Nelson's whole manner changed. I could see he was deeply touched.

"I don't know about Bible school yet, but I will come to help you translate again when you return from your country in November, Millie," he agreed. He and others began plans to build a house for Martha and me.

Nelson and I worked on a school book and some hymns together. But I noticed he didn't read his Scriptures. He prayed only before meals and generally avoided talking about God.

"Have you decided about going to Bible school?" I finally asked him.

"I have to wait to ask Esteban," he said.

"Will Julia go with you if you go?" I asked, hoping to get to his deeper feelings.

"No," he said. So I let it go at that and prayed that God would bring Nelson back to a right relationship with Himself, and that He would direct him and Julia about school. I only wanted him to go if it was God's will.

But I too began to feel depressed. One day I found myself thinking very negatively.

"Is it worth it, coming out here and all? The money of the trip out, the time I'm spending, the money to send Nelson and others to school? Maybe I should forget it all."

Immediately God drew my attention to Psalm 49 (THE LIVING BIBLE): "For a soul is far too precious to be ransomed by mere earthly wealth. There is not enough of it in all the earth to buy eternal life for just one soul, to keep it out of hell."

"Yes," I thought, "God doesn't think in terms of money. Money is never God's problem. People are His concern. Nelson and Julia are precious to Him."

Yet I felt as though I was in the midst of a great battle. It turned out that Nelson was feeling this way too.

"I feel like I'm fighting a great war," he said one evening. "It's all going on inside of me. I want to obey God, but I don't want to."

We turned to Romans 7 and read Paul's account of his own inner struggle.

"I know that if I don't go to Bible school now I will start down another trail which will be against God. I've got to choose, but I can't. If I don't go to school, I know that I'll go all the way in revenge, fighting and killing until I myself am killed. I can't stop myself, Millie."

At last I understood Nelson's struggle; it had taken me two weeks! The old feuds weren't settled. That's what was holding him back. But I didn't see where Esteban fit in.

The next day, Nelson's Uncle Wajai, the teacher across the river, brought me a letter that Nelson had written to Timias, the teacher at Kayamas. It was a very angry letter, full of the old hatred. Wajai had begged Nelson to stop trying to carry out the ways of the ancestors, to stop writing these letters. "As a pastor, you should be helping people to forgive each other, not stirring up hatred and revenge," he had told Nelson.

When I talked to Nelson about the letter, the whole story finally spilled out. Nelson had left Nueva Vida on the plane, with every intention of going to Yarinacocha and then on to Bible school. Then at the airstrip where they spent the night, some teachers told him that another group of teachers had gotten together and made plans to take revenge on Nelson's father-in-law. Family loyalty was his duty; it had to come first, before going to school or anything else. Besides, his father-in-law was his mother's brother, so he was doubly bound to defend him. Once back at Nueva Vida, Nelson tried to defend his family in the only way he thought he could without killing—by writing angry letters. These, of course, made the problem worse instead of better. Nelson had to discuss the feud with Esteban before he could think of leaving. But again he was stymied; Esteban had gone far downriver to teach in another community.

At last I could see the source of Nelson's depression and anger. But I didn't know how to help him, except to pray for God to intervene somehow.

Then Nelson's sister Elsa became sick. Nelson tried to minister to her so that she might be healed. But as he endeavored to help her, he came up against an unexpected barrier; he could not pray for her healing without asking forgiveness for his own sin.

36

Possessed

It was a dreary, rainy evening when Nelson sent word to me of Elsa's sickness. As I entered the dimly lit thatched hut, I heard the eerie rhythm of the shaman's song. Elsa was chanting the song in a high, falsetto voice. Her husband and stepfather were holding her down as she lay on a sleeping platform.

Suddenly Elsa sat straight up, swinging her arms and shouting. Nelson and other men moved in closer to restrain her. After her violent outburst, she settled down again and continued to sing.

"I see you over there by the edge of the jungle," she chanted. "There are many of you. Don't come any closer."

"She has a demon, Millie," Nelson said to me. "Last time she was sick like this we all prayed and confessed our sins, and I wrote a song for casting out demons."

While the others held Elsa down, Nelson prayed for forgiveness. He poured out his heart in genuine repentance, first for his own sins and then for everyone else's. Then he sang this prayer:

> Father, God, you are the one to be praised.
> There is no other so great on this earth.
> You are the only one who frees us.
>
> Father, God, you sent your Son.
> He suffered and died to save me.
> He has bought me by his blood.
>
> You are the truly perfect one who will free me.

Come here to me. Throw out the demons.
I renounce the demons that molest me.

Do not allow the demon to try me.
I am not strong.
Holy Spirit, live in me. I want to live with you.

Suddenly Elsa jumped up. The men grabbed her, but instead of struggling again, she sank back onto the sleeping platform. Her body became limp; her singing stopped, and she peered up, recognizing the men around her.

"I'm tired," she said. Then she turned over and fell asleep.

"They're gone now," Nelson said. "The demons have left her."

Back in my own house, this experience with Elsa pulled my thoughts back to a morning several years before, when we had been gliding down the swift Marañon River. We suddenly heard shouting from the far shore; the men in our canoe paddled furiously across the powerful current and tied up near another canoe.

In the middle of the canoe sat a young woman, groaning with pain, her eyes wild with fear, and her hair tumbled about her head.

"We have no medicines with us," was my first thought. But everyone was talking at once.

"She's been cursed; she's going to die; it's *tunchi*," they all said.

For a few seconds the woman looked straight at me, her eyes exploding with hatred. A chill slid down my spine. A demon-possessed woman was staring at me! For the first time in my life, I knew that demons were real and powerful. Did I have the courage to cast them out, as Jesus gave his disciples power to do? If I tried, and failed, would it do more harm than good? How did I know I could really exorcise a demon?

As I wasted time in doubt, the wailing, shouting, distraught family continued upriver, on their way to visit a famous shaman. We floated on down the racing river. A great sense of failure engulfed me as they disappeared from view.

"I have failed this woman who so needed help," I reproached myself. "And I have failed my Savior, who has power to help her— or does He? If I believed it, why did I fail to act? I don't really believe. I have always thought of demons as figments of the imagination of primitive peoples, as superstitions learned from their ancestors. My relation to God doesn't involve power over evil in such an active form. What is this Christianity I have come to share with the Aguaruna? I am translating Scripture into their language, but do I truly believe it myself?"

"Yes, I do." I argued with myself. "But somehow I have been brainwashed not to take too seriously the battle between Satan and God. Now I have been thrown into the battle, and being unpre-pared, I have lost."

Two weeks later, we heard that the young woman had died. "She's doomed to eternity in hell with real demons!" I agonized. The torment I had seen in her eyes haunted me. All this came back to me now as I thought of Elsa.

During the years that Jeanne and I had worked among the Aguaruna, we had believed medicine to be the all-powerful force that would overcome superstition and sorcery. If we could prove that all sickness had a natural cause, people would be free from their terrifying fears of it, related to supernatural sources as they considered it to be. Whenever someone claimed to be sick because of *tunchi*, we would try to show how it wasn't actually sorcery. It must be parasites, or some germ—and usually it was.

We had the all-powerful medicine as our weapon against sor-cery. Since it is a figment of the imagination, we reasoned, surely more education and more medical training will lead to its downfall. If pills didn't work, the illness was surely just psychological. Tran-quilizers ought to take care of a case like that.

But in spite of our disbelief, shamans kept healing some people; others died of *tunchi*. People still talked about and acted out re-venge against the curser. Even those who claimed to be be-lievers and wanted to obey God went to the shaman as a last resort. He could tell them, as Jeanne and I could not, whether they needed medicine or his own ministrations because they had had a curse placed on them. If he said they needed medicine, then they would buy medicine. If not, he could tell whose *tunchi* had caused the sickness so that they could take proper revenge if the patient died.

Many times since the encounter with the demon-possessed woman on the river, I had seen people that I knew must be pos-sessed like she was. But I felt no power to save these people from Satan's attack. With all my heart I longed for such power, but where was it?

Now, with Elsa's attack, I had once again seen demons in action. But this time I had also seen Nelson, with much more faith than I, win the battle against them.

That night, in the scanty privacy of my mosquito net, I cried out to God.

"Oh, God! Give me the faith and power you have promised," I

begged. "You have given my Aguaruna brother, in spite of all his struggles against hatred and revenge, faith to believe Your Word and to act upon it. I want the faith and power I see in his life to be real in my life too!"

A few days later, we received word that Esteban would return on the plane that was bringing Martha and Jeanne to Nueva Vida. Esteban, because there were too few students for a school, was being transferred. We were all relieved; now Nelson could talk to him and decide what to do about defending his father-in-law.

Nelson told Esteban everything that had happened since his departure.

"I don't know what to do, Esteban," he said. "What do you think I should do?"

"I have no doubt, Nelson. You must drop the feuding and go on to Bible school. Think about that."

So Nelson prepared to go with me to Yarinacocha. But I was still concerned about Julia. Finally, at the last minute, Nelson decided he wanted her to go along after all. We returned to Yarinacocha, and Nelson and Julia went on to Huanuco for Nelson's second year of studies.

On the flight home, I had plenty of time to think; the plane was too noisy to allow conversation. My thoughts were confused.

"Why is the enemy focusing so much attention on Nelson?" I wondered. " Surely there must be a simpler way for me to get the New Testament translated than to always be caught up in these problems." And then the truth dawned on me. "It's not because of Nelson, nor because of me. It's not who *we* are. It's the *work* we are doing! We have an enemy who is determined to stop the publication of the New Testament in Aguaruna!"

But I couldn't get away from another question. "Where is there power for Nelson to overcome his temper, to be truly free of his old nature, which constantly pulls him back? I keep telling him there is power in Christ. Yet I don't experience complete victory in my own life. Do I even believe what I tell Nelson? Life seems like such a vicious cycle of ups and downs."

Back at Yarinacocha, it was good to be away from the pressures and the oppression I had felt at Nueva Vida. But I couldn't free myself of my burden, the burden of hopelessness that I felt as I saw my own weakness and that of Nelson. "Is there no power available?" I kept asking myself. "I know there is. But why aren't we experiencing it?"

I returned to the U. S. to the summer linguistics course to teach young people preparing to go into translation—something I always enjoyed.

During my time away from Peru, I thought often of sorcery, demons, sickness, and the promises of Scripture that believers have power in Christ over these things. I began searching to understand my own weakness and inability to claim victory over Satan. I read several books about the Holy Spirit. Could it be that there was more to the Christian life than I had been taught or had experienced? I believed that as a Christian I possessed the Holy Spirit, but I didn't understand how His power could work in me. Then, suddenly I saw the difference. I possessed the Holy Spirit, but the Holy Spirit didn't really possess *me!* I needed to allow Him to live in me and to control me completely. I had seen how Elsa allowed the demons to possess and direct her—but with such a different result!

At that moment I wanted, more than anything else, to be totally controlled by God's Spirit. By faith I asked Christ to take complete possession of me, through His indwelling Holy Spirit. I yielded myself without reservation to Him. God gave me the faith to believe He had answered that prayer. With that assurance, a new joy and peace came into my heart and mind.

As I returned to Peru in late October of 1970, I knew that God would pour out His Spirit upon the Aguaruna. I also knew that this would not happen until I was united in a deeper way with my teammates and we could all pray *together* in spiritual power for the deliverance of the Aguaruna. We would have to resolve our petty criticisms and overcome our depression, our fears and discouragement and grow together in greater love before God could use us as clear channels of His power. I keenly felt my own weakness. Yet I returned excited because I now knew without doubt that God's power was available to each of us, to all of us. He had been strengthening us with fire, just as the potter fires his vessels to make them more durable. He knew precisely when to build His fire and how long to maintain the heat so that we would emerge tempered, ready for His filling.

Clockwise: Daniel Dantuchu, Alias's brother. Dantuchu's feathered head band and his trousers reflect both the old ways and the new. Here, he carefully records each man's rubber for the cooperative. Roman Shajian at the Summer Institute for Linguistics house in Lima. He often struggled with the implications of his university education in leading his people.

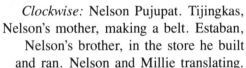

Clockwise: Nelson Pujupat. Tijingkas, Nelson's mother, making a belt. Estaban, Nelson's brother, in the store he built and ran. Nelson and Millie translating.

Part IV

Filling the Clay Pots

Exalted to the right hand of God,
He has received from the Father
the promised Holy Spirit
and has poured out
what you now see and hear.
Acts 2:33

37

Nelson's Light Side

My excitement at returning to Peru in October, 1970, was suddenly swallowed up by disappointment. Nelson and Julia were back at Yarinacocha, rather than in school at Huanuco. Julia had found it impossible to adjust in Huanuco, and Nelson had become discouraged and angry at her for thwarting his schooling. He was very disgruntled. It was hard to believe he was the same man who had so confidently been used of God to free his sister from demons a few months before.

Because of his change in attitude, the other members of our team felt he should not continue working on translation unless his problems, which led to many tensions in our own relationships, could be resolved.

I had been praying especially for greater unity on our team. Now it seemed that Nelson's perpetual struggles were dividing us. I couldn't help thinking of the controversy over John Mark, when Paul refused to allow him to continue and Barnabas had urged that they give him another chance. Our situation with Nelson was most perplexing. I had to examine myself. I had prayed for unity, but was I creating our lack of unity by insisting we keep working with Nelson? I could see that no one else thought Nelson should continue, yet I had no sense of freedom to suggest to him that he should no longer translate. The Lord seemed to say, "Keep translating with him. He needs the Word." God reminded me that even at our best we are all only clay in His hands, and that fire is an essential part of His process; surely this fire was of His making too.

On July 26, 1971, about fifteen years after I had begun working with the Aguaruna, Nelson and I translated the last verse of the Revelation. Every verse of the New Testament was now written in Aguaruna, at least in preliminary draft. Reaching this milestone was a great encouragement for all of us; we couldn't suppress our excitement.

As I waited upon God to help Nelson in his frustrations and problems, He began to work. Nelson again renewed his spiritual commitment. We had feared that his leadership had been spoiled because of his ups and downs, but the Aguaruna themselves began to ask him for his spiritual help.

The teachers invited Nelson to their 1971 conference.

"We want to learn about church organization," they told him. So he taught about the universal church and the local church. He instructed them about deacons and elders from Timothy, and led devotional studies from 1 and 2 Peter. The teachers, grateful for his help, took up offerings each day to help build the Bible school that Nelson, in his renewal, again hoped to start.

Then another invitation came, this time from Carlos and Doris Sachtler of the Swiss Indian Mission. Since 1961 they had been training Aguaruna pastors. Would Nelson come to speak for their conference for a week in early August, to again teach church organization and studies from 1 and 2 Peter?

As I watched Nelson's eager preparation for this time, I knew this was of God. "How good it will be for Nelson to renew his relationship with Carlos and to become involved with the other Aguaruna pastors, many of whom are already his close friends," I thought. And it was good.

As Nelson taught the other pastors more about baptism, he felt a great need to obey the Lord in this himself. He sent word to us at Nueva Vida that he was to be baptized on the last day of the conference. Nelson's mother, Tijingkas, and her husband also wanted to be baptized. So we made the trip together for this important event.

I was delighted to see that Carlos had trained the pastors, and then left them free to lead their own people in their own way. He and Doris and I watched as each Aguaruna pastor participated in the baptismal service. Nelson taught the Scriptures. Garcia baptized Nelson, his mother and stepfather, and eight others. Fernando served the Lord's Supper, using banana drink and manioc. God's presence was very real to all of us there that morning.

At noon, while we were eating the feast the people had prepared, a group of pastors from the Cenepa River asked to talk to me.

"Do you think Nelson could come and help us for a while?" they asked. "There are many strange rumors going around. Some people say, 'If you are baptized and punish your child, you will die.' Others say, 'If you were baptized by the priest and then are baptized again by an Aguaruna pastor, you will die.' We need Nelson and Garcia to come and teach about baptism and to help us organize our churches. There are many believers, but they need instruction."

Nelson and Carlos and I discussed the invitation. We all agreed that Nelson and Garcia should go for two weeks, even though I had to rethink my plans for polishing the translation.

The success of the men's trip affirmed that God had led them to go. Not only did Nelson and Garcia organize the churches and baptize the believers, but many new believers were added to the church in each community. God even arranged the weather to further their ministry. As Nelson was praising God for everything later, he concluded, "And God gave us good weather every day we had to travel. It rained only when we were in the villages."

After this success, even more requests came to Nelson to visit other communities. But this created a new conflict. He couldn't travel and help with revision. But Nelson himself settled the matter.

"Right now, we must finish the translation. Then I must start the Bible school and train the pastors so they can work better in their own communities."

As we continued revision, plans for the Bible school went ahead. The people of the community cleared the land. Esteban offered to direct the construction of the buildings. The teachers gave money to help buy sheets of corrugated aluminum—more durable than thatch—for the roofing. Other gifts also came in for the school. Many Aguaruna expressed a desire to attend.

Nelson did accept one more invitation, to help Alias in the Potro-Kaupan area downriver. Since he and Alias had never made their evangelistic trip, Nelson wanted to help him in this location. In October of 1971, Martha and I traveled with Nelson to Potro so we could continue revision. During the mornings we worked, and in the afternoons he taught the translated New Testament and did medical work.

People came eagerly to hear Nelson's teaching. Some made new commitments to Christ; many wanted to be baptized. Nelson helped them to choose elders. Then they planned a special day for baptism and the first communion service to be held in the downriver area.

Meanwhile, the teacher from just upstream, at Aichiaku, urged Nelson to help in their community also.

"Please, Nelson, can you come?" he begged. "Many people want to come to the meetings but are afraid because the shamans are coming, too, and might harm them while they're there."

"Okay, yes, I'll come—but I can only give you a week," he said.

Martha and I stayed at Potro. Nelson later told us what happened at Aichiaku.

"When I stood up to begin the first meeting, I noticed a woman outside. I suggested she come in, but she said, 'No, I'm afraid of the *tunchi.*'

"I was afraid, too. I was in a strange place. I knew those shamans were sitting there in front of me. I knew they were powerful. But when the woman said, 'No, I'm afraid of the *tunchi,*' it was just as though God touched me and filled me with courage. Right in front of them I said, 'These men can't hurt me with their sorcery. I belong to Christ. He is stronger than *tunchi.* Come in. They can't hurt you if you belong to Christ!'

"This was a crucial point for me. I knew I was standing against our enemy. I continued to teach, telling the people that God's power is greater than Satan's. When the meeting finished, all five shamans wanted to talk to me. So I met just with them. They all renounced the devil and committed themselves to Christ. They asked for His power. After three days, thirty-three of the believers in the community asked to be baptized."

Later Nelson spent two more months visiting the schools in the Potro and Kaupan area, working with Alias, Pancho, and the other teachers. God confirmed through many spiritual victories that He had indeed filled Nelson with His power.

38

It's Not Ugly!

L ove your enemies, turn the other cheek, go the extra mile..."
As we finished checking Matthew 5, Tomas sat back in his
chair.

"If we Aguaruna really did that, everybody would say, 'You're
crazy. You're not even a man! A man knows how to stand up for
his rights and to avenge,'" he said. Then, a couple of days later he
brought up the Sermon on the Mount again.

"You know, I've been thinking about what Jesus said. I've decided you really have to be more of a man to do what Jesus says
than to do what our people say."

In January, 1972, Tomas and several others were helping with
the final checking of the Aguaruna New Testament. Checking
every word through a committee of native speakers was the final
stage for translation of any New Testament. Nelson, Tomas, Kunyach and I had begun what I expected to be a long, tedious job.
We needed Kunyach on the committee because he was one of the
older generation; we wanted to be sure that even the grandfathers
understood the translation. Also, Kunyach was a teacher and a
respected leader. Besides, he had been the first one to help me
translate, and I wanted him to be in on "the last word" also.

Tomas was a pastor-evangelist who could keep any audience
spellbound with stories. I knew that he would make a good contri-
bution to the committee. With his keen imagination, he would
come up with some great answers to sticky translation problems.
But I also had another motive for having him participate. More and
more he was drifting away from the Scriptures and basing his

preaching on his dreams and the interpretation of dreams. It seemed that God had actually spoken to him through dreams, but I feared that he would get off center; he needed the balance of the Word itself.

Tomas constantly held up our progress because he wanted to go back to re-read some passage. I would become concerned, thinking something must be wrong. But then he would reassure me.

"There's nothing wrong. It's so good I want to buy it. Just let me think about it a minute." Then he would read the passage again, and finally say, "Okay, I've got it now. I'll not forget it."

One day we were reading through for the last time a passage which we had just revised.

"It's not ugly!" Tomas pronounced. In Aguaruna, that is even more emphatic than saying, "It's beautiful!"

As we read through Matthew, the committee soon got into the spirit of the verbal battle between Jesus and the Pharisees. Each time we got to a place where the text said, "And some Pharisees arrived," Tomas would start giggling. He could hardly wait to see what the questions would be now, and how Jesus would answer. Being specialists in oration and argument, they found it truly exciting to see how Jesus always came out on top in his arguments with the Pharisees.

When we read Matthew 25:40, "Inasmuch as ye have done it unto the least of these my brethren, you have done it unto me, (KJV)" Tomas became very excited.

"Can I go over to the Swiss Bible school and tell the Aguaruna there?" he asked urgently.

"Yes, of course," I said. "Why?"

"They really need to know this. They may have read it there in Bible school, but it's in Spanish and they'll not really understand it. I must go tell them what it actually says."

As we finished working on 1 Corinthians 13, describing the qualities of godly love, Tomas' comment gave me a start.

"Well, I've never seen anyone like that," he said. His words stung; I felt rebuked. "Yes, indeed," I reflected, "how far short I come from being an example of the loving person this beautiful chapter describes."

As we read about the gifts of the Spirit, Nelson, Kunyach and Tomas got into a discussion as to whether God still heals miraculously. I insisted that He did. Then, that very day, a Chayahuita man with tetanus was brought to the clinic, gravely ill.

"We could pray for that Chayahuita man," Tomas suggested. "If God still heals, He could heal him." So we agreed to pray, and each day the three asked for a progress report. When linguist George Hart told me the man was past the crisis and was sure to get well, I told the committee. Tomas jumped out of his chair, clapped his hands over his head and shouted with glee.

One day as Tomas was reading Corinthians through for the last check, he looked up and shook his head.

"We've really goofed on something," I thought. "What's the matter, Tomas?" I asked.

"Oh," he said, "even the apostles quarreled!"

As we continued, we came to Galatians 5: "The person who is controlled by the Holy Spirit loves others, is joyful, is peaceful with others..."

"I'll buy that," Tomas said. "It doesn't say a person has to finish grade school, or high school, or go to normal school. He doesn't need money. He doesn't even need to speak Spanish well. All he needs is to have the Holy Spirit. That's what I want." We talked about it further, and Tomas opened his life completely that very hour to the filling and control of the Holy Spirit.

Another morning, Tomas commented, "You know, brothers, God's Word is like a manioc garden. Somebody has to take a basket, dig up the manioc, bring it home, cook it, and feed it to the family. That's the way with God's Word. We need to dig it up, bring it home, and feed it to our families."

After we had been working for about four months, we finished 1 Peter.

"The New Testament is just all one word!" Tomas declared. "Paul, Peter, John, Luke—all of them wrote one word. It's all about love. I've got to tell my people. Many times when I have preached, I've told them things that weren't true. I had heard the Word in Spanish, but I didn't really understand it. Now I understand what the message is. It's all about God's love!"

After months of checking, Tomas summed up his feelings about the Word. "I never get tired of reading it, Millie," he said. "You must give me this copy! I must take this home to read to my wife and family. They will want to know about God's love too!"

I was most grateful that Tomas kept me encouraged during the months of the final revision, for Nelson hit a new low. After his six months or so of great victory, it seemed that Satan attacked him even more fiercely. He again became depressed. He saw only the dark side of everything. He was constantly angry at Julia; the translation checking was a trial to him, rather than a joy as it was to Tomas. Many times as we worked, Nelson sat passively, indifferent to the Word. At other times he was stubbornly resistant to suggestions made by the others. His misery was obvious to us all.

"I think a demon has gotten hold of me, Millie," Nelson told me one day.[24] I began to wonder if that were not the truth.

39

Freedom!

In spite of all his problems during revision, when we finished it Nelson returned to Huanuco in May, 1972, for his third year of Bible school.

"Maybe being away from Julia for a while will help him appreciate her more," I thought. "And contact with the other Christian students will help him too."

But every letter from Nelson during the term told of his problems —of how bad he was and of how he could not feel victory in his life. Clearly he wanted to obey the Lord, yet it was a constant struggle. I wrote back everything I could think of to encourage him and quoted every biblical passage I thought might help.

In November, a book about occult activities came into my hands. As I read it, I learned that even a Christian who gets involved in the occult opens himself up for demon oppression. The more I studied this book, the more I became convinced that this was Nelson's problem. "Perhaps he has gone to consult a shaman," I thought, little knowing how true this actually was.

I began to pray specifically that God would bring people into Nelson's life who would pray for his deliverance from oppression.

God answered my specific prayer specifically and dramatically. About ten days later, Nelson arrived at Yarinacocha, knocking on my door in the middle of the night. He was so overjoyed at what God had done that he couldn't wait until daylight to tell me about it.

"Just before exams, Millie, the director called me. 'What's wrong with you, Nelson?' he asked me. You're not like you used to be.

You've caused all kinds of problems this year. I want to help you find the reason. What sin is there that you haven't confessed? It's as though the devil has hold of you, Nelson.'

"I had to admit to the director that back in December, out of curiosity, I went to see a man at Chiriaco who practices black magic. He told me all about the devil and the various kinds of spirits and how to communicate with them. I also went to some astrologers' meetings, to see what they say and do. But I never thought of this or confessed it as sin. Then, as I talked to the director, I looked back on this and could see that this was the time at which my problems started up again. Ever since then, it had been as if some power was bothering me constantly, making me do all kinds of things I didn't want to do. This power just seemed to be growing over me. Less and less I was able to overcome my anger, lust, and depression.

"The week before the director called me in, I had talked with a pastor visiting from Argentina about my problems. After just a few minutes, he told me, 'You are oppressed by a demon, Nelson. You need to pray for deliverance from evil spirits.'

"I confessed these visits as sin, and the director and I asked God to deliver me. The next day was the worst day of my life, Millie, It was like being in complete darkness and confusion. I couldn't talk to anyone. Finally, about ten that night, I couldn't stand it any longer. I went to the superintendent of men for help. He called the director and another professor to pray with me.

"I renounced the evil spirits and asked God to deliver me from them. Then the other men prayed for me to be freed too. At about midnight, the confusion suddenly left. I felt free! I felt clean! It was like coming out of the darkness of the jungle onto a wide road in the sunshine. I had peace; my depression and hatred were gone. The first thing I wanted to do was to pray for one of the faculty members at whom I was angry. I felt such love for him. I also prayed for Julia, and I felt love for her. I could see that it was my fault that we have problems. I haven't helped her learn to follow the Lord as I should have.

"After the others left me, I went right to sleep. The next day we had exams, and even though I hadn't studied, I had such peace and could think clearly. I did better than I had been doing all year!

"I just couldn't wait to get back to Yarinacocha to tell you about this, my sister," Nelson went on. I could see that this had been tremendously liberating to him.

"One thing I've learned is to pray specifically, to confess specific sins. General prayers don't help. We have to tell God exactly what our sin is and exactly what we want Him to do for us. I am so thankful because, through all this time of struggling, Christ never stopped loving me. The Holy Spirit kept speaking to me all the time, drawing me back!"

The following Sunday morning, Nelson spoke to the Aguaruna at Yarinacocha. He turned to the passage in the Old Testament about Saul consulting the medium.

"The reason so many believers among the Aguaruna are weak and not following the Lord is because they have not turned away from sorcery," he exhorted them. "They just go ask the shaman if they'll get well or not, but they are really going to the devil for help, and not to God. When they do that, the devil begins to bother them and they are no longer free. The most important thing we can teach our people is that believers must never turn back to the devil, but only look to God for healing."

As I listened to Nelson teach that morning, I knew by faith that a new day was dawning for the Aguaruna. In some new way I now truly believed in the reality and power of Satan—and in the tremendous power of the Holy Spirit. Nelson seemed to know that he was now filled with the Holy Spirit, with the "Helper" who was from God, as Jesus described Him. He had traded the power of the spirit of darkness, who had helped him to do evil, for this new helper, God's own Spirit. I felt sure that God was about to manifest His power so that the Aguaruna would know that He is a power greater than the power of the shaman or of *ajutap* or other demons they fear so intensely.

When Nelson returned to Nueva Vida, he went with renewed vision. He was enthusiastic about the pastors' training course he planned to hold.

During the time that Nelson struggled, I too was in turmoil. I had wept and prayed and struggled with the opposing forces of the Aguaruna world. I tried to see God's plan and purpose in permitting such conflict. I wanted desperately to see His power at work in my own life, as well as in the lives of our Aguaruna brothers. The other members of our team—Jeanne, Martha, Dennis and Susie—struggled along with me. Then God began to open the eyes of all of us to the reality of spiritual battle, and our part in it. We began to recognize supernatural powers we had not been willing to acknowledge before. He met each one of us personally in a new, fresh way, as we allowed the Holy Spirit to control us more fully. The result was that we experienced a greater unity than we had known before. This unity enabled us to join together *with power* in prayer for the Aguaruna. Weekly prayer meetings, with the five of us and a small group of friends at Yarinacocha, became the most exciting time of the week for us all. We began asking God to do specific things for the Aguaruna; we saw God answer in dramatic ways. Our faith grew rapidly; we all had new hope and the expectation that God would truly act.

I shall never forget one prayer time in January, 1973. A pastor visiting from Florida met with us. We told him about the problems of demon possession and suicide among the Aguaruna. After discussing these, he prayed for us and with us about our ministry. That evening we all experienced great unity in Christ; and this, we discovered, gave us the power to claim a great victory against the forces of evil among the Aguaruna.

Jeanne told the pastor about Antun, then at Yarinacocha, who needed freedom from an evil spirit. Antun, in his last year of high school, was working with Jeanne recording Aguaruna myths.

"I'm afraid, Jeanne," he had told her just that week. "Some nights I can't sleep. Last night it happened again. Ever since childhood I have had visions at night. An evil spirit stands over me. It makes me so frightened, that I can't move or speak. It comes about every three months. Often, I have a premonition that it will come, and so I go to bed very frightened."

"But don't you pray, Antun?" Jeanne had asked him.

"I want to, but while the spirit is bending over me I can't do anything. I'm just there, immobilized," he said.

We knew that every Aguaruna man trains one son to be his avenger. Chief Kuji had chosen Antun for his avenger. Thus, as a boy, Antun had gone through all the proper ceremonies to obtain the power of the avenging spirit. Later Kuji came to believe in Christ. Antun had attended Dantuchu's school in Chiangus, and at the age of ten had received Christ. Both Antun and his father had long ago forgotten about Antun's training under the avenging spirit. In their new way of life, as Christians, this had seemed unimportant to them. Yet the spirit had apparently never left Antun. Through the spirit's occasional visits it reminded Antun of his commitment to it. It was as though the spirit would never allow him to forget, and would never release him.

"It was exciting for me to be a Christian, Jeanne," Antun had reminded her. "I really wanted to be one. Everybody was talking about Christ and wanting to be Christians. My brother and I decided to commit ourselves to Christ too. We were very happy. We didn't have much of God's Word then. We didn't know what to do, but we prayed and sang with the others, and we listened to Dantuchu preach.

"And now, after fifteen years, I am still not free from this evil spirit. Won't you pray for me again?"

Jeanne and I had prayed with Antun then; we prayed that he would have a good night's sleep, knowing that Jesus was with him.

"I didn't sleep at all last night," Antun told us the next day, to our puzzlement.

Jeanne related these experiences with Antun to the visiting pastor.

"Why don't we see results when we pray for something like this?" she asked.

"Don't just pray for him," he told her. "You must take the power Jesus gave you and cast the evil spirit out."

"Would you be willing to do that now?" we asked.

"Of course," he replied. So Dennis, Jeanne, and I went with him to the house where Antun was sleeping. Jeanne woke him up. The pastor asked me to translate so Antun could understand his explanation.

"I'm going to command the demon to come out of you, and then you will be completely free," he said. "You'll never have to be afraid again. It will never come back and bother you again."

But I found myself wondering, "But do I really believe that? Can I translate that for Antun and believe it's true?" Suddenly, I knew that this was absolutely true. Christ had already given us the power to send the demons away. Without hesitation, I put the pastor's words into Aguaruna for Antun. Then the pastor simply commanded the demon to leave him. He prayed and thanked God for His answer. Then he laid his hands on Antun and prayed for the Holy Spirit to fill his life. Antun prayed also. He asked that the Holy Spirit fill him and protect him from all evil spirits through the shed blood of Christ. We all praised God together and went home, elated.

The next day, Antun was so happy that he sang most of the day. On Sunday he shared a message on love, from 1 Corinthians 13. His teaching filled us all with anticipation of how God would use the Aguaruna to minister to each other by claiming Christ's power over demons. We prayed much that it would soon become a reality.

Our experience with Antun had suddenly given us the key to the question of living under the full control of the Holy Spirit. For thousands of years the Aguaruna had been enslaved to the demons they feared and the sorcery which haunted them. They were not so desirous of a Savior who promised them life in the distant future as much as of a Savior who had power to free them in this life from demons, to protect them from sorcery and to heal them of constant sickness.

Now that we could openly acknowledge that spiritual warfare was real indeed, and not a fiction or a superstition, and could demonstrate Jesus' power over demons, our Aguaruna brothers could discover more of His power too. Amazingly, when we at last understood how real Satan and his demons are, our Aguaruna friends opened up to us on a whole new level. "When you didn't believe these things, sister," they said, "we were ashamed to tell you much. But now that you too believe, we are not ashamed to tell you, because we need God's power."

40

How Different the Fruit

We began to discover that great spiritual progress is followed by adversity and testing, as God's enemy renews his attempts to gain control. When Jerry and Evie Elder and I flew out to attend the closing program of Nelson's short-term Bible school, we found that the enemy was indeed attempting to sabotage on every front the gains Nelson had made, even using nature itself as a weapon.

Nelson and his relatives all greeted us warmly, but Nelson himself was downcast.

"I am so glad you all could come," Nelson said, "but I feel very sad. Eight of the students insisted on leaving this afternoon, so we had the closing program without you. They heard a rumor that there were measles on the Marañon River, and they feared the people would stop bringing us food. I assured them that God would supply for us—and He did. Unexpectedly, someone brought manioc and bananas yesterday, so we had food for morning and noon. But even so, the students didn't want to stay all weekend with no more food in sight."

"Well, my brother, there must be some other purpose in our coming," I assured him. "I know the Lord wanted us to come." And then I asked, "Where is your mother, Tijingkas? She didn't come to the plane to meet us."

"She couldn't come. She has been sick."

"What's wrong with her, Nelson?"

"She has been hemorrhaging very badly off and on for several weeks. She has a large, hard lump in her stomach. She must have cancer to be so bad."

"And what about Esteban? I haven't seen him either."

"He is also very sick. He came home without finishing his summer school course."

"Oh! I'm so sorry! Was he able to get the buildings done for the Bible school?"

"No, the carpenter who was to help us didn't arrive in time. We had to use our old buildings for the course."

"But even if God takes my mother and my brother and we have no houses, I just remember Job," he said. "God is letting Satan tempt me. But I remember that Job said, 'Naked I came into the world and naked I shall return. The Lord has given and the Lord has taken away.'

"I told my mother, 'Your healing doesn't have to happen far away; it's right here. You don't need to go to Yarinacocha, nor to Lima. God will heal you here.' The students and I prayed for her and the hemorrhaging stopped a week ago. But she says she can still feel the lump."

I was amazed at Nelson's confidence in God in spite of all the disappointments.

I thought about this later as I hung my mosquito net and arranged my other sleeping gear.

"I think we should pray for Esteban, too," I thought. So I went to visit him for a few minutes.

"I have come, my brother. How are you? Nelson tells me you are sick again," I said.

"Yes, I am. My stomach ulcer hurts constantly. I always feel depressed. My headache and nausea are worse. I have been sick off and on for three years now." Esteban spoke glumly; it had been a long time since I had seen him smile.

The next morning, as we met to worship, Esteban sat with a painful, dejected look. As we worshipped, I reflected on Esteban's sickness. It had started three years earlier when he went to teach far from home, leaving his wife Victoria to tend the gardens. He had taken Lucila as a second wife, even though he had never intended to follow this custom of his ancestors. He had wanted very much to be a one-wife man, and so he felt guilty for succumbing.

Finally, because of his pain, Esteban had gone to a shaman. This only added to his feelings of guilt and he became more depressed. His headaches and stomach pains increased. He was angry with himself, but he worked out his anger on his wives. Many times Esteban prayed to be free of this anger, guilt and depression, but in vain. He began to doubt that God cared for him. Then Esteban saw the tremendous change in Nelson after he came back to Nueva Vida in November. This renewed his hope that he, too, would be free of oppression again.

Later, Esteban, Victoria, Lucila and I talked at length and then prayed. Esteban could barely express himself. He stopped during his faltering prayer and, to my surprise, he began talking to demons instead of to God.

"Leave me alone! Go away! Don't bother me anymore! Because of Jesus, I tell you to leave me!" Afterwards, he prayed again, sincerely reaching out to the Lord.

Then Tijinkas called me away abruptly to visit and to share the chicken she had prepared for lunch. But she didn't look well.

"Millie, when I first thought I might have cancer, I was afraid. But I prayed, and now I am not afraid to die. I know that I will be with Jesus, but I worry about my children. Now I have ten, counting Esteban and Nelson, and the youngest one is only two. Who will care for her if I die? But I believe God can heal me. Nelson says that if we pray, God will heal me. Will you and Jerry and Evie pray for me too?"

"Of course, we will, sister," I told her, feeling refreshed by her faith.

After dinner at Nelson's house, one of the children went to call Esteban so we could pray for him. But the boy returned without him.

"Esteban can't come. He's really sick," he said.

"How strange that Esteban should suddenly be so much worse," I thought. We all went over to Esteban's house instead. He lay under his mosquito net, groaning with pain. His headache, stomach pain, and nausea were so intense he could scarcely speak. With great difficulty, he told us what had happened.

"After I rebuked the demons, I got much worse, Millie. I was afraid to tell you, but as soon as you left I went right to my sleeping mat."

"That's just the way it is!" Nelson said. "That's the way it was at Bible school after they prayed for me and before the demons left! Then he looked at Jerry.

"You are the oldest; you should be in charge," he said.

Jerry asked the Lord to bind the demons that were bothering

Esteban, to free him, and to heal him. He commanded the demons to leave Esteban. Then we all placed our hands upon Esteban, and each of us prayed.

With our hands still on him, Esteban himself prayed. Then we all stepped back from Esteban, and looked at him, amazed. The agony was gone from his face. He was perfectly calm.

"How do you feel, Esteban?" I asked. He looked at me amazed, as if to say, "Has something been wrong with me?" It seemed as though even the memory of his pain had been wiped away.

"I just feel like laughing and laughing," he said. We all shared his joy.

Next, we turned our attention to Tijingkas. Nelson read the account of the woman with the hemorrhage who had touched Jesus' hem and was healed. Then we all gathered around Tijingkas, touching her as we prayed. I found it hard to pray, because of my love for Tijingkas and my intense feelings. But I managed a short prayer.

Suddenly, just as Evie began to pray, a violent wind hit us. Lightning flashed and thunder clapped. It seemed like all the elements let loose at once to distract us from prayer. The aluminum on one corner of Nelson's house ripped up; a tree crashed down right beside Esteban's house, where we were gathered. Nelson ran to his house, calling for a hammer and nails, and climbed up to secure the roof. Tijingkas yelled at her daughters to bring in the clothes swirling on the line. Everyone seemed to be dashing around. Jerry, without saying a word, walked back to the house where he and Evie were staying.

"Wow! Where did that come from?" Evie asked. The strong wind blew for only a few minutes and died down as quickly as it had come. It had lasted just long enough to break up our time of prayer.

Jerry told us later that as we were praying, he suddenly felt terrible nausea and weakness and intense pain in his stomach and head —the very symptoms from which we had just seen Esteban delivered. In all the sudden confusion of the storm, he went back to his mosquito net without mentioning it. There he prayed and read Scripture until he was released and felt normal again. In retrospect, we could see that such interruptions frequently occurred when we were united to pray for someone's release from evil power. It seemed Satan not only stirred up nature itself, but also our relationships at times, creating disagreements and tensions among us team members to prevent us from exercising God's power.

Later, I was glad to be alone with Julia. I knew she and Nelson were still having serious problems.

"I don't know why I always get angry about every little thing, my sister," she confided. "Every time Nelson tells me to do something, I get angry and answer badly. I know I believe, and I want to follow Christ, but no one thinks I am serious. They all say, 'Oh, you really aren't a follower of Christ. You just say that because Millie wants you to.'

"But I really am, Millie," she insisted. "It's just that I can't live right."

A month later, on my way to the U. S., I saw Nelson in Lima. He was on his way to Huanuco again.

"How is Esteban doing, my brother?" I asked him.

"He's fine, Millie. He has spent the last month working on the houses for the Bible school. He's very happy. He went out this week for the teacher orientation course. He'll start to teach again in April."

As I reflected on Esteban's illness and recovery I felt convinced that the power of *tunchi* would soon be gone—not just because of medicine and education, like I used to think, but because we were all discovering that the Holy Spirit is more powerful than evil spirits. "Christ has *already* won the victory over Satan," I thought.

I reflected too on the ways God was showing Himself to the Aguaruna. For generations it seemed that Satan had deceived them and, in grotesque ways, dominated them and controlled their lives. The "helping" *ajutap* they so eagerly and arduously sought seemed to me an evil substitute for the Holy Spirit, who could fill and control them. The confidence and personality strength they experienced seemed dark imitations of what the Holy Spirit would produce in them, once they were committed to Him. And the fruit—I shivered to think of it—how different the fruit! The *ajutap's* fruit was fear, revenge, killing, death—the exact opposite of the Holy Spirit's fruit of love, joy, peace, and life.

I hated to leave Peru, now that God had begun to show His power! I wanted to stay right there and watch to see what else God would do as He filled the Aguaruna more and more with His Spirit. But I needed to go to Mexico to check the typesetting and page proofs on the New Testament, which had been processed on a special computer. It would be hard to be satisfied with letters and tapes from my Aguaruna friends for a whole year!

Counterclockwise:
Alias and other
Aguaruna
teachers waiting
to perform for guests
at Yarinacocha.

David Cunachi,
Tomas Chamiquit and
Alias.

Alias and Millie
in the final phase
of the translation
process.

Shimpu (Gerardo
Wipio Deicat) and
Mrs. Cudney at the
SIL house in Lima.

Top: The view from Millie's house of the ridges of the Andes Mountains poking through the fog was not restricted by the windowless walls Aguarunas normally used to keep out evil spirits.

Bottom: Throughout Millie's years with the Aguarunas, she shared not just her skills, but her life with them, as they did with her. It was this mutual relationship of respect and love that formed the basis for the work of God with the Aguaruna.

PART V

Using the Clay Pots

Yet we who have this spiritual treasure
   are like common clay pots,
      in order to show that the supreme power
      belongs to God,
         not to us.
            2 Corinthians 4:7

41

It's Not Going to Leave Easily

During the time I was gone, Martha, Jeanne, Susie and Dennis traveled to Urakusa in July for the teachers' conference. They became more aware than usual that Satan's power was deeply entrenched in the village. Sorcery was prevalent. The small group of believers was weak; they cowered at the forces of evil, and felt no power to overcome. Many people were sick.

Nelson led the devotional meetings during the conference. He was eager to see others experience the deliverance and freedom he had found. One evening he asked another visitor, a man representing a philanthrophic organization giving practical assistance to the Aguaruna, if he would like to share. The visitor chose to read from Matthew 17, the passage about Jesus healing the demon-possessed boy with epileptic-like symptoms. He told how he himself, as a boy, had been freed from such a condition through prayer. He encouraged the people to believe that God still heals and delivers from evil powers.

When Nelson asked to meet with any who would like to pray, the response was overwhelming. Fifteen people asked for prayer, including a teacher who had had many near-fatal episodes of convulsions. Through the prayers of the believers that evening, he was freed from any further symptoms.

At the end of the conference, another man sought out Jeanne to tell her that his wife Emirita was sick. Jeanne didn't realize at the time what valuable insights and experience in exorcism this illness would provide, or what a key it would be into God's work in Urakusa.

Jeanne went to see Emerita and found her acting very strangely. She was an unusually pretty girl, about fifteen years old. But she rolled her eyes, only vaguely answered Jeanne's questions, and grinned senselessly. Jeanne was puzzled and frustrated, not knowing how to treat such symptoms. The next morning, the husband brought Emirita to Jeanne.

"She sings, Jeanne," he said.

This time, Jeanne was prepared. She had learned that many Aguaruna, especially girls, sing shaman songs which they have never been taught, and that they also prophesy. This was regarded by the people as a sign of a divining spirit having taken control of them. This spirit was often sought after, through the use of certain drugs, by women and girls who wanted to know the future.

"Emirita has been singing often, and the teachers and students gather around to listen to her prophecies," the husband continued. "Recently she has been trying to kill herself."

"We will pray for Emirita," Jeanne told the husband. "I don't think this is an ordinary sickness." So Pastor Pedro, Jeanne, Dennis and other believers met together in a small room with Emerita. Many other people listened through the slat walls, curious about the outcome.

First the believers prayed and read Scripture together, asking the Holy Spirit to lead them as they claimed God's power over the demons. Doing this was a new experience for most of them.

But as they prayed, Emirita started to sing. She sobbed, covering her eyes with her arm. She wouldn't look at any of them. Then she began dancing, and so they all formed a circle around her.

"We are more powerful than Christ," the demons sang.[25] "Nothing you can do will harm us. We are more powerful. All your efforts are in vain."

Pedro and Jeanne began to command the spirit to leave Emirita. Pedro had exorcised demons before and was better prepared for it than the others. As he commanded the demon to leave Emirita, in the name of Jesus, she became defiant. She continued to dance around and to sing, and tried to escape from the circle.

"I can't stand it here! I have to leave!" the demon said through her.

Someone suggested they make a path to let the demon leave.

"Let's go and take the girl with us!" the demon suddenly shouted. Emirita ran from the house with a robot-like gait, obviously propelled by some power besides her own.

Then the believers realized they had been deceived. The men ran after Emirita, to bring her back.

Martha and Susie, who were praying nearby, saw Emerita run out among some lemon trees, where she tried to hang herself. Julio, the health promoter, also saw her.

"That's a strong demon," said Julio, who many people said was himself a sorcerer. "It's not going to come out easily."

The men brought Emirita back to the small house. They continued to pray, as Pedro again commanded the demons to leave her. Emirita struggled frantically. Again Jeanne and Pedro commanded the demon to leave, but the demon harassed them.

"Stop! We're thinking on the wrong level," the visitor told them. "We shouldn't listen to the demon. Let's sing hymns for a while, concentrating on God." So they all sang and prayed together. But the demon again tried to distract them.

"Somebody here has had an affair with a woman," the demon accused. Since everyone knew that they must confess all sin in order to be channels of God's power over the enemy, each person looked around, but no one admitted being guilty. Emirita's husband, a non-believer, was also there. But he didn't admit to such a sin either.

Again, the Christians realized that the demon had deceived them to distract them from itself. They resumed singing. Suddenly, Emirita fell back, unconscious. After a few minutes, she looked up at them and smiled, her eyes sparkling. They all thought that she was free of the demon, so they prayed for her once more. She left feeling happy.

But in the afternoon, as Emirita was walking across the village, someone came up to her and snapped his fingers in her face. She immediately started singing again. The man who did this was one of the people who was fascinated by Emirita's prophecies. His own wife Rebecca had also been a singer, but she had committed suicide a year earlier.

Again the believers gathered around Emirita.

"Name yourself!" Jeanne told the demon.

"I am the spirit of Rebecca," the demon said. Rebecca had been a strong singer, and at one time Emirita had so envied her powers that she had asked her to transfer some to her. Rebecca had given her a hug, and had blown on her to pass on her power.[26]

Emirita was more violent during this second episode. She tore her dress, pulled her hair, threatened to hit the men, and climbed the cane walls in an effort to get away. Again they stopped her escape and continued to sing hymns. Finally, at about nine o'clock, Emirita fell to the floor, exhausted. She stopped chanting. She appeared to be all right, except for being stiff and sore from throwing herself about. She got up from the floor and lay down on a table.

"Do you want to tell us what hymn to sing for you, Emirita?" one of the believers asked. They sang the one she requested and then they prayed again. Domingo, the oldest member of the fellowship, prayed for her tenderly, in a touching and loving way. Then Emirita herself prayed, as the Christians laid their hands upon her. She was peaceful and coherent. She was free at last of the demons.

Emirita's deliverance had a powerful effect upon the people of Urakusa. The next day her husband came to confess his sins and to receive Christ. He became an enthusiastic and effective witness of the power of God, and expressed a desire to study to become a pastor. Several groups started meeting around the community for Bible study and prayer, also as a result of Emirita's deliverance.

But not everyone was impressed by Emirita's healing. Miguel, one of the teachers, made light of it. He had once been a strong believer in Christ, but had fallen away. One day soon after Emerita's healing, Miguel was abruptly attacked by such an intense headache that he had to leave school. Later he lost his vision. None of the medicine Martha offered helped at all.

"Miguel is dying! Miguel is dying!" his family shouted. "He's out of his mind. Everything he says is incoherent. His headache hasn't left, and he has started singing shaman songs."

Miguel lay on his sleeping platform, completely rigid, shaking from head to foot. With all his strength he sang the familiar *"Vi, vi, vi!"* of the shaman.

After the people sang hymns and prayed, Miguel's taut body relaxed. He calmed down and soon fell asleep. But later he woke up and started to sing again. He became blind and had a terrible headache.

"What do you think has caused this, Miguel?" Dennis asked.

"It's all this pressure," Miguel explained. "I've been working so hard trying to do a good job in school. I haven't had time to pray or go to church at all."

"Do you think this could be an evil spirit bothering you?" Weren't those shaman songs you were singing?"

"I don't want to think about that. That frightens me," Miguel answered.

But Dennis opened the Aguaruna Scriptures to Luke 17, and asked one of the believers to read the passage where Jesus' seventy disciples report that even evil spirits obeyed them when they used His name. He read, "Jesus told them, 'Yes, I saw Satan fall from heaven as a flash of lightning and I have given you authority over all the power of the enemy.'"

"Brother, it helps me to hear that," Miguel said. "Yes, I have been troubled by demons. Will you pray that God will release me?"

Martha, Dennis, Domingo and several other believers gathered around Miguel. Martha and Dennis prayed in English as a test; they didn't want to influence Miguel if this were just a psychological problem. They were amazed to hear an Aguaruna who understood no English pray precisely the same thing that they had prayed!

While the group prayed, Miguel's vision returned; his headache faded away.

"I see that I got my priorities turned around," he said. "I was putting school before the Lord. But He has done a miracle for me. Do you realize that several people in my family who had these same symptoms have all died? That's why they all shouted that I was dying. God has done a miracle. He has saved me from death.

42

Where Do I Fit?

God was using His Word in the hands of the Aguaruna. He was using their own leaders, now filled with His Spirit instead of with the old *ajutap* spirit, to meet the needs of the growing church; He would continue to use them. But one question still troubled me. Where did *I* fit in? How did He want to use *me*?

"What shall we talk to you about, Millie?" one of the teachers asked me in June, 1974, when I returned to Urakusa after my furlough.

"What do you mean?" I asked, surprised.

"Well, we talk to Jeanne about sick people, to Martha about school problems, to Dennis about community problems and all that, but what shall we talk to you about now?"

"That's the problem, precisely," I thought. "He has verbalized what I haven't been able to put into words—my feeling of being out of it. During my absence, the work has sped on. Before furlough my role was so clear—to get the New Testament translated. But that's done. What do I do now?"

I turned from my private thoughts to give the teacher an answer.

"Well, maybe we could just talk about God," I said.

"That's a good idea, Millie," he replied, and so we shared. He told me about the exciting events at Urakusa; God had delivered many people since I left. I shared what God was teaching me.

I soon realized that the Aguaruna had been discussing my problem among themselves. Now that the translation is finished, what is Millie going to do? I was certainly wondering too.

A few days later Shimpu[27], another teacher, brought up the subject again.

"Now that you have finished the New Testament, are you saying, 'Well, here's the New Testament; now my work is done!'? You can't say that, Millie. I've been thinking about this; I want to tell you what I've been thinking."

For three hours Shimpu and I talked. I was moved by his deep concern for the believers who were walking far from the Lord, and his desire to see the church grow in strength and holiness as well as in numbers.

"What is your solution to my problem of work, Shimpu?" I finally asked.

"That's what I want to tell you. Martha goes around from community to community studying problems in the schools and training the teachers and supervisors. Jeanne goes around studying problems of health and training the health promoters. Dennis goes around helping in community development. In just the same way, you should go around from place to place studying the problems in the churches. After you have figured out these problems, you should find some Aguaruna whom you can teach and then teach them how to handle these problems. Then give them the work of preparing others to handle problems."

"But Carlos and Doris Sachtler are already doing just that," I answered. "This is their job, not mine. Also, Nelson plans to open a Bible school at Nueva Vida next year, to pass on to the pastors what he has learned during translation and at Huanuco."

"That's wonderful, Millie!" Shimpu exclaimed. "But we still need *you* to go out and work in the communities."

That week the teachers gathered at Urakusa for their yearly conference. Tomas was making the most of what he had learned during translation checking. He not only spoke for the evening meetings, but he was also busy day and night counseling teachers who came to him with personal or church problems.

"Please, Tomas, come and help us," many of them begged him. So in the weeks following conference, he visited various villages, solving church problems.

Tomas was just one of the many pastors whom the Sachtlers had trained. They were doing a great job; I could see that the need for church supervision would be met through these pastors.

Antonio and Abel were two of them. Even with little education, they were very effective. Before Carlos had left for furlough in 1973, Antonio shared his desire to pass on what he knew of Jesus.

"There are so many villages up the Cenepa River where the people don't know about Jesus Christ. Could I go and teach in one of them?"

Antonio asked Abel to help him. Sixty people attended their classes, and at the end of the course twenty-two Aguaruna were baptized.

The response of the people in baptism created quite a stir. The village had been nominally Catholic, because the teacher had been sent by the priest at Nieva. When the priest of the area heard of the baptisms, he confronted Abel.

"Get all the people together," he told him. "I'm going to find out what's going on. Who has been teaching here? Where does this gospel come from? How do you know what it's all about?"

"The people here asked some believers to come and teach God's Word," Abel explained. "I'm a believer, so I said, 'Okay, I'll come.' We all love each other, so I came to tell them about God."

"Who sent you?" the priest demanded.

"The Apostle Paul said that Jesus Christ sent him to preach. And I was also sent just like that. Matthew 28:19 says, 'Go into all the world and preach the gospel.' Jesus said that." Then Abel added, "Who sent you?"

When Abel realized that he had offended the priest, he said, "My brothers make mistakes in their talking, and I guess I do too."

"Who teaches you?" the priest continued.

"I was trained to be a pastor by the Swiss and Germans in Bible school," Abel told him. "They taught me the New Testament there."

"Oh, they are just a small sect that works in secret," the priest said. "We are sent by the Pope and our church is well known in all the world. Their work is secret and they are deceiving you. Why, even the Scriptures say that deceivers will come—and these are the ones."

"What Bible do you have?" Abel asked. "How many books do you have in your New Testament?"

"Twenty-four," the priest said hesitantly.

"Count them," Abel said. So the priest counted, and found that there were twenty-seven.

"Mine has twenty-seven also," Abel said. "It seems our Bible is the same. So why are we quarreling? Who is it that you obey?"

"Jesus Christ," the priest answered.

"I also obey Jesus Christ," Abel said. "We both obey Him. Then we must not quarrel."

"You are right," the priest said. "Let's not quarrel. We are really brothers." And thus the walls between them were broken down. Abel and the priest became friends and visited often with one another.

When Abel returned to his own village, one of the men was very sick, to the point of being unconscious. Abel told us later about the unexpected things that happened as a result.

"We Aguaruna don't have medicine and we don't usually get well, but God will help us," Abel told his people. He opened his New Testament booklet to James and read chapter five. Then he anointed the man with oil, as the passage instructed, and prayed for him.

Just as Abel was praying, they were interrupted by wailing down at the river. A canoe pulled up with the body of a woman of the village who had just died. Abel went down to the river with the rest of the people.

"For people who are dead, it is too late to accept the Lord," Abel told the grief-stricken villagers. Then he opened his New Testament again, this time to Luke, and read the story of Lazarus and the rich man. He preached to them about what happens after death. Immediately, all those present turned to Christ.

Abel then returned to the house of the sick man. He found him sitting up.

"You are still alive. You were almost dead. You really need to follow Christ," Abel told him.

"Okay, I'll follow Christ," said the man, who had been a shaman.

A few days later, Abel was summoned to another village to visit Wajajai, another shaman who had committed himself to Christ through the witness of a young man who had been among the sixty in Antonio and Abel's short Bible course.

"I am afraid," Wajajai said. "Some people are saying that a shaman cannot become a Christian. I am not sure that God will accept me. Do you think God will heal me? I am old now, and I have been very sick and I can no longer turn to sorcery to heal me."

"Confess your sins, Wajajai," Abel told him. "Nothing is impossible for God. You are still alive." So Wajajai confessed all his sins, naming each of the many people he had killed or made sick by sorcery. Then Abel prayed for him and left.

But soon Abel heard wailing. He went back to Wajajai's house and found him dead. He prayed for him again. Later in the day he returned a third time. This time Wajajai greeted him enthusiastically.

"I am alive again, Abel!" he exclaimed. "I became thirsty, and came back. I want to tell you what I saw. There were two trails. One was a big trail. There were many people on it. The other was made of golden logs laid one beside another. Only two children were on this trail. I went with them a long way. I'm going back up that trail. I want to go back. But first I want to preach to the people."

The people eagerly crowded around to hear Wajajai. He sat up on his sleeping platform.

"Live well, and be at peace," he told them. "Tell my friend Chavez, the shaman, that we are working sorcery in vain. Our work isn't good for anything. Don't keep having seances. Tell him I'm going to heaven now. There is a dove in my chest and He is going to take me there when I die."

When he finished his messages to the people, Wajajai lay down. Immediately his spirit was gone; he was dead again.

"Our father was truly accepted by God! Let's follow Him!" said Wajajai's sons, who had been scoffers. They began to praise God, instead of wailing in the usual way. They kept saying, "Our father was a shaman, but God saved him!"

In Wajajai's village, the people continued to meet daily to worship together. They eagerly awaited every visit of Abel as he went to share the Word with them.

But the question about what God had in mind for my future still haunted me.

Then back at Nueva Vida in July, I made a startling discovery. The people there already had created a new role for me. Always before, Nelson and I had been so busy on translation that people were very careful not to disturb us. Now that I looked rather unoccupied, it seemed I was available to everyone. Each morning as the women came by on their way to their gardens, they would leave off their small children at my house.

"Why don't you stay here with Mother Millie today?" they told them. "We'll pick you up when we come back." One day I found myself with eight children for most of the morning! "Mother Millie, indeed!" I thought. "This certainly is a role I never anticipated!" Yet I thoroughly enjoyed the children, as I always had.

Translation had been my driving force for several years, so it was hard for me to make the shift to less demanding tasks. With translation, I always knew what had to be done. The next verse, and the next, and the next, was always there. But now, my days weren't laid out so clearly. I had to learn to trust God in a new way for each day, and how I was to spend it.

God began to fill my days with people—the people with whom he wanted me to talk. He began to lay burdens of prayer upon me that were lightened only when I laid them back on him. I, who had always been a doer, found it was not easy to learn to be quiet and to wait upon God.

43

Demon of Fear

One thing I had to wait upon God for was the outcome of Nelson's homecoming. He was returning to Nueva Vida for his July break from Bible school. As the boat pulled in, everyone excitedly ran down to meet him—everyone, that is, except Julia. Nelson climbed out of the boat and up the bank, greeting all his relatives and friends. But he kept looking around. "Where is Julia?" he asked, sensing that something was wrong.

I was fearful of their encounter because Julia had been unfaithful to Nelson. But I saw a miracle take place before me. When Nelson learned what had happened, he was upset. He wept a great deal, but he didn't lose his temper as he surely would have done in the past. He didn't beat Julia or slash her head with a machete—the usual punishment for adultery.

"Julia," he said, "I have just taken a course at Bible school on marriage and the family. I realized that I haven't treated you right in the past. I brought along the books from this course to share with you."

But Julia would not listen to Nelson or even to the New Testament. Nelson grew more frustrated.

"My sister," he confided to me one day, "Everybody says, 'Get rid of her. She's been unfaithful. Why do you keep her?' The Aguaruna custom would indeed be to get rid of her—to beat her up and to tell her, 'We're through!' But I just can't throw her out, Millie. Satan wants me to do that. Then he knows I'll never be able to have the Bible school. Why does God want me to suffer like this? Maybe God wants me to keep her."

Two nights later Julia disappeared. Nelson's family searched for her the rest of the night, and the next day. Finally at sunset, a relative across the river saw her come out onto the beach.

"Julia, come back home to your husband and the children," he insisted. "Why did you run away?"

"I don't know," Julia said. "I was afraid, and so I ran."

It seemed that God again used Grandmother Cudney to help in a crisis in Nelson's life. Nelson knew she was planning to bring her grandchildren to visit Nueva Vida. Several times when Nelson felt like giving up on Julia, he remembered Mrs. Cudney's forthcoming visit. Knowing how disappointed she would be if his family were not together increased his desire to work things out. The coming visit also helped Julia to stay at home, even though she wanted to run away out of shame.

Nelson's and Julia's perseverance paid off; we all had a wonderful time during Mrs. Cudney's visit. Then Nelson was to return with her to Yarinacocha and travel on up to Huanuco from there. After four years of school, he had just three months to go before graduation. To have to quit then would have been a victory for the enemy. Yet I could see it was harder for him to go than it had ever been; he felt torn between family and school. As they got on the plane, Nelson told Julia to stay well and to take care of the children. His concern for her was evident.

I stayed at Nueva Vida for two more weeks. During that time I became more and more convinced that Julia often did things without knowing why. Whenever I tried to talk to her or to pray with her, she always welcomed that, yet I never felt that she heard me. I felt very frustrated by her strange behavior. Then, suddenly, before I could help her more I had to leave.

A month later, I received a letter from Nelson. He was very upset over some teaching he had heard on the Hebrews 6 passage: "For it is impossible to restore again to repentance those who have once been enlightened...if they commit sin...(KJV)" Nelson gave me few details about how this had been presented, but it had caused him to relapse into the old fear, doubt and confusion:

> People are saying that if you know the Word of God, and then sin, you will never be saved. And I know I am the greatest of sinners. I know the Word, and yet I really don't obey it. Since that's the way I am, I'm wasting time here. If

I'm not going to be saved, why do I stay here suffering in order to learn?

Nelson's letter continued, full of doubts and fears for the future as well as about his own salvation.

The week after Nelson wrote me, he received a letter saying that Julia had run away again, leaving the sick children with Nelson's mother at Nueva Vida. He left school immediately and came to Yarinacocha to call home by radio and to arrange for a flight out.

Once again, Nelson seemed to doubt everything. He saw himself as too wicked to be forgiven. We talked at length about the problems at home, the problems at school, and the fears of which he had written, never guessing the dramatic events to which our conversation would lead.

"Nelson," I suggested, "I think that Julia is oppressed by demons, and that she can't help running away all the time. I wish I had talked with her about it more when I was there. Many people at Urakusa and in other villages have been delivered from demons. You know of some yourself and have been used of God to..."

"I feel all trembly inside and have a terrible headache, my sister," Nelson interrupted. "This happened at school last week when the visiting teacher started talking about freeing people from demons. Lately, whenever the topic comes up, I get like this. I really feel awful." He paused. "I think if some of the people here would pray for me, I would be freed."

"You're right, my brother. I'll call and ask if we can pray for you at Dr. Swanson's house tonight."

Dr. Swanson was happy to have Nelson come. He had taken care of several patients with symptoms like Nelson's, which seemed to be outside the realm of medicine. As Nelson and I left my house to go to the Swansons', Nelson's head suddenly started to ache again. He felt very shaky. He told me later that he almost refused to go, but with great determination he went anyway.

Nelson very openly and freely told Dr. Swanson about his early involvement with black magic, which he had confessed as sin when he was in Huanuco. He told how he had been freed at that time, yet recently had again experienced doubt and fear of inexplicable proportions. He felt these were from a source outside himself.

"Nelson, have you ever been delivered from demonic bondage when you have consciously severed all ties with the past?" Jack, another colleague in the prayer group asked. "I think you need to do this, including the influence that has been on you because your father was a shaman. Have you renounced all the times you have been involved with sorcery and demon activity?"

"No, I have never done this," Nelson said. "But I'm willing to."

We prayed together, Nelson asking forgiveness for all sins, especially those relating to sorcery, and for any influence his father's involvement in sorcery had brought upon him. He fully committed himself to Christ.

Jack ordered Satan to sever all ties with Nelson, in the name of Jesus Christ. He reminded him that Satan had no power over Nelson. Next Jack spoke to the demon that was bothering Nelson.

"Tell me your name," he ordered.

When he said this, Nelson felt very sick and was determined not to answer. But then he just couldn't help answering.

"I am Afraid," the demon replied.

"Demon of fear, I order you, in the name of Jesus Christ, to leave Nelson!" Jack commanded.

"I felt something move all through my body when he said that," Nelson told us later. "Then suddenly something was in my throat, and I couldn't breathe. My head felt like it would split. Then suddenly, I was free. I felt the demon go, right out the side of my head. The trembling, the feeling of smothering, and the headache all left. I was flooded with a sense of calmness."

The men in the prayer group placed their hands on Nelson and prayed for him again, this time asking for the fullness of the Holy Spirit in his life. Then we all praised the Lord together in song.

The next day, Nelson wrote another new song about Christ's power and victory over demons through the filling of the Holy Spirit:

> Christ was killed and buried,
> He rose again, defeating the demons.
> Therefore, by his Word
> Let us defeat the demons.
>
> The demons are completely defeated.
> Don't fear the demons.
> Christ guards us.
> He will send them away.
>
> The holy blood of Christ
> Protects us.

Encourage yourselves.
Let's send the demons away.

The Holy Spirit, the Holy Spirit,
Now has come to me.
Here he unites with all of us.

My Christ, my Christ
Is really strongest.
The demons are not strong.
Christ has been victorious.

A few days later, Jack read with fascination and gratitude a letter from a prayer group that prayed for him in the U. S. They had been praying very specifically the night of Nelson's deliverance:

> We had teaching on Ephesians 6:10-20 tonight.... Following this, we had intense prayer, supplication, and intercession for the breaking of bonds, for the "rending of chains asunder," for the "freeing of captives..."

God had indeed answered their prayers that night. We all felt excited at once again seeing God's timing in Nelson's life, but we had yet to see how God would solve the problem of Julia's dark side. Before Nelson could get a flight home, we heard from Carlos Sachtler by radio that Nelson's children were well and that Julia had gone downriver to her mother's. Nelson decided to go back to school. Since I was again going out to Nazaret, he asked me to arrange for Julia and the children to join him in Huanuco. He had just one month to go until graduation; he had to finish!

Mrs. Cudney traveled up to Huanuco for Nelson's graduation on November 15, 1974. One of the highlights was hearing Nelson's account of his struggles, defeats, and victories. He spoke in such a moving way that many people wept.

After graduation, Nelson, Julia, and the children returned to Lima with Mrs. Cudney. And once again, it seemed that God timed their stay in Lima perfectly. Julia and Nelson were delighted to find Jerry Elder, our prayer partner for several years, there also.

"Jerry, I need your help now," Julia said. "Will you pray for me? Every time anyone preaches the Word of God, I just can't hear.

Every time I try to pray I see a huge rock coming down to crush me. I know that if I pray I will be crushed completely, and so I can't pray."

"Sure, Julia, we'll pray for you if you want us to," Jerry assured her.

Jerry, another friend, and Nelson spent several hours talking, praying and singing with Julia. The demons in her manifested themselves in same kind of physical demonstrations that they by now recognized. They felt they were in an intense battle against the forces of evil. But finally, Julia was free. Though she felt exhausted from the hours of struggle, she prayed a beautiful prayer. Then she lay down and slept. Later in the day, she was radiantly happy. Even months later, when I again saw her in her home, I could hardly believe Julia was the same girl. Her physical disarray had disappeared, and she was taking good care of the children and Nelson. "She certainly has changed!" Nelson beamed.

44

I'll Kill Him

When Martha and I traveled to Urakusa in 1974, we again saw the Aguaruna believers being channels of God's power in situations of oppresssion. Miguel had relapsed after being delivered from demons; he had again opened his life to the enemy through hatred, resentment and revenge.[28]

"I'm so angry, I can't think. I can't pray. All I can think about is how I can kill my brother. I'll never live with Maria again. I hate her!" he told Martha and me.

As we talked, Miguel wept, realizing his disobedience to the Lord, but at the same time, being consumed with a hatred so strong that he could only say, "I'll never forgive him! I'll kill him if I ever see him!"

"Oh, my brother Miguel, I see that you are in terrible turmoil! What has happened to fill you with such hatred and anger?"

"One night I discovered that my brother Pijuchkun slept with my wife Maria while I was gone. When I found out, I was so angry I grabbed my gun and took off for his house. I perched on a stump by the river, and waited all night, watching his door. I planned to shoot him the minute he appeared.

"But before dawn, one of the men discovered me waiting. He tried to talk me out of my plans. Pijuchkun overheard us talking and ran out the back way, and fled downriver. When daylight came, I went home still terribly angry. I beat up Maria, and continued ranting around the village.

"When the news got out, Pijuchkun's wife became just as angry as I was. She took over Pijuchkun's store for herself. Now our

254

battle has been going on for several weeks. I've been fighting with Maria all the time and waiting for my chance to get even with Pijuchkun. Pijuchkun's wife is raising havoc with the store, and he is still hiding out."

As I listened to Miguel, I ached at the pain he must have felt, and I felt great sadness for Pijuchkun. He had been so successful with his store since Dennis had trained him. He had even trained others too. Now, he had brought disaster through his affair with Maria.

I shared the Scriptures with Miguel on our need to forgive if we want to receive forgiveness.

"I know all that, Millie," he said, "but I can't do it." I wondered if I would really be able to forgive in similar circumstances. What did I know of this kind of forgiveness? Who had ever wronged me so deeply? "Lord," I prayed, "please bring someone into Miguel's life who really knows what he is suffering and can minister to him." We talked, and shared, and prayed—yet Miguel persisted. "I'll kill him!" he insisted. It seemed clear that Satan had control of his life once more. I knew that God could free him—but Miguel didn't yet want to be free. He wanted revenge.

I left Urakusa, very saddened by Miguel's condition. I didn't see him again for about nine months. But in March of 1975 I received a letter from him from Jaen, where he was attending high school.

> My dear mother, do you stay well? I am here reading paper, but there is much suffering. Mother, I think of you often.
>
> Before, I used to serve the devil. But now Jesus has given me love. Now even when I suffer, I am happy. Jesus said that he came to heal the really wicked people.
>
> It's not ugly to live with Jesus. You know very well how I was living. I was so terribly angry that I was sick. Now I want to work as Jesus' servant. I thank Jesus because he helped me. Tell Nelson and Esteban that I thank them very much, because they helped me in prayer. I don't have time to write to Esteban now. You tell the people there that I say, 'My dear brothers, my dear sisters, I will tell you when I arrive how my angry heart has been changed.'

Later I learned more about the change in Miguel's life. In January, Miguel had gone to Jaen to attend summer school. But he couldn't study because he was still so full of hatred. Esteban was also there studying, and Miguel was so attracted by his joy that he asked him to pray for him. Esteban invited Miguel to join a small prayer group that he had started with several other teachers who were also in Jaen. Miguel joined them, but in spite of their encouragement to forgive Pijuchkun and Maria, he wasn't able to do it.

Then one evening Esteban and Cesar went with Miguel out of town, to a quiet place to pray. As they tried to pray, the power of evil enveloped them. Esteban and Cesar saw a huge, black form hovering over Miguel. At first Esteban was afraid, but then he called out to Jesus. "Protect us through your blood, Jesus," he pleaded.

Immediately the evil form became invisible to Esteban and Cesar. But Miguel still trembled with fear. The evil spirit was overcoming him. Then Esteban commanded the demon to leave. Instantly, Miguel was free. He prayed and wept, prayed and wept. He asked God to forgive him, but then realized that if he wanted to be forgiven, he must forgive Pijuchkun and Maria. Their adultery was no worse than his intention to murder. He too was a sinner.

God's Spirit cleansed Miguel as he prayed for forgiveness. He told God he was willing to forgive both Pijuchkun and Maria.

Miguel returned to school, a new man. He continued to study the Word and to pray with Esteban and the others every day.

Then Miguel wrote to Pijuchkun. "Please come to Jaen to see me, my brother. I want to talk to you. I forgive you."

But Pijuchkun was afraid to go. Perhaps Miguel was laying a trap for him. But finally he decided to go. Still afraid of Miguel, Pijuchkun first looked for Esteban.

"Let's go. I'll go with you," Esteban told him.

So together they came to see Miguel. The minute he saw them, Miguel ran to Pijuchkun, tears streaming down his cheeks, and threw his arms around him.

"Forgive me, my brother," he wept, "I almost killed you! I have sinned. But God has forgiven my sin, and I forgive your sin."

When Miguel left Jaen and went home to Urakusa at the end of March, he returned to Maria and their children. God healed their relationship through Miguel's forgiveness. When I visited Urakusa shortly thereafter, they were doing very well. Miguel glowingly told all the believers how God delivered him from sin, and from the enemy, once more.

45

The Old Ways Were Better

Not all the reports from the 120 teachers in summer school at Jaen in 1975 were as encouraging as the one about Miguel. Opposition to God's work came in unexpected ways. The "God-is-dead" philosophy had reached even into this small mountain town. Some of the professors of the Aguaruna teachers ridiculed Christianity.

"People who are really educated don't believe that any more. We know now that God doesn't exist," they said.

Esteban and others united in prayer groups in order to withstand the onslaught. But the teachers who were weak in faith or were living in sin succumbed. It seemed that even Roman, now coordinator of bilingual education for the area, let himself be drawn into the godless philosophy. He gave up reading Scripture. He ceased to pray. He allowed his old desires and the forces around him to control him.

"I don't believe in God anymore," Roman told his fellow teachers one day. "We must go back to the ways of the ancestors. The missionaries have deceived us."

At about that time, Roman was invited to the United States to participate in a conference of a radical Indian movement. This served to amplify his anti-Christian sentiments.

Because Roman's influence was so strong, many teachers reeled with doubt and confusion. "How can we know the truth?" they asked.

But others stood up to Roman. "What do you mean, go back to the old ways?" they challenged him angrily. "Shall we quit teaching and have the boys go to the jungle and drink drugs? Shall we go back to sorcery to heal the sick? Shall we stop using medicine? Shall we begin killing one another again?"

"I can't believe what Roman says," Miguel told them. God changed my life. I can't accept the idea that God doesn't exist. I know He does."

Many teachers' respect for Roman's superior education was shattered. Feelings crystallized on both sides of the issue. No one remained neutral.

The anti-God philosophy also crept into the Aguaruna area itself. In the education center where Dantuchu and David worked, it became strong. But at least in one official meeting, Dantuchu stopped the arguement cold. One of the participants from Lima was openly hostile to the teaching of Scripture.

"We must get rid of these men who are preaching from the Bible. They do much harm. We don't need them out here among the Aguaruna," he insisted.

Dantuchu got to his feet. Holding up a Spanish New Testament, he countered, "I don't know what kind of people *you* are, but we Aguaruna have souls. We need the Bible. Our souls need food."

I found that Roman was not the only one talking about "the good old days." After living in other villages, I had returned to Nazaret for the first time in ten years, again to feel the pulse of Aguaruna life. Alias had also returned after years away in more isolated areas. I was eager to talk to him, to Dantuchu, and to David. I wanted to reminisce with them and to assess what was happening with them.

I found the same lush, green mountains surrounding Nazaret, the same clear river rushing by, the same friendly, noisy Aguaruna. But I also found that the side of the mountain had been blasted away for the road to Urakusa, which cut through the center of Aguaruna territory. A bright orange metal bridge funneled the roar of traffic into the once quiet valley. These changes in the environment mirrored changes in the way of life. The Aguaruna now had little time to sit and chat. It seemed each one was caught up in the strenuous business of making a living in the new society.

"Some people would expect me to rejoice at the inroads of civilization,'" I thought. "But I just can't. Instead, I am nostalgic for the Nazaret of twenty years ago. The silence then was broken only by shouting, laughing or wailing—but never by bulldozers, cars and trucks. Now listen! Motors roar up and down the river as well as the road, carrying gasoline, supplies and beer."

Alias too was caught up in the new pace. He took time from dashing around to visit with me. We discussed the contrast between the old and the new.

"Everyone is talking about how much better the old Aguaruna ways are than the new ways of civilization, sister," he said. "But it's not the external things that worry me. I'm concerned about the complete lack of discipline that has come into our society. We were once governed by very rigid rules of behavior, especially for our young people. But now it's not that way."

As I listened to Alias, and later to Aguaruna leaders in other communities, I was amazed. The complaints were practically the same ones I had heard about my own society while I was on furlough in the United States! There was an increase in immorality, an increase in divorce, an increase in sorcery. Young people were involved in black magic, they were disobedient to their parents, materialism and stealing had increased, people were indifferent to God.

Many of the teachers complained about these changes, but did nothing to solve the problems. But one teacher put his concern into action. At Urakusa, Shimpu started "Project Investigation." He took his advanced students to visit elderly Aguaruna in their homes. He and the students interviewed them about the old Aguaruna culture and the changes they had seen take place. The young people, who had been making fun of these elders, began to appreciate them. They were amazed at their wealth of knowledge. They became interested in and excited about their heritage. The generation gap began to close.

Then Shimpu explained to his students that there were not just two alternatives—the old Aguaruna culture and the new "civilization."

"In the new there are both Christian and non-Christian people," he told them. "We do need a new Aguaruna culture," he said, "But we must choose an Aguaruna-Christian culture."

46

The ABC's of the Gospel

Through the work of the Holy Spirit, a significant conflict was resolved in 1975. God brought about a mutual change of attitude between us and Catholic missionaries who had been involved with the Aguaruna.

For twenty years, I had thought of the priests and nuns who worked with the people as "enemies." We had been working with different goals, approaches, and perspective. We worked for bilingual schools; just as fervently they worked for monolingual Spanish schools. In the past, I had seen the Roman Catholic church as a formidable foe, leading people into eternal destruction. Catholic priests had seen us as instruments of Satan, keeping the Aguaruna from fellowshipping in the true church.

A state of hostile co-existence had developed between us during the years. But God began to break down these barriers. It seems he started with me and other members of our Aguaruna team. In our prayer group at Yarinacocha, we began praying for the priests and nuns. We asked God to bless them and to change our attitudes towards them. We began to see them as people whom God loved and whom we should also love. God brought about many changes in us before He opened the way to fellowship with them.

We had concentrated our prayers on a certain priest who was in charge of the mission education program. When the school system had been decentralized, and the government had put all the Aguaruna schools under the education office in Jaen, this priest had been determined to see that the 130 bilingual school teachers trained at Yarinacocha would be allowed to teach only in Spanish.

We prayed earnestly that this would not happen, and God answered our prayers in an unexpected way. This priest was invited to attend an international conference on bilingual education in December, 1972. For the first time, he understood the government's program in bilingual education and saw its results. After the conference, he came to visit Yarinacocha, where, also for the first time, he got to know us. We continued to pray for this priest and his influence on our work.

In 1973 this priest left the priesthood and went to live in Lima to work in the Department of Education. He became a champion, not only of bilingual education, but also of our work. He developed an increasing desire to be involved in our efforts and offered to help us whenever he could. But the most notable change was that he enjoyed talking and sharing with us about God. We discovered that he was indeed a follower of Christ.

The choice of an alphabet for the Aguaruna language had been one source of our conflict for years. In 1954, based on my linguistic studies, I had devised an alphabet using one symbol for each sound, using Spanish symbols when possible to fit Aguaruna sounds. But since the sound systems differed, the alphabet didn't match the Spanish one.

The priests, with no linguistic background, heard Aguaruna through the sound screen of the Spanish system, and wrote it accordingly. Thus they would not accept our proposed alphabet. In 1974 Roman told me, "The alphabet is the problem, Millie. The government would like to make all the Aguaruna schools bilingual, but the Catholics will not accept the alphabet in the bilingual materials you have prepared."

In our prayer group we decided to pray consistently about the alphabet problem. Then one day in October, 1974, another priest who had worked among the Aguaruna appeared at Yarinacocha.

"Can you help us with a linguistic course in January?" he asked. "I want all the Catholic missionaries working in the jungle to study linguistics and anthropology."

We arranged for Dr. Olive Shell, a linguistics professor and translator of the Cashibo New Testament, to go into Lima to teach a course on sound systems and alphabet selection. We could scarcely suppress our excitement! We prayed especially that the priests and nuns from the Aguaruna area would attend. It seemed God was about to solve the problem of the ABC's.

God's answer surpassed our prayers. Not only did He make it

possible for six of the Catholic missionaries from the Aguaruna area to attend the course, but He also provided an Aguaruna youth studying in Lima to give practical language help to the participants. By the end of the course, the nuns were hearing the Aguaruna sounds and writing them down with the alphabet we had used. They were excited about learning to speak Aguaruna.

But our gains were more than linguistic. We all learned something about the ABC's of the gospel too. The nuns grew to love Dr. Shell and her SIL assistants. We all discovered that we could have fellowship together because of our love for Christ.

At the end of the course, we had a farewell supper at our guest house. The bishop, forty priests and nuns, and many SIL members came. We had a beautiful time sharing together as we abandoned our old stereotypes of each other.

One priest spoke from the book of Revelation, reminding us that "some from every tongue, tribe, and nation" will be in heaven.

Another said, "If we are going to be standing before the Lord and be accepted by Him, it's time we started accepting each other here on earth and working together towards the Kingdom."

"Yes," the bishop added, "I've always wanted to have spiritual fellowship with the members of SIL, but the time wasn't ripe. Now it is. God is doing a beautiful thing, visiting us with His Spirit."

Carlos and Doris Sachtler, of the Swiss Bible school, were also at the supper. A nun who worked up the Cenepa River near them stood up.

"Can you imagine it?" she asked excitedly. "Here I've just found out that Carlos has been working on the same river as I have for years. He has been telling everyone about the same Lord as I have, and we haven't been talking to each other! That's a shame. That's not going to happen any more. We're going to get together!"

We closed our evening with singing and prayer—prayers of thanksgiving for having gotten to know one another as people, as brothers and sisters also committed to Jesus Christ. We set aside our prejudices, and another barrier to the power of the Holy Spirit tumbled down.

Meanwhile, the other members of our Aguaruna team were making strides in their relationships with our Catholic brothers and sisters. Jeanne won respect and appreciation through her nursing activities. Dennis continued to develop his friendship with Father Pancho.

Because of their introduction to linguistics, the nuns working in the Aguaruna area wanted to learn the language. They asked me to teach a course in Aguaruna grammar. In March of 1975 I taught for a week in Nieva. The priest and ten nuns attended.

Martha and I shared a house with the nuns. Each morning and evening we all read Scripture and prayed together. All day, every day, I taught them Aguaruna. Through classes and our daily sharing we came to know and love one another. Trust between us grew. We realized that Christ was central to each of our lives. As members of His body, we learned to be members of one another. God continued to break down the walls I had built. To my own surprise, I found that I loved my Catholic sisters. This seemed, somehow, a fitting capstone on the completion of the New Testament, a necessary preparation for its dedication soon to come.

47

The Dream and the Battle

Nelson's dream of ten years was about to come true. But we didn't know how costly or complex its fulfillment would be. We never imagined all the ways in which opposition would come.

Martha and I flew to Nueva Vida on March 6, 1975, with carefully made plans. We would train two men to assist in the writers' seminar to be held in July and August, travel to Nieva for a week to teach the nuns, and be on hand for the opening of the Bible school on April 1. But we forgot to schedule time for the spiritual battle we would encounter. We didn't anticipate the fierceness of the struggle with Satan, who wanted to block the school.

"Everything is going okay," Nelson told us when we arrived. "The students will come March 15. Fifty men from thirty villages have already registered. They'll come two weeks early to cut back the jungle, put up walls, build the beds, and plant gardens. During the pastors' conference in December we chose a committee to help direct the work. Carlos Sachtler is coming the twenty-fourth. The inauguration will be April first. We're going to have a big program and lots of food!"

"Oh, I hope the copies of the New Testament we asked for by air mail arrive in time from the printer in Germany!" I thought. "I want everything to go perfectly."

But Satan had other plans. Immediately obstacles loomed up, creating confusion and doubt and distracting us all from the preparations.

The first problem was Julia—not the former problem of her old life, but another one caused by a new life. She was five-months pregnant. When her pregnancy didn't seem to be developing as usual, Nelson took her upriver to see a doctor. "If she were my wife, I'd leave for Lima and see a specialist immediately," the doctor told him. "I wouldn't wait even three days. If it is a baby, it is not developing properly. It has no heart beat and I feel no motion. Perhaps Julia has a tumor. Perhaps it is malignant."

Nelson and Julia had been getting along beautifully since her deliverance in Lima. Nelson agreed that she was completely different. But now his old fears were stirred up, as we requested a flight to take Julia to the doctor in Yarinacocha. Somehow he couldn't really trust her for this trip. The three of us prayed about whether Julia should go, and I asked God to heal her, no matter what they decided.

I could sense that Nelson still didn't want her to go. "Is there something else?" I wondered.

"I'm afraid of what I'll do if Julia goes," Nelson said. I'm not strong. Besides, if God wants her healed, He can heal her here. If He wants her to die, she will die even if she goes to the doctor—so she might as well die here. Let her decide. If she goes I don't know what I might do."

I felt completely confused by Nelson's comments. "What does he mean?" I wondered. "He's forcing Julia to decide, and she's not able to make a decision."

Later, Martha and I prayed for Nelson. How frustrated he must be feeling. It was the fifteenth already; the students were due to arrive. His wife was sick, his mother-in-law had a broken arm, and constant rain had muddied the gardens and the village. It seemed like a whirlwind had struck.

Through my devotional reading, the Lord reassured me that He would bring peace. Then I learned that there was more to Nelson's problem. A new young woman in the village had been after him. He feared that if Julia left, he would not be able to withstand her temptations. Then his sin would ruin the Bible school.

The next morning, Nelson left early for a short trip. But he didn't tell us Julia should go with the pilot, who was waiting.

"Julia, what did you decide? What are you going to do?" I asked.

"I'm not going. Nelson doesn't want me to go, so I'll stay."

"She is indeed changed!" I thought. "Obedience hasn't been her strong point. Now she'll obey her husband even if it means death."

Nelson returned at 9:30, just before take-off time.

"What are you planning to do, Nelson?" I asked. He was notably calmer and happier than he had been the day before.

"Just now, as I came up river, I asked God what to do. Now I know. Julia can't go today. Right now, I have to be here for the students. But when Carlos comes he can take care of them, and I will go to Yarinacocha with Julia. I must go with her. I don't want her to go alone."

"Thank you, Lord," I prayed silently. "I think he finally sees how to settle the conflict he feels between Julia's needs and the needs of the school. I think we'll see You work now!"

Nelson decided to take Julia along on the trip up river to the doctor to have her mother's arm set. The doctor decided to examine Julia again.

"But how can it be?" he asked Nelson in great surprise. "I know she had nothing but a hard lump in her uterus. I was sure it was a dead fetus. Now things are all okay. The baby's heart beat is clear. Julia is five months along!"

God thus took us over the first hurdle obstructing the opening of school. But others loomed ahead.

The teachers didn't arrive as scheduled. Students failed to show up. Finally someone tracked down the rumor that was keeping them away. They had heard it would cost 4,000 *soles* (about two months wages) to attend.

Then Nelson's dark side cropped up again; a small spark of bitterness was fanned into a fire by the old Deceiver. He started to dwell again on Julia's unfaithfulness. He lost the sense of freedom he had gained. A desire for revenge against the man who had wronged him grew. And with it grew a fear of his own behavior.

"I'll go ahead and teach this first term because I said I would," he confided. "But then I'm going away to work for the road company. I can't stay here. If I do I'll kill. I'm not fit to teach. It's better that someone else do it."

We all agonized with Nelson and spent hours in prayer. We searched our own hearts too, and God brought forgiveness and healing for more than just Nelson's sin. But the oppression didn't lift easily.

It seemed that even the storeroom that Martha and I shared as a bedroom was full of evil power. We constantly felt oppressed when we were there, especially whenever we tried to pray. When we left the building, we felt a release from darkness. We were happy to leave for our week with the nuns at Nieva. We chose another room when we returned.

Carlos arrived on schedule and moved into the vacant store-room. We were all glad to see him. With him there, surely prepa-rations would move ahead.

But we were wrong again. Carlos was concerned for an old friend, Angkuash and invited him to share the storeroom with him. Angkuash had a long history of epileptic-like seizures which the people attributed to demons controlling him. Carlos hoped to min-ister to him while they were together.

Carlos' first night with Angkuash passed like a nightmare. Each time Angkuash had an attack, Carlos prayed for him and attempted to deliver him. Angkuash would relax and lie down again. But soon he would become restless again.

"One minute, he would be on his bed. The next minute, he would fly, blanket and all, across to the other side of the room," Carlos told us next day. "I was afraid and could hardly wait for daylight."

At dawn, Carlos came to our house to radio his colleagues for prayer. We invited a group of believers to gather to pray with Ang-kuash. Esteban had just come home. He invited his prayer group from Jaen, including teachers Cesar and Cristobal, to come. The two local pastors and Antonio, who was to help teach in the Bible school, also joined in the prayer.

Esteban questioned Angkuash first. "Do you really want to be free? Have you denounced the demons?"

"Yes, I want to be free," Angkuash told them. "I have suffered very much. I will denounce the demons."

As Angkuash denounced the demons, Esteban and Carlos com-manded them to leave him. All the others prayed for him too.

That night, Antonio decided to sleep in the storeroom with Car-los and Angkuash. During the night, Angkuash had only one small attack, but as soon as they prayed for him, he was all right. All three went back to sleep, encouraged that he was fully free.

Thus the Lord cleared another obstacle that Satan had erected to block the opening of school. And then, as though the tests were past, He provided a special blessing. Nelson, Esteban, and others went out to hunt for meat the day before school opened. As soon as they stepped out of the canoe and into the jungle, Nelson's dog caught a scent. Almost immediately the men tracked down and shot a wild pig—the perfect meat for a community feast.

Opening day dawned beautifully. But more magnificent than the day was Nelson's delight at seeing the first printed New Testament. The first three copies, airmailed from Germany, arrived from Yarinacocha with Mrs. Cudney and my brother and his wife. Now each of the three Bible school teachers would have a copy for the course.

Nelson and Antonio pored over their New Testaments enthusiastically. Antonio immediately underlined some of his favorite passages. I could scarcely contain my joy, seeing those first complete books. I was overcome with a profound sense of gratitude to God for all He had done and for the hundreds of people who had helped in so many ways. That night, I had to pour out my thanks in a long letter to God before I could settle my thoughts and find rest.

Dear Heavenly Father,

Today I held in my hands a copy of the Aguaruna New Testament, printed and bound. And now I lay it at your feet and say, "thank you." Thank you for your mercy, for your patience, for your love. Thank you for letting me have a small part in this beautiful book.

I do not understand why you chose me. Why did you let me finish this New Testament while others became sick and had to go home? Why did you keep me from giving up and going back years ago? I wanted to, you know.

Oh, Father, I know it is not because of who I am. It is only because you are who you are. You chose. You chose Jacob the deceiver rather than his brother Esau. You chose Peter, and he denied you three times. You chose Paul when he was persecuting your followers. You chose my fellow workers in Wycliffe, many as weak as I. You use our frailties to show your greatness.

Thank you for letting me be one of hundreds of people whom you used to complete this book. Thank you for Kunyach and Misangkit who taught me the language and all the other Aguaruna who corrected and encouraged. Thank you for Alias, Tomas, and Nelson who suffered much to help put your Word in their very own language. Thank you for the bilingual school teachers who taught their own people to read this book.

Thank you for fellow team members—Jeanne, Martha, Dennis and Susie—for all the times they carried the extra load to keep me translating. Thank you for all the good instructors who taught me linguistics, for all those who gave me new insights into translation methods.

Thank you for wonderful pilots who fly me back and forth. Thank you for the men who keep the planes running. For radio men. For those in publications and the Peruvians who work there. Thank you for the people in the dining room and in the finance office, for the doctors and nurses, for the men at the maintenance shop who keep the water and electricity coming. Thank you for administrators who care. Thank you for "Grangran" Rich's love.

Thank you for the gang in Mexico who went the extra mile to get the New Testament typeset and pasted up. For the New York Bible Society who provided the funds. For the printer and his staff in Germany.

Father, there are so many. I can't name them all. But thank you especially for those who prayed. For my prayer partners at Yarinacocha, for Mrs. Cudney, my home church in Solway, my mother, friends around the world...

How many people does it take to finish a New Testament? I don't know, Father. You keep the records. I know that when I see your beautiful tapestry some day I will be only one small blue thread running through it. Thank you for choosing me.

From Millie, with love.

48

Books for Everyone!

The incomparable, living Word from Nazareth arrived in Nazaret in written form, in words every Aguaruna could savor and hold, on October l4, 1975. The message, almost two thousand years in transit, arrived clothed in the plastic wrappings of the twentieth century.

Eagerly, Alias and his relatives unloaded the 10,000 books, scurrying from the truck to the storeroom, where the boxes would be marked for distribution by air and river to a hundred other Aguaruna communities. How could they bear to wait for the day of celebration to rip open the boxes and pore over the exciting books they held?

As with the first-coming of the Word to earth, winged heralds proclaimed the arrival of the Word to scattered villages. Heliocouriers and the twin-engine Evangel carried invitations throughout the Aguaruna area. A twelve-day celebration, to cover fifteen villages, would be held. From these fifteen chosen communities, the New Testament would be distributed to all the others. Dates were set, the chosen communities were encouraged to prepare their celebrations and books were shuttled out to await the special day.

We knew we could keep to the celebration schedule only if the rivers and skies were right for flying. Could God give us perfect weather for twelve days in mountains where the weather was unpredictable and the rivers were precarious? We asked many people to pray that He would.

On October 17, a perfect flying day, Butch Barkman flew Martha, Carlos and me to the Marañon. Dennis, who had accompanied the books from Lima, Jeanne, and nurse Joy Congdon met us there.

On the way to Nazaret, where the first celebration would take place, we stopped at Nueva Vida to pick up Nelson. We wanted him to have the joy of presenting the New Testament to his people, since he and Alias had been the main co-translators. He and Tomas and Abel were to travel with us.

But Nelson was surprised to see us.

"Are you ready to go with us, Nelson?" I asked.

"I don't know. What are your plans? I didn't know about all this," he said. I could tell that he felt left out. "Why didn't you let me know?"

"We did! Didn't you get the letter weeks ago, asking you to join us on the trip? Or the one inviting all the villages to join in the celebration?"

"No, I didn't get either one. I can't possibly get ready for a celebration here in Nueva Vida and at the same time go with you. I'll just stay here and wait until you come down again, and then we'll see if I can join you."

As we taxied upriver without Nelson, I felt sick and sad. "Why did you let this happen, Lord?" I questioned. Then I remembered the reality of our spiritual battle. "The enemy is again trying to discourage Nelson and me," I thought. "We are his targets. He is angry at us for translating God's Word." As the plane lifted off the water, I prayed once more for God's special protection from Satan's attack upon us during the trip. I was comforted, too, knowing that our co-workers at Yarinacocha were praying around the clock.

Up at five the next morning, into the boat by six, we completed our trip to Nazaret by river. As the boat headed steadily into the current, I drank in the beauty of the morning—the rushing river, the familiar, lush mountains rimming the valley, the fern-draped, rocky banks and the flowering trees, the flowing vines, the chirping, colorful birds, a waterfall tumbling into the river. I read Psalm 98. My sadness and fear of the previous day fled and I was filled with joy and praise. The words were perfect for my mood.

> Make a joyful symphony before the Lord, the King! Let the sea in all its vastness roar with praise! Let the earth and all those living on it shout, "Glory to the Lord."
>
> Let the waves clap their hands in glee, and the hills sing out their songs of joy before the Lord...

We arrived at Nazaret in time for breakfast. Kunyach, my first language teacher, eagerly invited us to eat with his family. It was hard not to reminisce! Elisa, a baby when I first arrived twenty-one years before, served us while she skillfully kept an eye on her three children. Her mother Misangkit, wrinkled and almost toothless, had been my closest Aguaruna friend. She was very excited to have us in her home once more.

I shook off my reverie. "Don't sit here, dwelling on the past," I told myself. "This is a great day! We're back in Nazaret to give out the Word which we promised our friends so long ago."

Alias came in, all smiles of joy. His long hair was carefully pulled back and he wore special necklaces for the occasion. Later David joined us too.

The village was full of Aguaruna, eager to buy copies of their book—the first big book in their own language! They crowded into the school building, impatient for the selling of Scripture to begin. Handsome young Rodolfo was there. A naked little boy when I first knew him in 1954, he had helped with the final proofreading of the New Testament in 1972.

"Are you ready to buy your own copy?" someone asked him.

"Yes!" he beamed. "I have saved up enough money to buy ninety New Testaments. I will leave tomorrow morning to go by trail to the Chiangkus area. I want to take books to those who couldn't come out here to the main river."

"Fantastic!" I thought. "He's eager to hike with all those books over one of the worst trails. It's a tedious, twelve-hour trek up into those mountains."

After buying his copies, Rodolfo pitched in to help Tomas and Abel sell. Tomas was so enthusiastic that he was soon surrounded by a group of noisy young people asking questions about the New Testament. He began teaching them right on the spot. They had never seen the Gospel of Matthew; he opened up to chapter five and began reading to them. Immediately, they fished ballpoint pens out of their shoulder bags and began underlining the verses he was sharing.

As people bought books, they sat down and eagerly pored through them. Some sat outside under the trees to read, away from the loud hum of excited voices. The buying didn't slow down until about 700 copies of the New Testament had been sold. Then Alias led everyone in songs of praise and in prayer. Tomas read Scripture. A special dinner for everyone, with wild meat, fish, manioc and bananas, followed this very informal, short service of dedication. I noticed Jeanne happily eating her favorite—palm heart roasted in leaves with palm grubs.

As we said goodbye at noon, I realized I might never return to Nazaret. Yet I was so happy seeing each person with a New Testament in hand that I couldn't feel sad. I was overwhelmed with gratitude. As we floated back downriver, we passed a teacher who had bought fifty New Testaments for his community. The boxes sat in the middle of his tiny, five-pole raft, precariously near the water. "Well, God has protected His Word thus far," I thought. "I'm sure He'll keep those books safe too!"

After the success of the morning, our afternoon stop was sobering. We met mostly indifference in a community that had been invaded by the God-is-dead philosophy, which made Christians out to be second class. Only a handful of people were interested in the New Testament, including Jeremias. A teacher, he continued to follow Christ in spite of the negative pressures. He invited us to eat and pray with him.

Our next stop too was sobering and silent. In the morning we traveled on downriver to Uut. Just a few days before, men from Uut had gone upriver, beyond Nazaret, for a revenge killing. Besides killing the young man they wanted revenge on, they had mistakenly killed a five-year-old child and injured another man. Now they were all hiding, expecting retaliation. Only Roman's father, who was the teacher, members of his family, and a few women and children were there.

Our days began to melt together as we continued our tour. Each morning we were up at five and off by six. Most days we visited two villages, listened to two programs, had another big dinner, visited, slept a little. Then we would be up again at five, and off again by six.

But in each village something was memorable. At Chipi it was a choir, and the teacher reading from the Spanish New Testament. When he stood to read a passage from Romans, I thought, "Oh, no. Why is he doing that with the Aguaruna New Testament laying right there on the table?" But when he finished reading in Spanish, he laid the book down and walked over and picked up the Aguaruna New Testament. Opening again to Romans, he said, "Now let's find out what it says. I'm going to read it in our own language, so we can really understand."

At Nueva Vida, it was Nelson's new song: "The Word of Jesus

Christ, the Word of Jesus Christ, we receive it with joy." Early in the morning, he had practiced with the women and children for three hours, teaching the women one part and the children another.

Nelson joined us for the remainder of our trip. At Nieva, a mestizo community, Father Pancho had prepared the church by arranging copies of the New Testament in front of the altar. The ones with red covers formed a cross, surrounded and supported by the blue ones. He had invited all the school children and everyone from the mestizo town. The big church was so full that the school boys had to stand along the wall; the benches could hold no more.

"Do three things," Father Pancho urged the people. "Read this New Testament, meditate on it, and pray." Another priest taught the song, "I have a friend who loves me; His name is Jesus." Sister Carmen, who had been traveling with us for three days, led the children in singing. Sister Juliana read John 17, emphasizing Jesus' prayer that His followers would be one.

"Today, right here in this church, we see this becoming a reality," she said. "Here we have our protestant brothers and sisters in Christ united with us, praising God for this wonderful occasion when we can present the Aguaruna New Testament to the people."

My heart filled with love for Juliana as I listened to her, and filled with gratitude for the miracle God had done. He had changed both Juliana and me, and also our colleagues. His Holy Spirit was working in all of our lives.

Later, Juliana and Carmen traveled with us to the dedication in an Aguaruna village. "This has given me a whole new concept of the power of the Scriptures in the people's own language to change their hearts," Juliana said afterwards. Throughout our trip, God was graciously answering our prayers for the weather. We had so little rain, in fact, that by the time we wanted to land in the Potro and Kaupan area at lower elevation, the river was very low.

We circled the first village of the area, Aichiaku.

"I don't think we can land," our pilot Doug Deming said.

"But the people are all swarming down to the river," I told him.

"Well, let's drop a note and ask them to check the water." he suggested.

"Okay," I said. So I wrote, "If the river is too shallow to land on, stay up on the soccer field. But if it's deep enough, go down and show us the deepest part." We dropped the note, attached to a small parachute. The people all rushed up to the field to read it. We could see them discussing, trying to decide.

"God, don't let their eagerness to have us come outweigh their good judgement about the water," I prayed.

Then the decision was made. As a body, they turned and ran down to the river. We circled and came around again. By then a man had crossed in a canoe to the other side, marking the deepest passage. We had a narrow but sufficient channel to land on.

Doug left us there and flew on to check the water at Kaupan. We had another wonderful time of dedication, another tasty dinner—with ten kinds of meat!

Doug returned later than we expected. It was about 3:30 when he finally landed.

"I'm sorry, but we can't fly into Kaupan. The river is too low. I'll have to take you to a place five minutes on downriver from Kaupan. Some of the others are waiting there to go upriver by boat. That will take two hours, so we had better hurry."

"Goodness," I thought. "It's always pitch black by six. Why didn't we pray for rain last night to bring this small river up?"

Fourteen of us crowded into the rather small boat, already partly full of cargo. It was much smaller than the one we had been in on the main river, and it had only a ten horsepower motor. A palm leaf roof and side shades, meant to give shelter from the tropical sun, only made it hot and uncomfortable with so many of us aboard.

As we scraped bottom and made our way around grounded logs and other debris, I thought anxiously, "If the boat tips over, how do we get out?"

The limb of an old snag cut into our leaf curtains, but no one was hurt. We kept hitting sand bars and submerged trees. I felt sorry for Pancho, the director of the Kaupan school, who was manning the motor. I began to worry that we might ruin our borrowed boat.

We all felt hot and bothered. The trip seemed more dangerous all the time. Finally we decided to pray. We asked God to help Pancho to find the safest course. We prayed for rain—enough to make the river rise. By the time we finished praying, Martha said, "It's awfully dark." Peeking out, we could see that the sun had disappeared. Dark clouds were covering the sky. Five minutes later, sheets of rain beat down, cooling us through the leaky roof.

As we moved on, the river began to rise. Pancho's job became easier. But darkness settled while we were still an hour from Kaupan. Pancho could no longer see. One of the group decided that if God could give us rain, He could give us light too. So we prayed for light.

Lightning began to flash at regular intervals, lighting up the river all the way to the edges, exposing all the logs and debris. Even when we had to unload so the men could pull the boat through the rapids, the light kept flashing, so brightly that we women could see everything as we walked along the beach. Later I realized that I had felt no fear for our safety. The lightning hadn't crackled; it had just quietly flashed to light our way.

By the time we arrived in Kaupan and changed clothes, the stars were twinkling in a clear sky. People from many villages had crowded into Kaupan. They fed us another feast of wild meat, fish, manioc, watermelon, sugar cane, and bananas, topped off with a special dessert provided by Pancho: crackers, strawberry jam, and coffee with milk and sugar. While we ate, the young men sang to us. It didn't matter that they had their backs to us; reading their hymnals by the light of the one lantern was more important than that we see their faces.

We joined in another wonderful celebration, singing, sharing from the Word, and selling the precious books.

The next day, the river was high enough for the plane to land for us. Because God was so faithful to us in the physical realm, my confidence grew that He would answer our prayers in the spiritual realm, too. The impact of His Word would be great!

49

Celebration!

For more than two years before the arrival of the New Testaments, our prayer group at Yarinacocha had concentrated prayer on Urakusa. We chose this village because of the prevalence of sorcery there and because the people were so indifferent towards the Word of God. During this time, God steadily answered. Emirita and others were delivered from demons. Miguel renewed his relationship with God through his encounter with Him in Jaen. He told everyone that life is exciting when you follow Jesus and read His Word. Many believed because of these things.

About a month before the dedication was scheduled, we heard that all but one person in Urakusa had become believers. The day Butch landed to deliver New Testaments in preparation for the special day, only one man was on hand in the village. He couldn't help unload because of a bad back, but when Butch told him the books had come, he gave an excited shout. Immediately, women and children streamed down to the plane from all directions. They each grabbed a heavy box and trooped up the slippery, steep bank, singing praises to God. They wanted to open the boxes and to buy their New Testaments right then. "But you have to wait for the celebration day," Butch told them, grinning.

As the whole Aguaruna team and other SIL members from Yarinacocha pulled into port at Urakusa on the appointed day, crowds lined the steep banks. The singing people, lined up shoulder to shoulder, formed a path for us to walk along. It led to the church in the jungle at the far end of the village. As we walked down the path between them, they fell into place behind us, singing a new song composed for the occasion. We felt like leaders in a great procession of praise. Our hearts joined with theirs as our joy rang out through the still afternoon air.

People filled the church to overflowing. They squeezed into the benches, stood in the aisles and at the back, and sat on the platform, made of palm bark slats laid across supporting logs. Those who wouldn't fit inside watched over the cane walls or peeped through them.

Miguel's smile was as bright as the red shirt he wore. He took his place up front. In the first row sat his graying father, the leading elder. His faithful prayers had brought Miguel back to Jesus. Pastor Guillermo, a consultant in the final proofreading of the New Testament, also sat on the platform. He surveyed those sitting in front of him: several former shamans, a man who had once been driven from the village for sorcery, the whole village of Urakusa, and visitors from many surrounding communities.

Someone handed out mimeographed programs.

"Twenty-three items!" I chuckled. "They've taken advantage of our day of rest tomorrow and have planned a full twenty-four hour celebration! This afternoon will be for the dedication of the New Testament, this evening for the dedication of lives to Jesus Christ, and tomorrow morning for a dedication of lives to God through baptism!"

Guillermo led the people in singing. Then Miguel told again how God had delivered him, of the wonderful joy he now had in his home, and of his love for the Word of God.

Tomas explained about buying the New Testaments. "The covers are in three colors," he said, "red, blue and black. But on the inside they are all the same. There is just one message."

The moment Tomas finished and said, "It's time to buy now," the whole congregation surged to the front. People bought and bought. Tomas called for more boxes to be brought up from the boat. By sundown over 250 copies had been sold—mostly with red covers.

Martha and I squeezed in a quick bath in the creek before dark and returned just in time for the community meal. The village leaders had turned a huge oval dormitory into a dining room. A log table, seating about sixty, was covered with banana leaves. Two more long "tables," made of banana leaves laid out on the ground, reached the full length of the building. People squatted on both sides to eat the manioc, plantain and other foods heaped high in the center. The pastors and teachers of Urakusa dashed back and forth, serving enamel bowls of fish soup and a drink made of the tropical fruit, cocona, to the guests.

We ate by the light of one kerosene lantern hung in the center of the huge room. I sat across from an Aguaruna woman and Sister Carmen. As we visited, I marveled at God's grace in bringing us together from three very different worlds to fellowship in Him.

After eating, we all returned to the church. Tomas spoke from Scripture and then asked if anyone wanted to give his life to Jesus. If so, he would pray with him. People began to move forward; whole families squeezed through the crowded aisle to the front.

Amazed, I said to the young woman next to me, "I thought that all of you here in Urakusa were already believers."

"We are," she said. "These people are from Wachints, Warakai, Kayants and other places."

Over a hundred persons committed themselves to Christ, in true Aguaruna style. Everyone talked at once; the noise made them feel at ease. By families, they gathered around Tomas and other pastors to pray, as Guillermo led the rest of the congregation in singing. What would have seemed like cacophony to some people, rose up to God as the beautiful sound of repentance, thanksgiving and adoration.

When the last person had prayed and the noise died down, Tomas said, "I want to share something I read today in Luke." He turned to the passage about Jesus blessing the children.

"I think God wants us to bless the children tonight," he said.

I wondered what Tomas had in mind, as I had never seen the Aguaruna follow Jesus' example in this way. He discussed the passage and then invited the people to bring their small children to the front for prayer.

"If you bring them, it means that you are promising to teach them God's Word and never to take them to a shaman," he said.

Tears of joy flooded my eyes.

Mothers began moving up the aisle with their babies.

"Fathers, you must also stand with the mothers, since you will be responsible to fulfill the promise," he insisted. So the fathers stood and moved forward too. Tomas prayed for each child individually, with the parents as witnesses. Again, Guillermo helped by leading the others in song.

The leaders stayed on after the people left, to pray for Miguel's little sister, who was very ill. It was near midnight when we made our way through the dark and climbed under our mosquito nets. I thought my heart might burst for joy.

In the morning, more people gave their lives to Jesus; more parents brought their babies for prayer. Then it was time for the baptism.

After a suitable sermon, we all streamed down to the river. I was especially touched to see Miguel's father, one of the oldest Christians, be baptized. Twenty-nine whose names were on the printed program were baptized. Others wanted to join them, but the pastors decided to schedule another time for them later.

"What a wonderful problem to have," I thought. "Too many people to baptize all at once!"

During our twelve whirlwind days, 4,000 New Testaments were distributed among the Aguaruna. We knew that men like Tomas, Abel, Nelson, and Guillermo would take thousands more into dozens of other villages.

As I flew back to Yarinacocha, I was overcome with joy. "It's true that I might never work with the Aguaruna again," I reflected. "That should make me sad. But they don't need me any more. The job I came to do is done. It is time to leave. God has let me see the end of the work He gave me." Then, suddenly, a new thought filled my mind.

"This is not an ending; it is a beginning. My Aguaruna assignment is finished, yes. But, right now, a great outpouring of the Holy Spirit is beginning. I can see the Word, now in Aguaruna hands, powerfully changing more and more lives. I can see hundreds of men, women and children reading this Word and sharing it with one another. I can see persecution and opposition increase, as people learn more about being committed to Jesus Christ instead of following Satan."

I thought back to that gray day in Nazaret when I had stood weeping at the edge of the village. The Lord reminded me of the vision he had given me then, of the assurance He had placed in my heart about what He would accomplish.

"The most exciting part of the story is about to begin," I thought. "It may never be set down on paper. But it will be written in the records of heaven. I'll have the joy of praising God through all eternity for what His Word, by the power of His Spirit, has done in Aguaruna lives.

"Yes, God is still shaping His Aguaruna pots of clay. He is still drawing them through the fires of affliction and filling them with the treasure of His own Spirit. He will keep on pouring it out in a stream of love and power. But that will be a story for the Aguaruna to tell. They will have to write it, for it will be their task—and joy—to record the acts of God among the Aguaruna."

The New Testament in Aguaruna arrived on October 14, 1975. From truck to storeroom, then by air and river, the 10,000 books were delivered to the villages. Nelson joyfully participated in the celebrations

At Nieva, Father Pancho prepared a special display of books in front of the altar. Climbing steps was the beginning of the Urakusa celebration. The church was filled to overflowing. Twenty-nine were

while people of all ages eagerly read their newly purchased books. Nelson and Julia themselves, with their two children, were a witness to the power of God's Word. The team made its way between villages.

baptized. As the books were taken home by canoe or jungle trail, God's Word was truely in the hands of the Aguaruna pastors and people. The Potter was pouring out His Spirit again into common clay pots.

Supplemental Information

Epilogue

Nine years have passed since Jeanne and I completed our portion of the work with the Aguaruna. Martha has continued to give some assistance, particularly in training Aguaruna teachers in preparation of school materials. The Olsons continued with community development tasks until a change of assignment in November, 1982. Many significant changes have continued to occur during these years, both in the Aguaruna community and in the people's relationship to the outside world.

One hundred and fifty-six communities now have schools, with 250 teachers serving 7,500 pupils. Many of these teachers were influenced to enter teaching by the first Aguaruna men who entered the profession: fifteen are former students of Alias, thirty-five were taught by Dantuchu, and another thirty by David. All of the schools are bilingual schools, including the parochial Catholic schools.

Of the thousands of students who have been educated in the Aguaruna schools, well over 500 have graduated from high school; of these, 300 or so have gone on to post high school education. Most of these have returned to their home areas and continue to identify strongly with the Aguaruna culture. The decentralization of education by the Peruvian government for several years has given more autonomy to the Aguaruna and other indigenous groups, so they have not had to take total direction from Lima for educational matters. There may be a more recent trend, however, back to centralization.

All five of the bilingual education specialists and some of the other staff members at the *nucleo* level (equivalent to a school district) are Aguaruna men. Two of the three specialists in bilingual education above them at the zonal level (equivalent to the state level) are also Aguaruna. All of the teachers and the *nucleo* and zonal specialists are paid by the government. Through the help of SIL and other support organizations, the Aguaruna also now run their own print shop. In Urakusa, it is headed up by Shimpu, in addition to his work for the Zonal Office of Education. Last year, the Aguaruna printed a thousand copies each of eight different books.

Medical work has continued through the efforts of about eighty trained health promoters in sixty to sixty-five villages, trained under both SIL and the Aguaruna *Consejo* (Council). A few of these men are paid by the Peruvian Ministry of Health.

The church has continued to grow. There are more than 100 congregations, with well over 8,000 believers. About 120 pastors serve these congregations: most are self-supported, but churches now donate money, work or handcrafts to help with their expenses. All of the 10,000 copies of the Aguaruna New Testament printed have been sold and another 8,000 have been printed. Two systems of church organization are functioning, one under the Nazarene church and the other following the model of presbyteries. Both are autonomous, Aguaruna-governed. In addition, there are several Catholic congregations in the area. The Bible school at Yamakai, organized and taught by Aguaruna, met for the seventh year in 1984, with about a dozen students studying five months of the year for three years. A second Bible school downriver, below the gorge, is open part of the time to accommodate those students for whom travel is difficult. About 150 pastors or Bible school students have been trained by the Swiss Indian mission and the Nazarene mission.

In the next two years following the dedication of the New Testament, Nelson translated the Book of Genesis. He checked his work with Millie during one of her return visits to Peru in 1978. His excellent work was published and distributed, and he then planned to translate Psalms and Proverbs.

Alias has continued teaching in Nazaret, as well as doing further evangelization.

Other changes have continued to alter the life of the Aguaruna. A government sponsored oil pipeline passes through their territory. It has provided temporary jobs for many Aguaruna, who have taken the opportunity to learn welding, metal working, mechanics, and the use of machinery such as chain saws. Those who choose to work now earn a fair wage and are not so much exploited because of their ignorance of money; literacy helps them in this regard. The standard of living has increased because of this additional money in the economy. But problems have been created too.

Some men, during the building of the pipeline, neglected to keep up their garden plots and thus have sometimes faced a shortage of food. More colonists have come to the area. But the Aguaruna seem to feel the freedom to take only what they want of this outside life. They say, "We'll choose only the good changes," but sometimes find that even these have negative aspects. Most work away from their communities only temporarily, and return immediately to their homes. They do not regard this outside work as significant or long term.

The world increase in the price of gold has also had its effect on the Aguaruna. Many have returned to panning gold in the rich streams in their homeland, which the Spaniards once sought to exploit. (Few outsiders have come in to pan due to the ruggedness of the area and the temperamental nature of the water level in the streams.) Cacao has also become an important source of cash for the people. They now produce it by the truckload, and the villages above the gorge have even purchased their own truck for marketing. Below the gorge several boats have been provided through community development projects. By having their own resources for marketing their produce and other goods, the Aguaruna are receiving much more honest earnings, as well as avoiding the huge prices charged by local *patrones* for outside goods. Rice production has increased dramatically, adding much stability to the food chain of the Aguaruna because it can be stored for long periods.

Four regional councils of Aguaruna men govern the affairs of the people. They are vociferous and autonomous, and are actively trying to promote what they consider to be in the best interests of the people—to the point of expelling certain groups whose influence they do not like.

The Aguaruna identify strongly with the Peruvian national life. In 1981 during border skirmishes with a neighboring country, the people offered their help to defend the national borders and to serve as guides. They also transported troops and cargo in their canoes. The commanding general of the military in Iquitos commended them for their help and for their spirit of cooperation.

Certainly, change has come to the Aguaruna world, brought about by innumerable influences and forces. And as with the changes in any culture, there are both negative and positive aspects involved. Some work for the good of the people, and others lead to the weakening of their identity and self-respect. Fortunately for the Aguaruna, their ancestral patterns of pride and independence, coupled with new skills such as literacy, have helped them to confront rapid change and maintain their own identity and self-respect to a much greater extent than have many other indigenous groups.

The same fierce drive and energy which enabled them to resist the conquest of both Incas and Spaniards, now channeled into cooperation instead of hostility, help to conserve their cultural identity and sense of pride. Having their language preserved in writing and having the New Testament in their mother tongue has also helped to promote social stability and cultural identity. The roles of pastor and teacher have also been a unifying influence. For all of these, we can be grateful.

About the Authors

Dr. Mildred Larson is currently the international translation coordinator for the Summer Institute of Linguistics and the Wycliffe Bible Translators. She oversees the quality of translation work around the world by training and working with consultants, preparing training materials for new translators and promoting the preparation of helps for translators through biblical research projects.

Born in St. Laurence, South Dakota, she was educated at Wheaton College, in Illinois, earning a B. A. there. She earned a master's degree in linguistics at the University of Michigan and a doctorate in humanities at the University of Texas at Arlington. In addition to her linguistic and translation work with the Aguaruna for more than twenty years, Dr. Larson has often served as a professor in the bilingual teacher training course in Peru and on the staff of the Summer Institute of Linguistics (SIL) in various universities. She has been linguistic consultant and translation coordinator for many of her colleagues, and has often served in other leadership roles, such as on the executive committee of SIL in Peru, as a member of the board of directors of SIL International, and on the staff of the Latin America area director of SIL.

Besides completing the translation of the New Testament into the Aguaruna language, Dr. Larson assisted in the completion of the Huambisa New Testament.

Dr. Larson is the author of numerous scientific articles and books relating to linguistics, bilingual education, and translation, including training manuals and textbooks.

Lois Dodds, who organized and rewrote Dr. Larson's material, was born in Palmdale, California. She earned a B. A. in psychology at Westmont College, Santa Barbara, California, and an M.A. in education at Azusa Pacific University, also in California. Since 1969 she and her husband, Lawrence, a physician, have been members of the Wycliffe Bible Translators and the Summer Institute of Linguistics. They have served with SIL in Peru since 1971. Mrs. Dodds is the author of many articles and several books, including a volume of poetry, and has extensive experience in scientific writing and editing.

About the
Summer Institute of Linguistics
and
Wycliffe Bible Translators

From humble beginnings in 1934, when two students comprised the first trainees under William Cameron Townsend and L. L. Legters, the Summer Institute of Linguistics has grown into a highly respected and prolific linguistic organization working in nearly forty countries worldwide. Currently member linguists are involved with linguistic analysis, literacy, translation of the New Testament, and related work in more than 750 ethnic minorities which have never before had their languages written.

Seasonal SIL courses are given in about a dozen universities worldwide, and year round at the International Linguistics Center in Dallas, Texas.

Students may enroll for upper-division or graduate studies to prepare for linguistic, anthropologic, literacy, and community development work. SIL specializes in studying and reaching out to linguistic minorities around the world whose chances for survival physically, culturally, and linguistically are threatened by the pressures of twentieth century life.

Wycliffe Bible Translators, the sister organization of SIL, recruits workers and receives funds for the various field programs. Members of WBT and SIL sincerely believe that God's Word, offered to and freely chosen by indigenous peoples, is the best protection they can have against the forces that so often squeeze them into oblivion or cultural disintegration. Through coming to know the God of the New Testament, members of ethnic minority groups have opportunity to discover their own worth and uniqueness, and to find strength to be themselves with dignity and self-respect.

They can discover how to replace cultural characteristics which are destructive to both individuals and the society, such as hate and hostility, with those which are beneficial to both, such as harmony and mutual respect. They also gain skills such as literacy, and new knowledge, which help them bridge the gap and hold their own in complex national societies.

Anyone interested in SIL courses or further information about the work of SIL and WBT may write to Wycliffe Bible Translators or Summer Institute of Linguistics, Inc., Huntington Beach, California, 92647.

Historical Background on the Aguaruna

The Aguaruna are one of the largest indigenous groups in the jungles of Peru. They numbered about 22,000 in a census taken in the early 1970's and have increased about ten percent since that time. (A 1954 census counted 8,000.) They live in high jungle in the eastern foothills of the Andean range in the northern part of Peru, mostly along the Marañon River and its tributaries. Until recent years the only access to their territory was by trail from the coast or by river from the jungle city of Iquitos. In 1964 the Olmos-Marañon Road linked the area to other highways of Peru. The terrain of the Aguaruna is mostly rough, rocky, and mountainous, with peaks reaching up to 8,000 feet. Travel is difficult due to swollen rivers in the tropical rainy season and low water and rocks in the dry season.

The name Aguaruna most likely comes from early outsiders, who called the people by the Quechua words *awax* (weaving) and *runa* (man) because the men are the weavers in this culture. The Aguaruna call themselves *aents* (people) or *pata* (family) and designate as *uma* (sibling) other related groups with whom they have friendly relations. These groups include any of the *Jivaro* (named for *ji*, fire, and *varo*, man) in Peru and Ecuador, such as the Achuar, Huambisa, Candoshi, and others like the Bracamoro, who no longer exist. All of these groups have a common history and are related linguistically and culturally. At times they have been at peace with the Aguaruna, serving as their allies or trading partners, and at other times they have warred fiercely against them.

Women outnumber men about two to one, mostly because of the tradition of wars and revenge killings. Thus many men have more than one wife, particularly the very capable and respected, such as shamans, who have had up to five wives. Mortality up to the age of five was usually forty-five to fifty percent as late as the 1960's. Aguaruna population has been adversely affected, like that of virtually all of the jungle populations, by periodic epidemics of measles, smallpox, tuberculosis and other "white man's" diseases, particularly around the turn of the twentieth century during the rubber boom and the search for pelts. (Even in the last decade there have been many deaths due to epidemics.) The Aguaruna were exploited terribly by *patrones* during this period.

In general, there is not abundant historical data about indigenous groups of South America. Compared to other groups, the history of the Jivaroan groups is well documented, though some of what has been published is either unreliable or contradictory. During the Spanish colonization of Peru, as early as 1549, explorers entered the Aguaruna and other Jivaroan territories in search of gold. But the fierce Jivaro were the only group known to have successfully resisted conquest by both the Inca and the Spanish empires. Catholic missionaries also entered the area very early. The first settlement of outsiders on record was established in 1552. Most contacts with outsiders, however, were short-lived and hostile.

The Aguaruna area is rich in chalk and salt, which have served as sources of trade with outsiders for at least 300 years. Oil seepage in the foothills and streams has also led to exploration of the area by outsiders, as has the continued search for gold.

The Aguaruna have been mostly hunters and gatherers, who cultivate small plots of manioc, banana, peanuts and wild potatoes. They have a reputation for fierceness and bravery. Like other Jivaroan groups, their tradition and history is rich in wars, raids, revenge killing, headhunting, and sometimes head shrinking, all based on their beliefs relating to the supernatural.[29]

For the Aguaruna, as for most of the "traditional" peoples of the world, the spirit world is the real world. The focus of his life is his belief in and appeasement of supernatural forces; no aspect of life is unrelated to the spirit world. Traditionally, every Aguaruna youth has been arduously trained in seeking supernatural power and cultivating and maintaining it through revenge killing. At times, one of every four adult men has been a shaman—either a "curer" or a "curser." To the Aguaruna, no death occurs by natural causes. All accidents, disease, and death are considered to be caused by someone, through their spirit power or sorcery. Thus, every death requires revenge of some kind; to avenge the death of his relatives is the duty of the Aguaruna. Death and the fear of death and the afterlife (in which one becomes an evil spirit) are powerful forces dominating the thinking of the Aguaruna. It is through the spirit realm that the Aguaruna derives and maintains his life force (he has three souls), develops his personality, and gains status and respect.

Pronunciation Guide

The following consonants are pronounced with a sound quite close to the most common English sounds: *b, ch, d, k, m, n, ng, p, s, sh, t, ts, w,* and *y.*

The *a* is pronounced like the *a* in "father" except before *i* and *u.* The combination *ai* often sounds like the *ai* of "tail" and the combination *au* is pronounced *ou* as in "Oh." When not preceded by *a,* the *u* is pronounced like *oo* in "boot."

The *i* of Aguaruna has the sound of the *ee* of "beet." The *e* does not have an equivalent in the English sound system. It is made by saying the sound of *u* (see above) but with the lips unrounded.

The *j* of Aguaruna is pronounced like the *h* in "hot."

Glossary of Terms and Names

Alias (A-lée-as) Dantuchu. The brother of Daniel Dantuchu.

Amuesha (A-muái-sha). Another native Amazon group, located south of the Aguaruna in the Andean foothills.

Apajui (A-pa-huée). The Aguaruna name for God, the creator and supreme being. The Aguaruna believed in him before the Spaniards came; many of their legends pre-date that time. However, there has been some shift in the content of belief since the coming of the Spaniards.

Candoshi (Kăn-dó-she). A group closely related to the Aguaruna geographically, culturally and ethnically. They are both subgroups of the Jivaroan.

Chicais (Chee-kāys). Located on the Marañon River, it was the center for collecting rubber and hides for the Aguaruna cooperative.

Chiriaco (Chee-ree-á-kou). A mestizo village at the crossing of the Chiriaco River and the government road.

Cudney, "Grandmother" Elizabeth. The SIL worker who managed the SIL house in Lima, where members went for vacation, rest, etc., and where Aguaruna and other indigenous peoples could stay when in the city.

Dantuchu (Dón-too-chew) Daniel. The brother of Alias and the first Aguaruna teacher.

David (Da-véed) Cuñachi. The principle Aguaruna teacher in Nazaret, a supervisor of schools and coordinator of the bilingual teachers' conferences. The father of Kunyach.

Elsa (Él-sa) Pujupat. Nelson's sister who was delivered from demons.

Emerita (E-me-reá-ta). A young woman who was demon possessed.

Esteban (Eh-stáy-bon) Pujupat. Nelson's brother.

Huanuco (Wá-new-kou). A mestizo town in the central Andes area on the western side of the mountains. The surrounding area is populated mostly by Quechua people, descendants of the Incas.

Indigenous group. A group of people that originated in a particular region or country.

Iquitos (Ee-kée-toes). A city in northern Peru at the juncture of the Ucayali and Amazon Rivers. Iquitos is a principle place of trade for many groups in the upper Amazon area. During the rubber trading days at the turn of the century, Iquitos was a major city, the farthest navigable point on the Amazon by sea-going vessels.

Japa (Há-pa). Alias' uncle.

Jeanne Grover. The SIL nurse who was Millie's partner.

Jerry Elder. Leader of the prayer support group for the Aguaruna, who often served as the director of the Peru branch of SIL.

Julia (Whó-lee-a) Pujupat. The wife of Nelson Pujupat.

Kaupan River (Cow-páwn). This was the area pioneered for schools and the gospel by Alias.

Kistian (Kéys-tea-ann). A white person, especially one who speaks Spanish. (See footnote 17.)

Kuyach (Cúe-yach) Silas Cuñachi. The son of David Cuñachi. One of Millie's Aguaruna language teachers during her early years at Nazaret.

Leishmaniasis. A parasitic disease spread by small sand flies. The bites first result in ulcers on the skin, and many years later the organisms cause the break down of soft tissues in the nose and throat, resulting in ultimate death by choking the victim or making it impossible for him or her to breathe and swallow. The disease is endemic in the Amazon basin.

Mamai (Mom-áye). Millie's good friend.

Marañon (Ma-rah-nýon) River. The principal river in Aguaruna territory.

Martha Jakway. Millie's co-worker from SIL who specialized in the educational needs of the Aguaruna.

Mestizo (Mess-téa-so). The term used in Latin America for people of mixed Spanish and Indian blood.

Nazaret. The village of Alias and Dantuchu, where Millie and Jeanne lived during their first five years among the Aguaruna. It is located on the Chiriaco River.

Nelson Pujupat. One of the two principal co-translators of the Aguaruna New Testament.

Olson, Dennis. The SIL colleague of Millie who specialized in community development work among the Aguaruna.

Olson, Susie. An SIL medical technologist and the wife of Dennis.

Palm heart. The germinal bud of a palm tree, eaten as a delicacy.

Patrones (Pa-tró-nays). As referred to in this book, men, usually of mixed Spanish and Indian blood, who make a living by selling merchandise to the jungle peoples, usually in exchange for produce, lumber or labor. They often travel from village to village or set up a store or farm in one community to which the people come to trade. The people often go deeply into debt to the *patrones,* who usually charge exorbitant prices, and are thus virtually enslaved by them.

Roman (Row-mon) Shajian. An unusually talented Aguaruna who studied at the University of Trujillo and held important posts in the Aguaruna educational system.

Sachtler, Doris and Carlos. Members of the Swiss Indian Mission who trained Aguaruna pastors and other indigenous peoples.

Shaman. The traditional medicine man who worked either as a "curer" or a "curser."

Shipibo (She-péa-bow). A native Peruvian group who live along the Ucayali River in the Pucallpa area, near Yarinacocha.

Sol de oro (plural *Sóles*) (Soul, Sóul-lays). The Peruvian currency or "dollar." It means "sun of gold."

Tomas (Toe-móss) Chamiquit. A teacher at Nazaret who also assisted Millie in early translation efforts of the New Testament. He is the cousin of Alias and Dantuchu.

Tomas Daate. Helped with the final revision of the New Testament.

Townsend, William Cameron. The founder of SIL and WBT who lived for many years as director at Yarinacocha.

Tunchi (Tóo-n-chee). The Aguaruna word for sorcery.

Yarinacocha (Ya-ree-na-kó-cha). This word means "palm lake." It is the name of a lake, as well as of a small town and district which border it, near Pucallpa, in central Peru. It is also the name for the SIL work center in Peru.

Wynans, Roger. A Nazarene missionary who lived among the Aguaruna from 1925 to 1947.

Footnotes

1. The Aguaruna prepare the leaves of the guayusa shrub as a tea, and use this to wash out their stomachs each morning. See Steward, Julian H., editor, Handbook of South American Indians, U. S. Government Printing Office, Washington D.C., 1949, Vol. 5, p. 547.
2. The *ajutap* (a-hoo-tap) is a spirit sought by all Aguaruna males from early childhood. It is believed to impart great power and invincibility to the one who encounters or receives it. A man may accumulate *ajutap* power through killing, by having visions, usually through the use of hallucinogenic drugs, and by acting bravely. Once having entered the man, the spirit shows itself through the man's personal force, loud speech, bravery, and power to kill.
3. Belladonna is a poisonous plant, *Atropa belladonna*, used by the Aguaruna as an anesthetic, either by wrapping the affected part of the body in the leaves or by having the patient drink a solution made from the plant.
4. *Datem* is the Aguaruna name for the Spanish *ayahuasca*, the vine *Banisteriopsis caapi*, a species belonging to the *Malpoighiaceae*. For more details regarding its use, see *Hallucinogens and Shamanism*, Michael J. Harner, ed. New York: Oxford University Press, 1973.
5. *Baikua* is another variety of the same family of drugs as *datem*. It is stronger in its effects.
6. The Aguaruna often take on Spanish names in addition to their native ones, to accommodate the Spanish-speaking Peruvians

who cannot readily pronounce Aguaruna names. This practice fits into their own custom of having many names for a person. Certain Spanish names change according to the sound system of the Aguaruna language—i.e, "Arias" becomes "Alias."

7. See Historical Background section on page 295 for more detailed information.

8. Yarinacocha means "palm lake." It is one of several lakes formed by the changing course of the Ucayali River, a major source of the Amazon River. Yarinacocha is also the name of a mestizo community near Pucallpa, and the name used for the center of the Summer Institute of Linguistics, in the state of Ucayali (formerly Loreto). From the SIL center at Yarinacocha, linguists and other personnel travel back and forth to work in more than forty indigenous groups.

9. In bilingual schools students are first taught to read and write in their own language. Then they are taught the national language. For information on bilingual education in the Peruvian jungle area, see the book *Bilingual Education: An Experience in Peruvian Amazonia*, by Mildred L. Larson and Patricia M. Davis, published in 1981 by The Center for Applied Linguistics and The Summer Institute of Linguistics.

10. Manioc (man-ee-oc) (Spanish *yuca*) is a tuber which serves as the staple food of most jungle peoples. It is used in various forms: boiled, dried and roasted as a grain, and as a beer made by fermenting the mash in water, often after mastication.

11. The Aguaruna make blowguns by boring out the center of strips of hard palm wood, split open and grooved. The two halves are bound together by wrapping "aerial root" vines around them. They are then coated with resin. The mouthpiece is made of bone. The darts for the gun are made of bamboo slivers, usually tipped with the poison *curare.* Kapok or wild cotton is usually used as a wad to wrap the dart before it is blown. The Aguaruna are accurate with the guns at thirty to forty-five yards. *Curare* is a poison having a paralytic action. Made of various plant and animal ingredients, it usually depends for its effectiveness upon aqueous extracts of plants of the genus *Strychnos.*

12. *Achiote* (a-chee-oh-tay) is the seed of the *annotto* tree. The seeds are covered with a greasy red substance which is used as a face paint by the Indians of northern South America. It is also sometimes used to color food.

13. The Spanish *barbasco*, or joewood in English, is *timu* to the Aguaruna. The scientific name is *Verbascum* or *Tephrosia toxicaria*. This plant is used by Indians of northern South America as a fish poison. Though it stuns the fish, and allows them to be easily caught when they surface for air, its effects are not passed on to those who eat the fish.

14. *Suwa* is the Aguaruna name of a tree (Spanish *huito*) of the genus *Genipa* of the family *Rubiaceae*, bearing yellow flowers and succulent edible fruit with a thick rind. The fruit is used as dye for painting the body black before going on raids. It is also used as a shampoo to clean and dye the hair. Some groups use it as an insect repellent.

15. Japa called his nephew "grandchild," a term of endearment used for any younger relative.

16. The round shields were made of wood, a solid cross cut of a tree, varying in size according to the diameter of the tree.

17. The word *kistian* (keys-tee-ann) is an Aguaruna version of the Spanish word *cristiano*, meaning Christian. When the first white people (Spaniards) came into Aguaruna territory, probably four hundred years or more ago, they identified themselves to the Aguaruna as *cristianos*. The Aguaruna applied this name to any white person, especially those who speak Spanish. The Spanish language is called *kistian words* by the Aguaruna.

18. The crime of rape was unknown among the Aguaruna, even in revenge raids, before the coming of the white man.

19. The Aguaruna consider that the spirits of all dead go to a place called "the devil's place." The concept of and word for heaven came into their culture through the Spaniards, probably about 1560 or 1580 A. D.

20. Because the Aguaruna culture, like that of many indigenous groups in the Amazon basin, has no social place for a non-married woman, this was a grave offense as well as a social oddity. Women derive much of their identity, their social standing, and their material resources from their husbands. To leave a woman and her children without husband and father in the Aguaruna culture is to threaten their very survival, as well as to make them misfits and outcasts. For these reasons SIL personnel believe it is most fitting for a man to continue with whatever wives he already has when he becomes a Christian, trusting the Holy Spirit to bring awareness of the New Testa-

ment preference for one wife to those not yet responsible for more than one.

21. Japa was bitten by a *jergon*, or bushmaster, a deadly poisonous snake.

22. The agouti (a-goo-tee) is a rodent of the genus *Dasyprocta*, called *majas* by the Spanish and *kashai* by the Aguaruna. It is about the size of a very large rabbit and grizzled in color. The meat is considered very delicious by the Aguaruna.

23. A lieutenant governor serves in the hierarchy of Peruvian government as the overseer of a community or local area.

24. If you wish to read about demon influences, two books will be of help: Merril F. Unger, *Demons in the World Today*, Tyndale House Publ., Wheaton, Illinois, 1971; and Hal Lindsey, *Satan is Alive and Well on Planet Earth*, Zondervan Publ. House, Grand Rapids, Michigan, 1972, especially page 159 and following.

25. Though I can not say specifically how one recognizes the voice of a demon, all of the people involved in the accounts recorded here recognized and identified certain voices as being those of demons. Also, see Mark 1:21–28.

26. When I heard about this later, I was fascinated to compare it with the incident in John 20:22, when Jesus breathed on the disciples and said, "Receive the Holy Spirit."

27. Shimpu's official name is Gerardo Wipio Deicat. In 1978 he wrote an article called "La Educacion en el Pueblo Aguaruna," published first in Spanish and then as the fifth chapter of the book by Larson and Davis referred to in footnote 13. The title of the chapter in English is "Education Among the Aguaruna." Shimpu is currently director of bilingual education for the state of Amazonia in northern Peru.

28. According to the Scriptures, Christians give Satan a "foothold" into their lives through sins of attitude, such as resentment, unresolved anger, pride, and non-forgiveness, and through other sins such as lying, deception, sexual immorality, etc. (See Ephesians 4:26, 27, I Peter 5:5-9, James 3:14-16, Acts 5:3, I Cor. 7:51, I Tim. 3:7 for some examples.) For more information about this, see *Making God Visible*, by Lois Dodds, Wheaton, Illinois: Harold Shaw Publishers, forthcoming.

29. For a highly descriptive account of the Jivaro belief system and practices, see *The Jivaro: People of The Sacred Waterfalls*, by Michael Harner, Garden City, N. J.: American Museum of Natural History, Doubleday Natural History Press, 1972. Also see the

life story of a twentieth century Candoshi chief, *Tariri, My Story*, by Tariri, as told to Ethel Wallis. New York: Harper and Row, New York, 1965.

Left top: The name Aguaruna most likely comes from the Quechua words *awax* (weaving) *runa* (man) because the men are the weavers in this culture.

Right top: Aguaruna houses (approximately 75' × 30') have tightly thatched roofs. *Below:* Sleeping platforms also store clay pots.

Above: Clay is rolled, molded, fired and painted. *Below:* Jeanne Grover, Millie Larson, Martha Jakway, Dennis and Susie Olson.